KEY TO THE BIBLE

VOLUME 1

> *"I am convinced that modern scholarship has opened the Bible to us in a marvelous manner, and my sole desire is to place that key in the hands of those who seek it."*

The words of Wilfrid Harrington, O.P.—eminent Scripture scholar and author of this acclaimed theological work. According to Fr. Harrington, the majority of people who read the Bible find it difficult to understand. Many are discouraged and give up Bible reading altogether. They need a guide to help them understand it and to get the most out of their Scripture reading. *Key to the Bible* is the answer to their problem; it helps them enjoy it and benefit from it.

After publication of the first volume of this three-volume series came these raves from other noted contemporary scholars:

"Record of Revelation is a very readable and interestingly written general introduction which I should be happy to recommend to anyone." —*Bruce Vawter, C.M.*

"In *Record of Revelation* Father Harrington extends . . . his gift for simplified clarifying of issues that are still in ferment." —*Robert North, S.J.*

". . . up-to-date in its factual information, admirable in its clarity of expression, and sure of its grasp of basic theological issues." —*W. L. Moran, S.J.*

And about the other volumes, critics have applauded:

". . . an excellent work . . . should serve a useful purpose." —*Emmanuel*

"The reader who lacks any special preparation, but who wishes to make a study which will give him a grasp of what the Bible is and what it contains, should welcome this work." —*Our Sunday Visitor*

". . . is useful as an introductory survey along the lines of mainstream academic biblical criticism and as an example of where contemporary Catholicism stands." —*Christianity Today*

KEY TO THE
BIBLE

Wilfrid J. Harrington, O.P.

VOLUME 1

RECORD OF REVELATION

Foreword by Roland de Vaux, O.P.

IMAGE BOOKS

A Division of Doubleday & Company, Inc.

GARDEN CITY, NEW YORK

Image edition by special arrangement with
Alba House Communications
Image Book edition published September 1976

NIHIL OBSTAT: *Very Rev. Gilbert J. Graham, O.P.*
Censor Librorum

IMPRIMATUR: ✠ *Most Rev. Cletus F. O'Donnell, J.C.D.*
Administrator, Archdiocese of Chicago

ISBN: 0-385-12205-5
© *Copyright* 1974 *by* Alba House Communications,
Canfield, Ohio 44406
PRINTED IN THE UNITED STATES OF AMERICA

FOREWORD

The Bible is both historical and doctrinal, containing the revelation which God made to men through his own deeds and words. The Bible tells the history of our salvation, the gradual unfolding of the divine plan of redemption all through the two Testaments or Covenants, first in the Old Covenant concluded between God and Israel and maintained by God in spite of the unfaithfulness of his Chosen People, and then in the New Covenant, open to all mankind and sealed by the blood of a son of this people who was also the Son of God. Moreover, the Bible shows how each man must enter into this Covenant and abide within it, thus achieving his personal salvation. It tells us what we must know about God and Man, and what man must do to become acceptable to God.

This word of God is meant for each one of us as it was meant for our remote ancestors in the faith. It is the source of our faith, as it was of theirs. To reach man and transmit the message of salvation, this word became "incarnate," even as the Word of God became flesh to achieve man's salvation. God's word became "the Book," or rather "the Books" of the Bible. And just as the Word made flesh took upon himself our entire human condition, except for sin, so too God's word was subject to the conditions of human language, except for error. It was transmitted through human authors in whom divine inspiration suppressed none of the traits which belonged to them as men of their own times, of their own environment, and of their own culture. These distinguishing characteristics vary from one sacred author to another, and they are different from ours.

The writing of the books of the Old and New Testaments took place during a period of a thousand years, and the last of these books was written nearly two thousand years before our day. During these three thousand years, the face of the world has changed many times. God spoke to the ancient Israelites in the language of their time, and he spoke differently to those who came out of Egypt with Moses and to those who returned from the Exile with Esdras. Jesus spoke to the Jews of his day. And we are different from both the ancient Israelites and from the Jews of the time of Christ. Biblical writers who received and transmitted the sacred message were Semites who thought and spoke like Semites. Our thinking is not the same as theirs and we speak in different terms.

The Church was constituted by God as the guardian and interpreter of the word; but the Bible, considered as a book which contains that word, has not been preserved from the accidents that affect the transmission of any human text. It was copied, and the copyists made mistakes or introduced changes. It was translated, and the translators were not always accurate. It was expounded, but the commentators did not always understand it very well. In spite of all this, the message of the Bible is everlasting and is valid for all men of all times and all places. Indeed, the Bible has always been the most widely read book in the world, and men of the most diverse origins find the teaching of truth and a rule of life in its pages. It is because the Bible comes from God that it has this universal human value, and bears within itself the grace of light for all men of good will.

However, the mystery of the divine message itself and the dissimilarity of the times and concepts of those who first transmitted it and those who receive it today constitute serious obstacles. The Bible reveals its full richness only through the combined work of the exegete and the theologian, and since the Bible's richness is inexhaustible, this task is never finished. There will always be efforts to find a purer text or a more accurate translation, or to understand it better by placing it again within the human context in which it was first written, and to penetrate more deeply its divine meaning by the light of faith. Even as meditation on the life and deeds of Jesus will never elucidate the whole mystery of his Person, the study of the Bible will never quite exhaust the content of God's word.

Biblical study is a duty for every student who makes use of holy Scripture in developing his own theology, or who seeks his spiritual nourishment within it, and who will be preaching it to the faithful. It is also of interest to the laity who have acquired a taste for holy Scripture because of the biblical revival of our time and who now participate more intimately in the liturgy of the Word as the result of recent reforms. Both groups need to be introduced to this study and guided in this reading. It is for both of them that Father Harrington has written these three volumes on the record of revelation. It is a pleasure to be able to say that he has admirably achieved his purpose. He has clearly delineated a sound theological introduction to the entire Bible. He has made use of the conclusions best established by modern research in introducing the books of both the Old and New Testaments. Readers will readily see how these positions established by biblical science accord with the mind of the Church, the guardian of the Bible. By following this guide, they will proceed from the books of the Promise to the books of the Fulfillment, and the written word will give them a better knowledge of the Word Incarnate, "Jesus Christ, the focal point of both Testaments, of the Old as its hope, of the New as its model, and of both as their core" (Pascal).

Roland de Vaux, O.P.

Harvard University

PREFACE

After some years of teaching experience, I am more conscious than ever that we lack an introduction to the Bible in English that might form the basis of a Scripture course for students of the Bible. At the same time, there is no fully-satisfactory work that may be recommended to interested layfolk. It would be presumptuous to claim that this introduction fills both needs, or either of them, but it is an attempt to grapple with these needs. It is designed as a textbook which will provide the student with a clearly-defined foundation and will leave the professor a little more time to get on with the essential task of expounding the text of the Bible. Since it is meant to be self-explanatory, or largely so, it is hoped that it may also serve as a "teach yourself" book for those who do not have the advantage of a professor. Such, at least, are the aims, and time alone will show whether or not they have been attained.

When I say that no suitable work is available, I am not disdaining the admirable *Guide to the Bible*.[1] Yet it will be admitted, I believe, that this work can rather bewilder the student, who prefers to have the matter presented more succinctly and arranged more systematically. The *Guide* (or its French original, *Initiation Biblique*) has been supplanted by the massive two-volume *Introduction à la Bible*[2]—easily the best introduction to the Bible by Catholic scholars. The reader will quickly observe that I have leaned heavily on this splendid work. I think I can say that, as a consequence, this introduction to the Bible faithfully presents the views of some of the finest biblical scholars of our day.

The most important section of the whole introduction is

formed by Chapters Three to Six of this first volume, which treat inspiration, inerrancy, and the senses of Scripture. In these chapters I have been content to follow exclusively one who is an acknowledged authority in this field: Father Pierre Benoit, O.P., professor at the École Biblique and editor of the *Revue Biblique*. Father Benoit has, over the years, built an imposing synthesis. I believe that the more profitable approach—the alternative would be to present and evaluate different opinions—is to place this synthesis before the student. He can be sure that every step has been carefully worked out by a master. Other solid opinions will be found in the Appendix at the end of this book, and will be indicated in the footnotes and Bibliography.

It remains for me to thank Father Thomas C. Donlan, O.P., of The Priory Press who commissioned this work; without his invitation and encouragement I should never have undertaken it. I owe a special debt of gratitude to my colleagues, Fathers Liam G. Walsh, O.P. and Thomas P. McInerney, O.P., professors at St. Mary's, Tallaght, Ireland, for their painstaking reading of my manuscript and for their valuable criticism and suggestions.

I am grateful also to Father Kevin A. Lynch, C.S.P., who has kindly granted me permission to make free use of material in *What is the Bible?* published by the Paulist Press and copyrighted by the Missionary Society of St. Paul the Apostle.

W. J. H.

---

[1] A. Robert and A. Tricot, *Guide to the Bible,* trans. E. P. Arbez and M. R. P. McGuire (New York: Desclée, 1960[2]), I-II.

[2] A. Robert and A. Feuillet, *Introduction à la Bible* (Tournai: Desclée, 1957-59), I-II.

CONTENTS

Foreword   5

Preface   9

Abbreviations of Sacred Scripture   15

ONE: *The Written Word*   17
  1. THE BOOKS OF THE BIBLE   18
  2. THE FORMATION OF THE BIBLE   20
    1) *The Old Testament*   20
    2) *The New Testament*   30
  3. THE BIBLICAL WRITINGS IN CHRONOLOGICAL
    ORDER   31

TWO: *Scriptural Inspiration and the Truth of*
  Scripture   36
  1. THE FACT OF SCRIPTURAL INSPIRATION   36
  2. INSPIRATION IN THE BIBLE   38
  3. REVELATION IN THE BIBLE   41
  4. THEOLOGY OF INSPIRATION   47
  5. THE TRUTH OF SCRIPTURE   49

THREE: *The Interpretation of Scripture*   52
  1. THE WORD OF GOD TO MEN   52
  2. LITERARY FORMS   53
  3. THE PEOPLE OF THE WORD   54
  4. THE BIBLE IN THE CHURCH   57

FOUR: *The Canon of Scripture*   60
  1. CANON AND CANONICITY   60
  2. DEUTEROCANONICAL AND APOCRYPHAL
    BOOKS   61

3. THE FORMATION OF THE CANON   62
  1) *History of the Canon of the Old*
    Testament   62
  2) *History of the Canon of the New*
    Testament   65
4. THE NATURE OF CANONICITY   70

FIVE: *Biblical Criticism*   73
  1. TEXTUAL CRITICISM   74
    1) *Verbal Criticism*   74
    2) *External Criticism*   75
    3) *Internal Criticism*   76
  2. LITERARY CRITICISM   76
    1) *The Language*   77
    2) *The Composition*   77
    3) *The Origin of a Writing*   78
  3. HISTORICAL CRITICISM   79

SIX: *An Outline History of Israel*   83
  1. THE WORLD OF ISRAEL'S ORIGINS   84
    1) *The Ancient World in the Third*
     Millennium B.C.   84
    2) *The Eve of the Patriarchal Age*   85
    3) *The Patriarchal Age*   86
  2. THE PATRIARCHS   92
  3. EXODUS AND CONQUEST   94
    1) *The Background*   94
    2) *The Exodus*   97
    3) *The Conquest*   98
  4. THE PERIOD OF JUDGES   100
    1) *The Background*   100
    2) *The Amphictyony*   100
    3) *The Period of Judges*   101
  5. THE RISE OF THE MONARCHY   108
    1) *The Institution of the Monarchy*   108
    2) *The Reign of David* (*c. 1010-970* B.C.)   111
    3) *The Reign of Solomon* (*c. 970-931* B.C.) 114

6. THE DIVIDED MONARCHY ... 117
   1) *The Schism (1 Kgs. 12; 2 Chr. 10)* ... 117
   2) *The Background of the Divided
      Monarchy* ... 118
7. THE KINGDOM OF ISRAEL ... 127
   1) *Dynasty of Jeroboam I* ... 127
   2) *Dynasty of Baasha* ... 127
   3) *Dynasty of Omri* ... 128
   4) *Dynasty of Jehu* ... 130
   5) *Dynasty of Menahem* ... 132
8. THE KINGDOM OF JUDAH ... 134
9. EXILE AND RESTORATION ... 148
   1) *The Background* ... 148
   2) *Judah after 587 B.C.* ... 150
   3) *The Exiles in Babylon* ... 151
   4) *The Restoration* ... 151
10. THE WORK OF NEHEMIAH AND EZRA ... 153
    1) *The Background* ... 153
    2) *Chronology of Ezra-Nehemiah* ... 154
    3) *Nehemiah* ... 156
    4) *Ezra* ... 157
    5) *The Elephantine Colony* ... 159
11. FROM EZRA TO ANTIOCHUS IV ... 160
    1) *The Background* ... 160
    2) *The Jews under the Ptolemies* ... 162
    3) *The Jews under the Seleucids* ... 163
    4) *The Jewish Diaspora* ... 164
12. THE MACCABAEAN REVOLT AND THE
    HASMONAEAN DYNASTY ... 166
    1) *The Background: Antiochus IV to
       Antiochus VII (175-129 B.C.)* ... 166
    2) *The Maccabaean Revolt (1,2 Mc.; Dn.)* ... 167
    3) *The Hasmonaean Dynasty* ... 173

SEVEN: *An Outline History of New Testament
        Times* ... 179
   1. THE GRAECO-ROMAN WORLD ... 179

1) *The Roman Empire* 179
2) *Philosophical Trends* 182
3) *Religious Trends* 184
2. THE JEWISH WORLD 187
  1) *Palestine under the Romans* 187
  2) *Jewish Religious Sects* 195
  3) *The Jewish Diaspora* 206
3. CHRONOLOGY OF THE LIFE OF JESUS 210
  1) *The Birth of Jesus* 210
  2) *The Public Ministry* 212
  3) *The Death of Jesus* 213
4. THE APOSTOLIC AGE 214
  1) *The Jerusalem Community* 215
  2) *The Spread of the Church* 218
5. ST. PAUL: CHRONOLOGY AND MISSIONARY
  JOURNEYS 224
  1) *Chronology* 225
  2) *The Missionary Journeys* 226
  3) *Chronological Table* 232

Bibliography 236

ABBREVIATIONS USED FOR
THE BOOKS OF THE BIBLE

Gn.: Genesis
Ex.: Exodus
Lv.: Leviticus
Nm.: Numbers
Dt.: Deuteronomy
Jos.: Joshua
Jgs.: Judges
Ru.: Ruth
1,2 Sm.: 1,2 Samuel
1,2 Kgs.: 1,2 Kings
1,2 Chr.: 1,2 Chronicles
Ez.: Ezra
Neh.: Nehemiah
Tb.: Tobit
Jdt.: Judith
Est.: Esther
Jb.: Job
Ps(s).: Psalms
Prv.: Proverbs
Qoh.: Qoheleth
    (Ecclesiastes)
Ct.: Canticle of Canticles
Wis.: Wisdom
Sir.: Sirach
    (Ecclesiasticus)
Is.: Isaiah
Jer.: Jeremiah
Lam.: Lamentations
Bar.: Baruch
Ezek.: Ezekiel
Dn.: Daniel
Hos.: Hosea
Jl.: Joel

Am.: Amos
Obad.: Obadiah
Jon.: Jonah
Mi.: Micah
Na.: Nahum
Hb.: Habakkuk
Zeph.: Zephaniah
Hag.: Haggai
Zech.: Zechariah
Mal.: Malachi
1,2 Mc.: 1,2 Maccabees
Mt.: Matthew
Mk.: Mark
Lk.: Luke
Jn.: John
Acts: Acts
Rm.: Romans
1,2 Cor.: 1,2 Corinthians
Gal.: Galatians
Eph.: Ephesians
Phil.: Philippians
Col.: Colossians
1,2 Thes.: 1,2 Thessalonians
1,2 Tm.: 1,2 Timothy
Ti.: Titus
Phm.: Philemon
Heb.: Hebrews
Jas.: James
1,2 Pt.: 1,2 Peter
1,2,3, Jn.: 1,2,3, John
Jude: Jude
Ap.: Apocalypse

ONE

THE WRITTEN WORD

THE BOOKS OF THE BIBLE
THE FORMATION OF THE BIBLE
THE BIBLICAL WRITINGS IN CHRONOLOGICAL ORDER

The Bible may be described as the collection of writings which the Church has recognized as inspired; often this collection is also called the Scriptures, Holy Scripture, the Sacred Books, and, especially, the Testament. The word "Bible" comes to us from the Greek via the Latin. The Greek expression is *ta biblia* ("the books"); in later Latin the borrowed word *biblia* (neuter plural in Greek) was taken to be a feminine singular Latin noun meaning "the book." Hence, for us, the Bible is the Book par excellence.

Although there is a true sense in which the Bible may be considered as one great work—the work of a divine Author—yet, from the human standpoint, it is not a book; it is not even *the* book; it is a library or, better still, it is the literature of a people, the Chosen People, God's people. This, as we shall see, is a very important observation, a fact that must be grasped if we are to have a proper understanding of the Bible.

We find that Scripture is divided into two parts: we speak of the Old Testament and the New Testament. The word "testament" is an approximate translation of the Greek *diathēkē;* it indicates a fundamental feature of revelation, the Covenant or treaty which God made with a people whom he had chosen, the people of Israel. This treaty (in Hebrew *berith*), which was renewed more than once, was also a contract, since the people too, on their side, accepted certain conditions, especially the obligation of being faithful to him, the one true God. The Old Testament is the story of this people in the light of the Covenant, a story largely of infidelity on their part—inevitably bringing just punishment in its train—and of unfailing fidelity on the part of God.

God's purpose, the redemption of mankind, was to be achieved by sending his Son into the world. The coming of the Son of God naturally marked the beginning of a new era. God made a new and final treaty, sealed in the blood of Christ, with a new people—yet directly descended from the old—the Church. The New Testament tells of the fulfillment of God's plan. This plan, however, was there from the beginning, for the Testaments, although distinct, are closely linked. The Old Testament leads up to and is the preparation, God's preparation, for the New. Indeed, the Old Testament can be fully understood only in the light of fulfillment.

1. THE BOOKS OF THE BIBLE

The Jews, very wisely, had an elastic division of their Bible; they spoke of the Law, the Prophets, and the (other) Writings. The Law, which in their estimation took pride of place, consisted of the five books of Moses, the *Pentateuch*. Among the Prophets they listed not only the books that we term prophetical, but also Joshua, Judges, Samuel, and Kings, called by them the Former Prophets. Significantly, they did not number Daniel among the Prophets (as we do), but placed it in the third division, the Writings, which grouped the remaining books. The Hebrew division has much to recommend it, especially the fact that it does not (and this is particularly true of the Writings) seek to fit the various books into predetermined categories. We may indicate it more clearly thus:

The Law (*torah*): The Pentateuch.

The Prophets (*nebiim*) { Former: Joshua to Kings.
Latter: Isaiah, Jeremiah, Ezekiel, and the 12 minor prophets.

The Writings (*kethubim*)

1) Psalms, Proverbs, Job—the "great" writings.
2) Canticle of Canticles, Ruth, Lamentations; Qoheleth (Ecclesiastes), Esther—the "scrolls."
3) Daniel, Ezra, Nehemiah, 1, 2 Chronicles.

Since the thirteenth century, Catholics have divided the Old Testament into *historical, didactic,* and *prophetical* books. The division is a convenient one and does, in the main, give a good indication of the general character of the different books; but it must not be pressed too far because, in certain cases, it may be quite misleading. However, it will be useful to give a list of the biblical books according to this division.

1. *Historical:* The Pentateuch (Genesis; Exodus; Leviticus; Numbers; Deuteronomy); Joshua; Judges; Ruth; 1 and 2 Samuel; 1 and 2 Kings; 1 and 2 Chronicles; Ezra; Nehemiah; Tobit; Judith; Esther; 1 and 2 Maccabees.

It should be noted that in the Vulgate and Douay:

1,2 Samuel = 1,2 Kings
1,2 Chronicles = 1,2 Paralipomenon
Ezra, Nehemiah = 1,2 Estras

but the names given in the list above are now almost universally accepted. Note further that since 1,2 Sm. = 1,2 Kgs. in the Douay, then 1,2 Kgs. in the list above = 3,4 Kgs. in the Douay.

2. *Didactic* (and poetical): Job; Psalms; Proverbs; Qoheleth (Ecclesiastes); Canticle of Canticles; Wisdom; Sirach (Ecclesiasticus).

3. *Prophetical:*

Four major prophets:	Isaiah; Jeremiah (plus Lamentations and Baruch); Ezekiel; Daniel.
Twelve minor prophets:	Hosea; Joel; Amos; Obadiah; Jonah; Micah; Nahum; Habakkuk; Zephaniah; Haggai; Zechariah; Malachi.

In Catholic versions of the Bible many of these names are usually spelled differently, and the same is true of most other proper names. The reason for this is simple. Proper names in the Douay are based on the Vulgate which, in its turn, has accepted the Greek forms of the names as they occur in the version of the Old Testament known as the Septuagint. The King James Version (1611), and all subsequent Protestant versions, have adopted the Hebrew form of the names. Conformity in this matter would be very welcome and there is a steadily growing movement among Catholics to accept the Hebrew forms.

The New Testament is sometimes, on the model of the Old, divided into historical, didactic, and prophetical books.

1. *Historical:* The Four Gospels; Acts of the Apostles.

2. *Didactic:* Epistles of St. Paul: Romans; 1,2 Corinthians; Galatians; Ephesians; Philippians; Colossians; 1,2 Thessalonians; 1,2 Timothy; Titus; Philemon. The Epistle to the Hebrews. The Catholic Epistles: James; 1,2 Peter; 1,2,3 John; Jude.

3. *Prophetical:* The Apocalypse.

2. THE FORMATION OF THE BIBLE

1) *The Old Testament*

The formation of the Old Testament was a lengthy process. Sacred history begins with God's choice of Abraham sometime during the nineteenth century B.C.; and the origins of the Old Testament, the traditions built around the patriarchs, go back in germ to Abraham, the man of the divine promises, and to his immediate descendants. But it was Moses, the born leader and the lawgiver, who, in the thirteenth century, forged a motley crowd of refugees into a nation, set on foot a mighty religious movement, and gave the impetus to the great literary achievement that is Israel's—and ultimately God's—gift to mankind.

The *Pentateuch* bears the stamp of Moses, but the work as we know it took its final form many centuries later than Moses: in the sixth or, more likely, in the fifth century

B.C. The prophetical literature began with Amos and Hosea in the eighth century and closed with Joel and Zechariah 9-14 in the fourth century B.C. The historical books range from Joshua (based on traditions going back to the thirteenth century B.C.) to 1 Maccabees, written about the beginning of the first century. The fifth century, which saw the final form of Proverbs and the appearance of Job, was the golden age of the wisdom literature, but the movement had begun under Solomon in the tenth century, while the Book of Wisdom emerged a bare half-century before Christ. This is enough—even though nothing has been said of the complex genesis of individual books—to indicate that the shaping of the Old Testament was unhurried and involved.

We have to realize that most of the books of the Old Testament are the work of many hands, a work that has grown over a long period, perhaps over centuries. All who have collaborated in the production of each book, whether they have written the substance of it or have merely added some details, have been inspired. Most of them were quite unaware of being moved by God; hence for the moment we too shall consider the human side only of the Bible and view it as a collective effort, the work of a whole people which has deposited in the Bible, through the centuries, the treasures of its tradition. It is the literature of a people, enmeshed in the history of that people. We shall sketch briefly that literary activity from its beginnings and not it against its historical background; in this way we shall obtain a view of the Old Testament that will greatly facilitate our understanding of it.[1]

Much of the Old Testament is based on oral tradition. That part of it which comes first in our Bible—the *Pentateuch* to Samuel—is based on many oral traditions centered mainly around the patriarchs, Moses, Joshua, the Judges, Samuel, David, and later, in a section of Kings, Elijah and Elisha. These traditions, even before they were set down in writing, formed a true literature. "Literature" is, primarily, an art form; in a sense it is incidental that most literature has been set down in writing because, principally, it is a matter of words and language (whether written or not). Although, as we shall see, the biblical books as we know them took final shape at a relatively late date, this only marks the definitive setting down in writing of traditions that had begun, and in many cases had reached full development, many centuries before. The date of a biblical *book* is, very often, no indication of the date of the material contained in the book; and when we speak of "traditions" we do not exclude the possibility—indeed the certainty—that many of them may have been written down quite early. In fact, as will become clear, later literary activity in Israel was, to a large extent, concerned with the re-editing of earlier writings. We do not, then, by any means ignore or underestimate the contribution of previous centuries when we set the beginning of biblical literature, strictly understood, in the reign of Solomon.

In the face of Philistine aggression which, in the middle of the eleventh century, had overthrown the Israelite amphictyony (the confederation of twelve clans united in covenant with Yahweh), Israel made her first bid to organize herself as a monarchy. Despite initial promise, Saul proved a failure, but the idea of monarchy was not abandoned. A new beginning was made with David who succeeded in establishing a kingdom, and even a modest empire; a situation that was maintained and exploited by his son, Solomon. In order to handle the administration of kingdom and empire a class of scribes, educated men, emerged. Royal annals were kept and the business of state was recorded and filed away in archives. This provided the raw material of historical writing. Very early in the peaceful reign of Solomon (c. 970-931 B.C.) a writer of exceptional gifts produced the prose masterpiece of the Old Testament, the court history of David: 2 Sm. 9-20 and 1 Kgs. 1-2. A contemporary writer, of hardly less literary skill and endowed with a keener mind, working on old traditions, wrote a theology of history which forms one of the four main strands of the *Pentateuch*.[2] David (c. 1010-970 B.C.), whose skill as a poet is given abundant testimony, was the author of some of the psalms. These form the nucleus of the Psalter. The whole work, receiving its original impetus from him, was traditionally attributed to him. In quite the same way, the Wisdom literature, which developed in the following centuries, was attributed to Solomon, the proverbial wise man, who had begun the movement among the Hebrews or, at least, had provided the atmosphere for its emergence.

After the death of Solomon, the kingdom, united by David, broke apart, and Israel (or the Northern Kingdom) and Judah henceforth went their separate ways. A religious schism followed the political division, Judah alone remaining true, not only to the dynasty of David, but to a purer form of the authentic religion. In Israel one *coup d'état* followed on another and the worship of Yahweh—at the schismatic shrines of Bethel and Dan—was much affected by foreign influences. The Book of Kings gives us the parallel religious history of the two kingdoms.

It was in Israel that Elijah and Elisha, the champions of Yahweh, appeared; around them grew up the traditions that we find in 1 Kgs. 17–2 Kgs. 1 (Elijah) and 2 Kgs. 2-13 (Elisha). It was in Israel too, during the reign of Jeroboam II (783-743 B.C.) that the first of the so-called "writing" prophets, Amos and Hosea, carried out their mission, even though Amos was a Judean. About the same time, another strand of the *Pentateuch tradition*, parallel to the *Yahwistic tradition* that had evolved in Judah, took definite shape. This Northern tradition—in its final form the work of the Elohist, as we now name this author—faced with the abuses in the worship of Yahweh current in Israel, was understandably more conservative than the other, setting up as its ideal the religion of the Exodus and of the desert. Shortly after Amos and Hosea, the Prophets Isaiah and Micah arose in Judah. However, only the first part of the Book of Isaiah (i.e., chaps. 1-39)—and not even all of that—can be attributed to this great Prophet of the eighth century. Isaiah himself tells us of disciples who had gathered around him (8:16). It was these who published his prophecies; the inspired writers who later added to the work of their master came from that same school which continued through the centuries.

Meanwhile, the terrible scourge of Assyria had begun

to make itself felt and the days of the Northern Kingdom
were numbered. Samaria, its capital, fell to Sargon II in
721 B.C.; the population of the land, in accordance with
Assyrian policy, was deported; and Israel, as a separate
entity, disappeared from history. Before the final tragedy,
some refugees, religious men who had seen the writing
on the wall, fled to Judah, taking with them their sacred
traditions. As a result of this, under Hezekiah (716-687
B.C.) the two earliest strands of the *Pentateuch* (the
Yahwistic and Elohistic traditions) were combined. Another heritage of the North, brought to Jerusalem at the
same time, was the legislative part of Deuteronomy (the
deuteronomical code, Dt. 12-26). This was to have a powerful and far-reaching effect—but not just yet.

The great power which had destroyed Israel menaced
Judah too, but the latter, thanks in great measure to the
efforts of Isaiah, managed to survive. A century later, Assyria, while apparently at its apogee, collapsed and disappeared with dramatic suddenness. In the short period that
covered the decline of Assyria, before its successor the
Neo-Babylonian Empire could assert itself, Judah was
granted a brief respite and the young and pious king,
Josiah (640-609 B.C.), was able to begin a religious reform. One of the first works to be undertaken was the
restoration of the Temple—which had been sadly neglected
—and during the work of renovation the "book of the
Law" was discovered (2 Kgs. 22:8-10). This was the deuteronomical code which had been brought to Jerusalem
by refugees from Israel one hundred years before and
which had been deposited in the Temple, to be disregarded
and eventually forgotten. Now providentially coming to
light again, it became the charter of the reform and was
published in the framework of a discourse of Moses; this
first edition of the work corresponds to chapters 5-28 of
our Deuteronomy. It was later re-edited during the Exile
when the other discourses of Moses were added, one at the
beginning and the other at the end.

Deuteronomy (or, more precisely, the first edition of it)
gave the impulse to a very important literary work. The
deuteronomical outlook was profoundly religious and

striking in its singlemindedness: the nation stood or fell by its fidelity or unfaithfulness to Yahweh and to his Law. The history of the Chosen People was measured by this yardstick and the result provided the answer to a perplexing problem. The problem was this: on one hand stood the divine promises, which could not fail, and on the other hand one catastrophe after another had befallen the nation—Israel had disappeared and Judah had only just survived. The deuteronomists (as we may conveniently term them) saw very clearly that all these evils had come upon them because the people had been consistently unfaithful to their God; this was the one obvious lesson of their history. These men set about editing the older historical traditions, in the process giving to that history their own special religious slant. But they were careful not to do violence to the material, making their point either by means of modest insertions or by providing a distinctive framework. For example, in the Book of Judges the cycle of infidelity, punishment, repentance, and deliverance in which the story of each of the great Judges is set, is the work of these editors. During the reign of Josiah, the books Joshua-Judges-Samuel-Kings were edited, with Deuteronomy (chaps. 5-28) as an introduction. 2 Kgs. and Dt. were completed during the Exile (587-538 B.C.), and early in this period the history Joshua-Kings was edited for the second (and last) time. The Prophets Zephaniah and Nahum flourished during the reign of Josiah; Habakkuk was a little later than Nahum: both were contemporaries of Jeremiah.

After the untimely death of Josiah (609 B.C.), the Kingdom of Judah moved quickly to destruction; its last tragic years were reflected in the life and person of Jeremiah. The preaching of this great Prophet had gone unheeded —except to the extent that he had been persecuted for it —but after his death it had a profound influence. His message was recorded and published by his faithful disciple Baruch. In 587 B.C. Jerusalem fell to Nebuchadnezzar, as Jeremiah had emphatically declared it would, and its inhabitants were deported to Babylon. This must have seemed the end, but in God's unfathomable design the

Exile was to be the crucible in which the religion of Yahweh was purified of all dross; it marks, too, a decisive moment in the formation of the Bible.

Side by side with the deuteronomical movement there was another, of which the Law of Holiness (Lv. 17-26) is representative. This movement was inspired by the outlook of the priestly class who insisted on the holiness of Yahweh and who pictured the nation as a priestly people whose whole life was a liturgy. Ezekiel, who had been transported to Babylon with other Judeans sometime before the fall of Jerusalem, probably in 598 B.C., was a product of this school; whereas his contemporary, Jeremiah, was more in the line of Deuteronomy. During the Exile, the priests, now cut off from the Temple and its cult, turned to the old traditions, especially to the Mosaic legislation, and edited and presented these from a marked cultic viewpoint. Almost all the legislation in Genesis to Numbers belongs to this tradition, although it includes much narrative besides; and, after the Exile, it was the priests who gave the *Pentateuch* its final form.

Not all Judeans had been deported; some few remained, and from time to time these came to weep over the ruins of the Temple. It was in these circumstances that Lamentations took shape. It is universally recognized that this is not the work of Jeremiah, although the writing is attributed to him by the Vulgate—but not in the Hebrew Bible. Baruch, placed immediately after Lamentations in the Vulgate, is of uncertain date. In Babylon the exiles were comforted by an anonymous prophet, a late, but authentic, disciple of Isaiah; his work, composed in the years before 538 B.C. (when Cyrus the Great, having taken Babylon, permitted the Jews to return to Palestine), is contained in Isaiah 40-55. These chapters mark a theological (and poetical) summit of the Old Testament. Very soon after the return to Jerusalem, chapters 56-66 were added to Isaiah by other members of the Isaian school. Nor was this the end, because in the fifth century chapters 34-35 and 24-27 finally closed the work that had begun in the eighth century. But with Second Isaiah (as we name the unknown author of Is. 40-55) prophecy had reached its climax; it would gradually decline, to disappear in the fourth century, until the time of fulfillment.

The first of the exiles returned to Jerusalem from Babylon in 538 B.C.; eventually the Temple and the city were rebuilt. The work of restoration was encouraged and supported by the Prophets Haggai and Zechariah (only Zech. 1-8 belong to this period). Early in this period—at the latest early in the fifth century—the Torah was finally fixed. Deuteronomy, because it completed the story of Moses, was detached from the great historical work (Joshua-Kings) and attached to the first four books of the Bible. The *Pentateuch* came into being. The little Book of Ruth was probably written soon after the return (though it may possibly have appeared before the Exile). The last of the prophets appeared in the fifth and fourth centuries: the author(s) of Is. 34-35; 24-27; Mal.; Obad.; Joel; and the author of Zech. 9-14.

At this time too, that is to say, in the fifth century especially, another type of literature flourished: the wisdom literature. This was not altogether new by any means, because already under Solomon a practical outlook had found expression in sayings and maxims governing everyday life. "By 'wisdom' one must understand not only an encyclopedic knowledge of everything under the sun, but also the concise definition of all forms of human behavior, in particular the art of being the perfect gentleman. This art, so indispensable for the attainment of a successful career, had been practiced for centuries in Egypt."[3] In Israel, however, this practical wisdom was, to a certain extent at least, always inspired by faith in Yahweh, a tendency very marked after the Exile. In the fifth century the Book of Proverbs (parts of which go back to the time of Solomon) took final shape and, shortly afterwards, the poetic masterpiece of the Bible appeared: Job.

The Book of Job is by no means the only poetical work in the Bible. In the first place there are the psalms: David undoubtedly composed some of these and the number continued to grow steadily. The building of the Second Temple (after the return from the Exile) and the re-establishment of the Temple cult, gave a new impetus to the composition of these liturgical poems and to the adaptation of older psalms. By the end of the fourth century it is very likely that the Psalter, as we know it, was complete. In that same century the Canticle of Canticles made its appearance.

The writing of history did not end with the Exile, and the restoration, dominated by the figures of Ezra and Nehemiah, found its historian too. The books 1,2 Chronicles, Ezra, Nehemiah (four books in our Bible) really form only one volume, the work of a single author whom we conveniently call the Chronicler. In the first part of this writing (1,2 Chr.) the author follows, to a large extent, the Books of Samuel and Kings. In the second part he depends on the memoirs of Ezra and Nehemiah and on other documents of the same period. The differences between 1,2 Chr. and Sm.-Kgs. are marked because, whereas the latter is a religious history, the Chronicler has written a theology of history. Rather like the deuteronomists, he has drawn a religious message from the history of his people; but he uses that material much more freely than they. He wrote for his contemporaries and pointed out to them once again that the existence of the nation depended on its fidelity to its God; he would have his people be a holy community in which the promises made to David might at last be fulfilled. The work was written in the fourth century, just before the advent of Alexander the Great. Somewhat earlier, in the days of Ezra, and in opposition to a narrow nationalist outlook, the author of Jonah, a brilliant satirist, stressed the universal providence of God. And about the same time the Book of Tobit, in form not unlike a modern novel, extolled the daily providence of God.

In 333 B.C., with Alexander's conquest of Syria and Palestine, the Greek period began in Judah. For the Jews, or for those at least who were faithful to their traditions, this meant, not the assimilation of Greek culture, as it did elsewhere, but resistance to the Greek way of life. An indication of this perhaps may be seen in the emergence of a typically Hebrew literary form, the *midrash*.[4] The form already influenced the work of the Chronicler, but it is early in the Greek period that we find the first developed biblical *midrash*. In this period also (about the middle of the third century) we may date Qoheleth (Ecclesiastes), and sometime afterwards, about 180 B.C., another wisdom writer, ben Sirach, wrote Sirach (Ecclesiasticus).

Soon the Jews had to face a great crisis. When Antiochus IV (175-163 B.C.) came to the throne of Syria, he determined to force his Jewish subjects to adopt the Greek way of life. The consequent religious persecution provoked the Maccabean revolt, which began in 167 B.C. Towards the close of the first part of the struggle (167-164 B.C.), the author of Daniel published his work in order to encourage his countrymen. The first part of the work (Dn. 1-6) is a *midrash;* and in Dn. 7-12 we find a perfect example of a Jewish literary form then in vogue: the apocalypse. Daniel appeared just before 164 B.C. (At a later date the book was supplemented by the addition of 3:24-90 and chapters 13-14.) Esther was written shortly after Daniel.

The last historical works of the Bible capture the spirit of the stirring Maccabean times. About the year 100 B.C., 1 Maccabees was published. 2 Maccabees, composed in Greek and adapted from the work of a certain Jason of Cyrene, is a little earlier, about 120 B.C. It covers much the same ground as 1 Mc. and, like it, it is a historical writing, but it is oratorical in style and tends to handle details with some freedom. The Book of Judith, a *midrash*, appeared early in the first century.

If the Palestinian Jews had effectively resisted Hellenization, some Jews in the important center of Alexandria successfully assimilated Greek throught without sacrificing their Jewish heritage. The last work of the Old Testament, the Book of Wisdom, was written by one of these. However, although it is a product of the Alexandrian school and was written in Greek, the Greek influence should not be exaggerated; its author was not a philosopher but an authentic "wise man" of Israel.

2) *The New Testament*

The New Testament differs from the Old in many important respects, but it is like the Old Testament in being closely linked to the life and development of a people, the new people of God: the early Church. Similarly, although the whole of the New Testament took shape within the first century of the Christian era, nevertheless its genesis is also complex. And just as the Jews regarded the five books of Moses, the Law, as the first and most important part of the Old Testament, so also Christians regard the four Gospels as the heart of the New Testament. These have their origin in the apostolic preaching, but the first three Gospels, as we know them, did not appear for a generation or more after the resurrection: Mark is dated 64-65 A.D., and Matthew and Luke to a time immediately before (or, perhaps, just after) 70 A.D.—the date of the destruction of Jerusalem by the Romans. St. Luke wrote the Acts of the Apostles soon after his Gospel.

In the meantime, between the years 51 and 67, St. Paul had written his epistles, or letters, to various churches, often dealing with special problems. In these epistles we find the beginning and the first development of our specifically Christian theology; reading between the lines we learn about the Christian life and the difficulties of the early Church. The Epistle to the Hebrews was written shortly before 70 A.D. by a disciple of St. Paul. James appeared in the year 50 A.D. or, more likely, in 58 A.D.; St. Peter wrote his epistle (1 Peter) about 64 A.D. Of the other "catholic" epistles (so-called because, for the most part, they are addressed to Christians in general) Jude and 2 Peter were written in the decade 70-80 A.D., and 2, 3 John, followed by 1 John, were written in the last decade of the century. Apocalypse, a book that is not quite as mysterious as it seems, in its final form dates from about the year 95 A.D. The most eventful century in history had nearly ended when the Fourth Gospel was published.

All that has been said about the formation of both Testaments is in no way irrelevant, but has a practical bearing on our study of inspiration. It is not merely (this concerns the Old Testament especially) that we cannot name the authors of most of the books; if the problem were simply this, it would not trouble us because we can say that the eventual author—whoever he may have been—was inspired. In practice, however, we can rarely point to any individual as the author of a whole book. We have remarked, for instance, that Isaiah contains material ranging from the eighth century to the fifth century. Our notion of inspiration must be supple enough to accommodate this situation and others like it.

It ought to be abundantly clear by now that the Old Testament is the ultimate result of a collective effort. The same is proportionately true of the New Testament, especially of the Gospels. The work of an evangelist was not a private undertaking; in reality he was the last link in a chain. The Gospel, founded on the works and words of Christ, was first lived in the Church; and the evangelist, although himself directly inspired by God, was also the spokesman of a Church guided by the Spirit of God. Thus the New Testament, no less than the Old, bears witness to the truth that God's written word, like his Incarnate Word, came quietly among us, growing and developing until the moment of its manifestation to men. The sacred writers were moved by the Spirit in a special way, but the long preparation which their labors crowned was all part of God's saving plan, his solicitude for his Chosen People, the Old Israel and the New.

3. THE BIBLICAL WRITINGS IN CHRONOLOGICAL ORDER

It is convenient to give a schematic view of the biblical writings, indicating the approximate date of each. The correct sequence, which will manifest the steady development within the Bible, is, of course, essential for an intelligent reading of Scripture.

With regard to the Old Testament books, the title "Other Writings" suggests that the works listed under that heading do not really belong to the categories in which they are

traditionally placed. It is better, then, to list them apart,
because each of them must be studied by itself and its
particular literary form established. In the New Testament,
the heading simply groups the writings that do not come
under the other titles.

---

[1] The date of a biblical book is generally difficult to establish.
The dates given in this chapter are always approximate. However, within limits, there is a definite consensus in this matter
among leading Catholic scholars of the day.

[2] The *Pentateuch* is a combination of at least four distinct
traditions; literary analysis has unravelled the four strands.

[3] L. H. Grollenberg, *Shorter Atlas of the Bible,* trans. Mary F.
Hedlund (Camden, N.J.: Nelson, 1959), p. 94.

[4] *Midrash* is a method of exegesis which developed rather late
in Judaism; it is fully explained in W. F. Harrington, *Record of
the Promise: The Old Testament* (Chicago: The Priory Press,
1965).

CENTURIES B.C.	HISTORICAL WRITINGS	PROPHETICAL WRITINGS
13th	Moses: Beginnings of *Pentateuch* literature. Joshua: Traditions of the Conquest.	
12-11th	Judges: Traditions of the Judges.	
10th	Solomon (c. 970-941) *2 Sm.* 9-20 and *1 Kgs.* 1-2. Yahwistic tradition fixed.	
9th	Elijah and Elisha Traditions underlying 1 Kgs. 17— 2 Kgs. 13. Elohistic tradition fixed.	
8th	Deuteronomical Code fixed.	*Amos* *Hosea* *Isaiah* (1-39) *Micah*
7th	Under Hezekiah (716-687), Yahwistic and Elohistic traditions combined. Under Josiah (640-609), first edition of *Deuteronomy* (Dt. 5-28). First edition of deuteronomical history, *Joshua-Kings*.	*Zephaniah* *Nahum* *Habakkuk*
6th	Before the Exile During the Exile (587-538) Second (and final) edition of *Deuteronomy*. Final edition of *Joshua-Judges*, *Samuel-Kings*. Priestly tradition fixed after the Exile.	*Jeremiah Ezekiel* *Lamentations* *Second Isaiah* (40-55) *Haggai; Zechariah* (1-8) *Isaiah* (1-39)
5th	*Pentateuch* fixed	*Isaiah* (34-35; 24-27) *Malachi* *Obadiah*
4th	*Chronicles-Ezra-Nehemiah*	*Joel* *Zechariah* (9-14)
3rd		
2nd	*2 Maccabees*	
1st	*1 Maccabees*	

CENTURIES B.C.	WISDOM AND POETICAL WRITINGS	OTHER WRITINGS
13th		
12-11th	David (c. 1010-970) Beginning of the *Psalms* Solomon	
10th	Beginning of *Wisdom* literature	
9th		
8th		
7th	Many Psalms	
6th		
5th	*Proverbs* *Job*	*Ruth* *Jonah* *Tobit*
4th	*Psalter* complete *Canticle of Canticles*	
3rd	*Qoheleth*	
2nd	*Sirach*	*Baruch* *Daniel* *Esther*
1st	*Wisdom*	*Judith*

	NEW TESTAMENT WRITINGS		
A.D.	GOSPELS AND ACTS	EPISTLES OF ST. PAUL	OTHER WRITINGS
51		1,2 Thessalonians	
56		(Philippians?)	
57		1 Corinthians 1 Galatians 2 Corinthians	
57/58		Romans	
58			
61-63		(Philippians?) Colossians Ephesians Philemon	James
64	Mark		1 Peter
04-05			
65		1 Timothy Titus	Hebrews
67		2 Timothy	
68-70	Matthew Luke Acts		
70-80			Jude 2 Peter
90-100			Apocalypse 2 John 3 John 1 John
	John		

TWO

SCRIPTURAL INSPIRATION AND THE TRUTH OF SCRIPTURE

THE FACT OF SCRIPTURAL INSPIRATION
INSPIRATION IN THE BIBLE
REVELATION IN THE BIBLE
THEOLOGY OF INSPIRATION
THE TRUTH OF SCRIPTURE

1. THE FACT OF SCRIPTURAL INSPIRATION

Though there is no explicit mention of inspiration in the pages of the Old Testament, there are many passages which hint at it. We learn, for example, that it was at the divine bidding that Moses wrote the book of the Covenant (Ex. 24:4 f; 34:27) and that Jeremiah set out in a book the oracles of the Lord (Jer. 30:2; 36:2). The Jews had a three-fold division of their sacred books and they believed that all of them came from God. Thus the Torah was regarded as the Word of God, and the Prophets spoke the Word of God; these, with the Writings, constitute the "sacred books" indicated in 1 Mc 12:9. The Christian Church inherited these Scriptures and accepted their sacred character. Jesus had already quoted them as the Word of God (Mt. 22:31; Mk. 7:13; Jn. 10:34 f.). The apostles had done likewise (Acts 1:16; 4:25; 28:25). Arguments could be based on Scripture as on divine authority (Rm. 3:2; 1 Cor. 14:21; Heb. 3:7; 10:15). There are two classic texts, 2 Tm. 3:16 and 2 Pt. 1:21 which, with reference to the Old Testament, consider respectively the extent and nature of inspiration.

The Church's belief in the divine inspiration of Scripture is clear too, for the earliest times, in the tradition of the Fathers and in the teaching of theologians of all ages, quite apart from any special pronouncements. The earliest Fathers, those of the second century, named the Scriptures the "oracles of God" which were "dictated by the Holy Spirit" who used the sacred writers as "instruments." Later writers spoke of the Holy Spirit as the "author" of Scripture and asserted that both Testaments were inspired by the Spirit. The teaching of the Fathers on inspiration may be summarized in two statements: (a) God (the Holy Spirit) is the author of sacred Scripture; (b) the human writer is the instrument of God.

Along with this tradition of the Fathers we have a whole series of pronouncements on the part of the Church and in these we may trace a steady development and a growing precision. Until the fifth century the Church was principally engaged in defining and defending the extent and content of the Word of God, and lists of the sacred books were drawn up. From the sixth century to the thirteenth century it was repeatedly stated that those books are sacred because God is their author and also, in view of certain heresies which minimized or rejected the Old Testament, that God is the one same author of the Old Testament and of the New. At the Council of Florence (1441) a reason (found already in the Fathers) for this last statement was brought forward: God is the author of both Testaments because the sacred writers of both Testaments have spoken under the inspiration of the same Holy Spirit. This is repeated by the Council of Trent and the First Vatican Council, and the latter also makes clear what inspiration is not. The encyclical *Providentissimus Deus* gives a positive definition of inspiration and certain aspects of it are further developed in *Spiritus Paraclitus* and *Divino afflante Spiritu*. Finally, chapter three of the Constitution *De Divina Revelatione* of Vatican II draws attention to the inspiration of the Holy Spirit and the consequent divine authorship of Scripture as well as to the "divinely inspired realities" which it contains. And it stresses the freedom enjoyed by the men chosen by God as his instruments in writing these books.

2. INSPIRATION IN THE BIBLE[1]

Apart from the *theopneustos* of 2 Tm. 3:16, the term "inspiration" does not appear in the Bible. But, something far more important than the occurrence or non-occurrence of a specific term, the reality of "Spirit-possession" is met with very frequently. At the same time, the manner in which this is described is extremely varied. It will be well to examine, briefly, the broad pattern of God's way of moving men in the context of his saving plan for mankind. We shall readily see that "inspiration" is much wider than the particular charism enjoyed by the biblical writers.

In the Old Testament the "Spirit of Yahweh" is a mysterious force which enters mightily into the history of the chosen people and accomplishes the works of Yahweh, savior and judge. It seizes upon and transforms chosen men, empowers them to play exceptional roles, and by their instrumentality guides the destiny of Israel and the stages of salvation history. In the earlier texts the action of the Spirit is brusque and transitory: the Spirit of Yahweh "stirs" (Jgs. 13:25), "falls upon" (Ezek. 11:5), "carries away" (1 Kgs. 18:12; 2 Kgs. 2:16), "comes mightily upon" (Jgs. 14:6). It can awaken, in those whom it touches, extraordinary physical strength which is employed in the service of God's people (Jgs. 13:25; 14:6-19; 15:14), it can stir men to deeds of prowess in battle (Jgs. 6:34; 11:29; 1 Sm. 11:6 f). In short, many of the judges, without preparation or predispositions, were abruptly and totally changed, were rendered capable of extraordinary actions of boldness and of strength, and were endowed with a new personality which made them leaders and saviors of their people. The Spirit also stirs up prophetical enthusiasm and ecstasy (Nm. 11:24-30; 1 Sm. 10:5-13; 19:20-24), the power to work miracles (1 Kgs. 17:14; 2 Kgs. 2:15; 4:1-44), the gift of prophecy (Nm. 24:2; 1 Chr. 12:19; 2 Chr. 20:14; 24:20) and the explanation of dreams (Gn. 40:8; 41:16,38; Dn. 4:5; 5:11; 6:4). In all these cases the Spirit "comes upon" men as a supremely free gift of God.

Later texts present the Spirit of Yahweh as resting, in an abiding manner, on charismatic leaders. It comes to rest on Moses (Nm. 11:17-25), on Joshua (Jos. 27:18; Dt. 34:9), on Saul (1 Sm. 16:14) and on David (1 Sm. 16:13; 2 Sm. 23:2). The kings, unlike the judges, were charged with a permanent function and the rite of anointing which consecrated them, manifested the imprint of the Spirit and invested them with a sacred majesty (1 Sm. 10:1; 16:13). But the Spirit rested, too, on Elijah (2 Kgs. 2:9) and Elisha (2:15); and the prophets were the privileged bearers of the Spirit.

The prophets were aware that a sovereign pressure—even overcoming their own inclinations—constrained them to speak (Am. 3:8; 7:14 f; Jer. 20:7-9). They speak—and the word may cost them dearly, may be wrung from them —but they know it did not originate with them: it is the very Word of the Lord who sends them. For it is through the Spirit of Yahweh that the prophets receive Yahweh's Word (Is. 30:1; Zech. 7:2). The Spirit turns the prophet into a "fortified city, an iron pillar" (Jer. 1:18; cf. 1:8; 20:11) and makes his brow as "adamant harder than flint" (Ezek. 3:8 f; cf. Is. 6:6-9). In the messianic age all of Israel will enjoy prophetic inspiration from a general outpouring of the Spirit (Jl. 3:1 f; cf. Is. 32:15; Ezek. 39:29).

Turning to the New Testament, we find that in the Lucan writings the concept of the Spirit is close to the Old Testament idea. Almost all the persons mentioned in Lk. 1-2 are said to be moved by or filled with the Holy Spirit: John the Baptist from his mother's womb (1:15-18), his parents, Zechariah (1:67 ff) and Elizabeth (1:41 ff) as well as Simeon (2:27 ff) and Anna (2:36). In all these cases the Holy Spirit is presented as a supernatural divine power (cf. 1:35). Jesus as Messiah is the bearer of the Holy Spirit—this is a truth emphasized by Luke. After the baptism and temptation it is "in the power of the Spirit" that Jesus returned to Galilee and began his messianic work (4:14) and his first words were a quotation of Is. 61:1 f—"The Spirit of the Lord is upon me, because he has appointed me to preach the good news to the poor" (Lk.

4:18). The whole public ministry is thus put under the sign of the Spirit and all the works and teaching of Christ must be seen in the light of this introduction. And, at the end, the risen Lord guaranteed that he would send the "promise of the Father," the "power from on high," upon his disciples (24:49; Acts 1:8), for the Holy Spirit is the gift of the risen and ascended Lord (Jn. 7:38 f; 14:26). From Pentecost onward the Spirit is the guide and motive power of the Christian mission. The Spirit which moved the Messiah is now poured out by the risen Lord upon his Church (Acts 1:8; 2:4) and the prophecy of Joel 2:28-32 is fulfilled (Acts 2:17-21).

In Paul the Spirit is basically the divine and heavenly dynamic force, which exists in a special way in the risen Christ and pervades his Body, the Church. The Spirit is not obviously and explicitly conceived of as a distinct personal being. An isolated text in Matthew (28:19)—a post-resurrection baptismal formula—is an explicit declaration of the personal character of the Spirit. And John tells us that the Holy Spirit is a Paraclete, an Advocate, just like the Son (14:16).

Our rapid survey has, at least, indicated that in the Bible, the action of the Spirit is varied; yet it may be classified under two general headings. In the first place there is an *inspiration to act*, that is, an efficacious movement of the Spirit which takes hold of a man in order to make him accomplish certain deeds. Nor are these only sporadic exploits or symbolic gestures, but also enterprises of great moment and of decisive historical import; for, as we have seen, the Spirit of Yahweh raises up and stimulates those whom God has charged with the conduct of sacred history. Then there is, especially in the prophets, an *inspiration to speak*. The prophets are the interpreters of the Spirit and the effect of their inspiration is the proclamation of these "oracles of Yahweh" which teach and direct the people.

It is surely not by chance that though the Spirit is thus said to move men to speak or to act, the Bible has no instance of the Spirit laying hold on a man in order to move him to think or to write. Of course, we may still speak of "scriptural" inspiration but, in view of the evidence, we must be careful not to make of it the absolute and exclusive manifestation of inspiration in Scripture. We may legitimately speak of scriptural inspiration because the Bible is indeed the term, willed and directed by God, of the events of sacred history and of the oral teaching which it preserves in written form. But it is necessary not to restrict inspiration to this ultimate stage but to extend it, as the Bible does, to the earlier and no less important stages of the word lived by the pastors and leaders of the people of God. When, however, we say that the Bible never shows us the Spirit coming upon a man in order to move him to think we do not mean that Scripture has no place for thought or knowledge. The fact of the matter is that in the Bible "knowledge" is never speculative only—it is a matter of the heart and of action as much as of the intellect. Inspiration, in the Bible, is a movement of the Spirit which touches the whole man and makes him think or know only by first urging him to act or speak or write.

Thus we end up with three forms of inspiration. The "inspiration to act" noted above may be described as *pastoral inspiration,* which moved the "pastors" or leaders of the people of God. Then there is *oral inspiration,* enjoyed by the speakers of the word: prophets and apostles. Finally comes *scriptural inspiration,* the prolongation and completion of the other two. All three together form what we might describe as "biblical" inspiration. For this reason it is very important to connect scriptural inspiration to its antecedents and to see it in its historical setting.

3. REVELATION IN THE BIBLE

We begin to understand the biblical idea of "revelation" when we have grasped the meaning of *dabar* ("word"). For the Hebrew the word was more than the verbal expression of thought; he saw the spoken word as a dynamic entity—it is power-laden. Then, too, *dabar* means not only "word" but also "thing" or "deed"; more precisely the "background of a thing wherein resides its deepest meaning." But *dabar* also, of course, expresses an idea. It is evident that *dabar,* signifying a "word-thing" goes beyond the meaning of the Greek *logos;* except where it renders *dabar.* If, then, the human "word" has a power and an efficacy, it will be readily appreciated that, above all, the word of Yahweh is efficacious.

In the Old Testament Yahweh reveals himself, he speaks to men, by the prophets, in the law and in nature and history. Israel was certainly conscious of three types of divinely appointed spokesmen, prophet, sage, and priest, and of the distinction in their manner of speaking: "the law (instruction) shall not perish from the priest, nor counsel from the wise, nor the word from the prophet" (Jer. 18:18). Yahweh puts his word in the mouth of the prophet (Jer. 1:9) who cannot resist the divine call (Am. 7:5; Jer. 20:9), and the prophet, in his turn, proclaims God's word to the people. The prophetic word is a decisive force in the history of Israel (1 Sm. 9:27; 15:13-23; 2 Sm. 7:4); its effective power cannot be gainsaid (1 Kgs. 2:27; 2 Kgs. 1:17; 9:36), it is a consuming fire and "like a hammer which breaks the rocks in pieces" (Jer. 23:29). Differing in its action from the divine Word which comes powerfully upon the prophet, the divine wisdom can come more gently upon men, to teach them (Prv. 8:1-21, 32-36; Wis. 7-8). But in neither case is it a human phenomenon: prophets and sages, both, are in communication with the living God. And in that communication what they learn is not for themselves alone: it is a message to be transmitted to the whole people of God.

The prophet spoke in a given situation and to his own contemporaries—though, afterwards, his words were seen to have a relevance far beyond their immediate context. But, from the first, the Torah—the "teaching," the "law" —was the Word for all the people and for all time. And Israel received the Torah "the words" (Ex. 34:28; cf. Ps. 147:19) from Yahweh (Ex. 20:1; 22). Yahweh expects that Israel will hear and conscientiously live according to the word which it has accepted (Dt. 13:1). His word is near at hand: a spoken word which can enter into the heart of man and bear fruit (3:11-14). It opens up

the way of life or death, setting before Israel two ways
(30:15-20).

The divine Word is creative. But it is necessary to see
this fact or, more precisely, the realization of this truth,
in proper perspective. In studying *how* the Hebrews understood creation we must begin by noting that their experience of God was first and foremost an experience of
salvation and that their concept of God and of his activity
was founded on the events of salvation history, on the
fact that God had drawn near to his people. Gradually,
by reflection on the divine action on their behalf, the
Israelites became aware of their God's sovereignty over
other peoples and over all men, and they began to see
themselves as creatures vis-à-vis the Creator. They had
come to realize that Yahweh, the God of Israel, is the
Creator-God; but he remains the God who has called Israel
into being and has surrounded her with his love.

The Word of Yahweh is revelation. In speaking to men,
God reveals himself; his Word is a law and rule of life,
an unveiling of the meaning of things and events and a
promise for the future. At Sinai, Moses had mediated to
his people God's religious and moral charter, the "ten
words" (Ex. 20:1-17; Dt. 5:6-22). Beforehand, Yahweh
had spoken to the patriarchs and had made himself known
in a special way to Moses (Ex. 3:13-15; cf. 6:4); and to
the people: "I am the Lord your God, who brought you
out of the land of Egypt" (Ex. 20:2). The Word of God
reveals the significance of the history of the people (Jos.
24:2-13); and not only that, it enlightens Israel on the
immediately approaching stages of the divine plan (Gn.
15:13-16; Ex. 3:7-10; Jos. 1:1-5, etc.). And beyond the
immediate future, which is often painted in sombre colors,
it reveals what will happen in the "last days" when God
will fully accomplish his plan.

At once creative and revealing, the Word of God is a
dynamic reality, a power which infallibly achieves the results God has in view. Sent by God into the world as a
supremely efficacious agent—"My Word that goes forth
from my mouth shall not return to me empty, but it shall
accomplish that which I purpose and prosper in the thing

for which I sent it" (Is. 55:11)—it does not weaken or
fail (40:8). It directs the course of history (44:7 f, 26, 28)
and it carries out the divine vengeance: "Your all-
powerful Word leaped down from heaven . . . carrying
the sharp sword of your authentic command and stood
and filled all things with death" (Wis. 18:15 f; cf. Ap.
18:11-16). Such power, observable in nature and in history, assures the efficacy of the oracles of salvation. Indeed
"the word of our God stands forever" (Is. 40:8); from
age to age it continues to be a revelation and a vital force.

In the New Testament the Word of God is frequently
the message of salvation, the Gospel (Lk. 8:11; 2 Tm. 2:9;
Ap. 1:9). It was spoken by Paul (Acts 13:5; 1 Thes. 2:13)
and by the other apostles (Acts 6:2) and by Jesus himself
(Mk. 2:2; Lk. 5:1). But the Gospel that Paul and the
apostles preached was in reality Christ (1 Cor. 1:23; Gal.
3:1; Acts 2:36; 4:12). This was inevitable in view of the
Christian realization that in him God had spoken his definitive Word: "In many various ways God spoke of old
to our fathers by the prophets; but in these last days he
has spoken to us by a Son" (Heb. 1:1 f). And it is on the
person of Jesus that John, too, focused his attention; he
saw very clearly that Jesus is himself the message of salvation, the Word—the Logos, God's perfect self-revelation.
But in speaking of the Logos as the Word made flesh, in
declaring that all things were made by him, in stressing
his power to make men "sons of God," John underlines
the truth that God's Revelation in the Logos is *for us*.

The concrete, existential use of "word"—the dominant
aspect of the term throughout the Bible—points the way
to the understanding, in a biblical context, of the correlative notion of "revelation." The Bible is not a sum of
abstract "truths," a body of doctrine. What Scripture reveals is God himself, a living person: the Creator who
governs the world (Is. 45:12), the holy one who summons
men to a service of love (Ex. 20:1 ff; 34:6; Hos. 11:1 ff),
the Lord of history who guides times and events towards
a goal of salvation (Ex. 14:18; Am. 2:9 f; Jer. 32:20;
Is. 45:1 ff; 52:10). God reveals himself by his impact on
the life of individuals and of his whole people. And in the

full revelation of the New Testament what Jesus made known was not a system to be grasped but a way to be followed (cf. Jn. 11:6). He spoke, but his person and his actions spoke louder than his words; and his message was a message of salvation. "Biblical scholars agree more and more in affirming that revelation comes to us essentially in the framework of history and that it is essentially 'economic' or 'functional': there is no revelation of the mystery of God and Christ except in the testimony handed on about what they did and are doing *for us,* that is except in relation to our salvation."[2]

It is clear that if we are to be true to the data of the Bible we may not understand "revelation" only in the sense of declarations of abstract, purely speculative truth; we must take it to include the whole field of God's self-manifestation, it must embrace actions as well as words— for God is no abstract essence but a living person. And the mediator or interpreter of this revelation is not alone the "prophet" who has "received" a vision, or an oracle, and then has faithfully passed on to others what he has learned; he is, first and foremost, a man who has had an encounter with God, one who has come to recognize the Savior and Creator, one who has experienced the creative and salvific love of God.

To restrict revelation to "prophecy"[3] strictly so called would entail the risk of neglecting all the existential context of action, of history and of personal intervention which surrounds the spoken Word of God with a living and lived Word. To fail to recognize revelation in the events of sacred history just as much as in the enlightenment granted to the prophets would mean a dangerous impoverishment of the extreme richness of that encounter which God offers to men in the Bible. To pay attention only to the teaching of Jesus and not to the significance of what he did and what he was, would be to condemn oneself to be numbered among those who do not know him. Not to realize that the person of the Incarnate Word dominates the New Testament is to miss its message. Christianity is not founded on the Sermon on the Mount but on the living Lord.

Because biblical religion is basically and essentially historical, events will always speak louder than words. That is why the sacred writers are so preoccupied with the significance of events; that is why they are so concerned with the past. And their Spirit-guided meditation and analysis bring forth a message for the present and hope for the future. There is no neat and logical development of doctrine by the accumulation of "propositions"; the process is as complex as history itself. The Bible is not a manual of theology.

Our study of the biblical evidence has brought home to us that from one end of the Old Testament to the other, the Spirit of God and the Word of God do not cease to operate together. If the prophet bears witness to the Word, it is because the Spirit has seized him; if Israel will one day be capable of adhering (in her heart) to this Word it can only be in the Spirit. And, in the New Testament, the preachers begin to proclaim the Word only when the Spirit had come upon them. We may believe that the relationship between revelation and inspiration may be clarified by an examination of that existing between Word and Spirit. Revelation is the manifestation of the Word, inspiration the movement of the Spirit: two distinct but inseparable divine powers; or if one prefers, correlative aspects of the divine power.

We may conclude that, when seen in the perspective of the Bible, it would be misleading to regard inspiration and revelation as two quite separate charisms. In fact, inspiration and revelation in Scripture, are distinct, but they operate simultaneously. A man is raised up and moved by the Spirit to direct a phase of salvation history, to speak as a prophet, or to write down the essentials of this divine pedagogy; but all of the activity is "revelation," the personal manifestation of a living God. God reveals the truth which he himself is in terms of the lived, spoken and written experiences of his people and to that end he inspires leader, preacher, and writer who perceive this truth and who pass it on to the people by living it, by speaking it and by writing it.

4. THEOLOGY OF INSPIRATION

There has been no dearth of writing on the theory of scriptural inspiration since the last century. The field has been competently researched by J. T. Burtchaell.[4] A major tendency has been to invoke the scholastic notion of instrumental causality and to see God as the principal author of Scripture and the human writers as the instrumental or secondary authors.[5] In our day this scholastic synthesis centered on the notion of instrumental causality is largely abandoned. In an important book[6] Bruce Vawter has studied the development of a theology of inspiration in both Roman Catholic and Protestant traditions. His final chapter, "Towards a Synthesis," presents his suggestions regarding a desirable theology of inspiration.[7] We indicate his main points.

1) Inspiration should be thought of primarily as one of the qualities bestowed upon the community of faith by the Spirit of God that has called it into being. That Spirit works in the community, the people of God; and thus, the scriptures of that people are, in a real sense, the work of the Spirit. Where the older theories of inspiration conceived of God as acting upon an individual directly in favor of the community, we should rather think of God as working through the community by affecting an individual. Scriptural inspiration was primarily a community charism, even though exercised through individuals.

2) Karl Rahner's conception of the New Testament as a constituent of the nascent Church, and of inspiration as an exercise of the divine constitution by which the Church came into definitive form, is most helpful. The entire self-disclosure of God is given in Jesus Christ in the form of the final eschatological salvation of the whole human race. Anything that happens from the time of Jesus Christ must be referred back to this beginning of the end which is given in Jesus Christ. "By inspiration Scripture becomes the work of God precisely in its role of the objectivation of the faith of the primitive Church understood as the permanent norm of the faith of all later ages, and

this is a pure norm."[8] The Bible of the very earliest Church, however, was exclusively the Old Testament. Thus, the Old Testament, as constitutive of the Church from its beginnings, was also produced through the action of the Spirit in a community that was also the people of God. The Bible, Old Testament and New Testament together, is the record of the one history of salvation.

3) We should not conceive of scriptural inspiration as being exactly the same in every part of Scripture.[9] No part of Scripture falls outside the influence of inspiration. The least text of the Bible, is part of an individual book (and part, too, of the ensemble which is the whole Bible) and it has its part to play in the complete work. When he adds a secondary fact here or a colorful detail there, the author acts as a writer conscious of his art; he knows that these less important elements will help in the presentation of the special truth he wishes to convey or in the general effect he wishes to produce. We should recall that the biblical author is inspired to write a *book* and it would be ridiculous to argue that any one sentence or any one passage of a book is just as important as any other. Besides, in many cases, the authorship of the biblical writings is a complex matter; for many books have been retouched and developed over long periods, even over centuries. We see more and more clearly that the Bible is a complex work built up by successive generations; it is the achievement of a whole people. Scriptural inspiration must have been as diverse as the human efforts that conspired to produce the Bible. However, it is never a question of one biblical work being less inspired than another; rather it is that one book is inspired *differently* from another; each conveys the word of God in its own proper fashion.

4) Scriptural inspiration, after all, is a reality; we must acknowledge a divine intent in the writing of the Bible. But it is not possible to specify the precise kind of divine causality that is present in each book or section; we may not classify types of inspiration. We should think of inspiration as always a positive divine and human interaction, wherein God displays his condescension. "God has inspired a literature: he has infused into it his word, not by de-

priving it of anything human but rather by utilizing all of its meaning and diverse human qualities. He has accommodated himself to the ways of man: not an ideal, unhistorical man, but man in his only historical condition, precisely the man who needs to hear the saving word of God. This is the man we find in the Bible, and this word has come to him."[10]

5) Inspiration has a permanent and dynamic quality which accounts for the continued power the word has to evoke response in the believer. "Without denying the obvious once-for-allness involved in the literary fixation of the Bible, we must at the same time acknowledge that it is the continuous reinterpretation of the biblical word in the life of the believing community that constitutes it effectively God's word to men. By inspiration we should understand not only the spiritual influence responsible for the Bible's origins, but also that which sustains it as a medium of speech."[11] Conceived of in this way, biblical inspiration continues to reside in the belief and understanding of the communities of faith, communities still guided by the Spirit.

5. THE TRUTH OF SCRIPTURE

One may, with reason, complain of a negative and defensive approach to Scripture due to a preoccupation with the "inerrancy" of the Bible; it would surely be more rewarding to speak of the "truth" of Scripture. Now we find that the Dogmatic Constitution on Divine Revelation of Vatican II does just that. It does more than that; it asserts that the divine authorship of Scripture guarantees that the truths taught and the realities described in the Bible provide the sure way of salvation without error: "The books of Scripture, firmly, faithfully, and without error, teach that truth which God, for the sake of our salvation, wished to see confided to the sacred Scriptures" (art. 11). This text echoes the view of some who, in recent years, have studied the problem of biblical inerrancy and the nature of revelation. For, indeed, the message of the Bible is essentially religious and is altogether concerned with

what is pertinent to salvation. Besides, Scripture can be
positively inerrant only where something is taught; for,
when we speak of the truth of Scripture we do not imply
that truth must be positively taught in every part of Scripture. Or, to put it another way, just because Scripture is
everywhere inspired it does not follow that it is always and
everywhere inerrant—in a positive sense. Inspiration and
inerrancy are co-existent, but under either of two aspects:
positively when truth is at stake; negatively in the fore-
stalling of any teaching of error.

We have seen that *scriptural* inspiration governs the
composition of a book and that much of what a writer
says is, or at least can be, accessory to his leading ideas,
and it is abundantly clear that the sacred writers are not,
at all times, and in every detail of their work, teaching
something. Instead of "teaching" his readers a writer may
seek to touch their hearts, to stimulate, to console or please
them. Even when his appeal is to their intellect he can
take steps to present his message in an accessible and
agreeable manner. The sacred writers have not acted
otherwise. Among the qualities of their work—beauty,
charm, persuasion—truth stands high; but it is by no means
the only quality and it is not present in every passage. But
each book puts before us an aspect of the one, true living
God, and the whole Bible is a revelation of living, existential truth, a personal encounter with God, Creator and
Savior.

---

[1] For inspiration and revelation in Scripture see relevant articles in X. Léon-Dufour (ed.), *Dictionary of Biblical Theology*
(New York: Desclée, 1967); J. B. Bauer (ed.), *Encyclopedia
of Biblical Theology*, 3 vols (New York: Sheed and Ward,
1970); J. L. McKenzie, *Dictionary of the Bible* (Milwaukee:
Bruce, 1965); also P. Benoit, *Aspects of Biblical Inspiration*
(Chicago: The Priory Press, 1965); "Inspiration and Revelation," *Concilium*, 10, no. 1 (December 1965), 5-14.

[2] Y. Congar, "Christ in the Economy of Salvation and in Our
Dogmatic Tracts," *Concilium*, 1, no. 2 (January 1966), 8 f.

[3] Scholastic theology has tended to see revelation (and inspiration) in the light of St. Thomas' specialized study of prophecy in *Summa Theologiae*, II.II, qq. 171-75.

[4] *Catholic Theories of Biblical Inspiration since 1810* (Cambridge: The University Press, 1969).

[5] See W. J. Harrington, *Record of Revelation: The Bible* (Chicago: The Priory Press, 1965), 35-53.

[6] *Biblical Inspiration* (Philadelphia: Westminster Press, 1972).

[7] *Op. cit.,* 156-70.

[8] K. Rahner, *Theological Investigations,* VI (Baltimore: Helicon, 1969), 90; see *Inspiration in the Bible* (New York: Herder & Herder, 1961).

[9] The truth is that inspiration is not a univocal concept but an analogical concept. "Human nature," for instance, is a univocal concept because all men possess it in the same way. "Life," on the other hand, is an analogical concept, for it may be predicated of men, animals, and plants. We may speak of life, in a true sense, in each case, but it is clearly not the same in each case. Similarly, all the parts of Scripture are truly inspired, but not all are inspired in quite the same way.

[10] B. Vawter, *op. cit.,* 169.

[11] *Id.,* 170.

THREE

THE INTERPRETATION OF SCRIPTURE

THE WORD OF GOD TO MEN
LITERARY FORMS
THE PEOPLE OF THE WORD
THE BIBLE IN THE CHURCH

1. THE WORD OF GOD TO MEN

A parallel drawn in article nineteen of the Constitution on
Divine Revelation is a helpful pointer to an understanding
of the fact of God speaking to men, a parallel between the
two incarnations of the Word of God: in human language
and in human flesh. Just as we know that the Son of God
became like men in all things, except for sin (Heb. 4:15)
so we can say that the written Word of God is like human
language in every way, except that it can contain no formal error. We can, and indeed we must, push the parallel
further. Christ is not only *like* men, he is truly man and
truly God; Scripture is not only *like* human language, it is
human language in the fullest sense, while all the while it
is the Word of God.

It is a matter of first importance, then, to determine the
precise meaning which the sacred writer had in mind. Subject as he is to the limitations of human language, he will
treat of things and speak of them from one aspect only.
It is also well to remember that not everything an author
writes is a categorical statement. Balanced exegesis of any
scriptural passage will determine, in each case, just how
far the writer guarantees his ideas, and the truth of what
he says will be involved to that extent and no more. He
may venture an opinion or he may even express hesitation
and doubt. It behoves us to respect these qualifications because God, who speaks through him, has condescended

to accept them. We may go a step further and say that a writer can affirm something which he does not put forward as a fact to be believed; in other words, he may write fiction. A sacred writer, too, may use fiction, because fiction can be a vehicle of revelation, of divine truth. The Gospel parables bear this out, and indeed, there are fictional works in the Old Testament, e.g. Jonah, Esther, Judith. It is evident that such writings must be judged according to the intention of the authors and not according to our preconceived notions. But this brings us to the question of literary forms.

2. LITERARY FORMS

All literature is cast in types or species distinguished from one another by distinct form or structure: these are literary forms. The basic distinction is that between prose and poetry; but, in practice, a given literary unit is not just "prose" or "poetry" as such but some particular species of either. There is plenty of room for wide variety and different forms have evolved in different cultures and in different ages. Diversity of literary forms, even within a given culture, is due to a desire to give more meaningful expression to a subject and to bring out different aspects of a truth. A single event may well be the subject of a variety of forms—for instance, prose narrative, epic poem, drama, philosophical treatise; and each form will have its own "truth." "The truth of poetry is not the same as the truth of the drama. All of these forms are different efforts to express the truth; but because the truth is larger than any single form, the truth expressed, while it is a conception of the same reality, is often quite different in one form from what it appears to be in another."[1]

In practice, the existence of literary forms in literature is one of these things we take for granted. Still it is a fact that as regards the Bible—precisely because its human aspect was not fully appreciated—the application was very restricted. Now at last the situation has been rectified and it is admitted that Scripture does contain a variety of types. At the same time it is realized that literary forms cannot

be determined *a priori;* often we have to be well aware of
the literary conventions of an age in which a writing took
shape before we can establish its form.

It is clear that the sacred writers may have employed
any of the literary forms in use among their contemporaries "so long as they were in no way inconsistent with
God's sanctity and truth." Some have felt that this would
exclude fiction—a singular conclusion in view of the parables. Only very few literary forms, past and present, could
be excluded on this score and even then it would, perhaps, be by reason of the content than because of the
form. It has been said that whereas we could very well
imagine God inspiring a novelist like Dostoevski we could
never dream that he would inspire a pornographic novel.
That is so, but the observation is not altogether relevant
since, in either case, the form might be the same. We can
hardly ever decide, in the abstract, what is becoming or
unbecoming to God, for the divine condescension goes
deeper than we know. When studying the Word of God it
is well to have in mind the stark reality of the Incarnation
and the scandal of the Cross.

3. THE PEOPLE OF THE WORD

We have seen that we may not ignore the human condi-
tioning of God's Word under peril of misinterpreting God's
message. This means, for one thing, that we should learn
to identify and rightly evaluate the literary forms employed by the biblical writers. But it also means that, as a
more fundamental step, we must strive to understand and
appreciate the Semitic origin and the Semitic cast and
background of the Bible—for all this is an essential part of
it. We may not measure the Scriptures by our Western
standards but we should, rather, seek to understand the
mentality of its writers. This, obviously, calls for a certain
reorientation. Our Western culture has its roots in Greece
and Rome and the Greek heritage, especially (though most
of us are unaware of it) has influenced our ways of
thought. We, quite spontaneously, use abstract ideas and
abstract terms, but the biblical writers, and our Lord him-

self, used concrete terms and imagery. Our manner of thought comes naturally to us, but we have to realize that the Semitic mind works differently and, consequently, that Semitic outlook and culture are different from ours. A few examples will help to clarify this point.

For us "to know" means to grasp an idea, but for the Semite it involves much more than that. "Knowledge" of God in biblical language is not primarily a speculative notion of God: it includes the acceptance of all he stands for, it includes the service of God, it involves a commitment. The man who "knows" God is one who lives in the presence of God, one whose "knowledge" is a rule of conduct. In the eyes of the Semite, God is not an abstract essence, a pure spirit—he is Creator, Judge, Father. The very idea "pure spirit" does convey something to us; we understand, vaguely at least, that God is immaterial. To the people of the Bible the expression would be meaningless simply because they did not have our distinction (which is entirely Greek) between spirit and matter.

We are inclined to regard the Bible as a sort of textbook in which we look for a set of doctrines and we are somewhat ill at ease because the teaching is not neatly arranged in logical order. What we should seek is the living image of a God who acts, who enters into our history, who speaks to our hearts. Then we shall understand why the Old Testament can speak of God as the shepherd of his people: "I myself am the shepherd of my sheep" (Ezek. 34:15)—words that are echoed by the Son of God: "I am the good shepherd" (Jn. 10:11, 14). We shall realize how it is that God can be presented as the spouse of Israel: "Your maker is your husband, the Lord of hosts is his name" (Is. 54:5) and how in the New Testament the Church is the bride of Christ (Ap. 21:9). We have boiled down the doctrines of the faith, and set them out in precise, technical language—but Jesus taught in parables. He took striking examples from everyday life and spoke the language of poetry.

We do not seek to disparage systematic theology, but it should be kept in mind that our theology, as a system, grew up later than the Scriptures. It has its roots in the

Bible, in the New Testament especially, but it speaks another language; it translates the striking, sometimes daring, images of Semitic speech into precise carefully framed formulas. In doing this it renders a necessary service, but we should not expect to find the same scientific terminology in the Scriptures any more than we ought to regard the Bible as a theological treatise—while recognizing that there are a number of theologies in the Bible. We lose the whole flavor of the Word of God if we want to have its teaching parcelled out in neat, clearly labelled compartments. In short, we must strive to understand the Bible as it is, and not try to force it into our categories of thought.

This Semitic cast is not confined to the Old Testament but involves the New Testament also. Except for St. Luke, the New Testament writers were Jews, but even he is not really an exception because his writings are still fundamentally Semitic. All four Gospels especially have this quality. They are in no way speculative but are always vivid and concrete. In them we read of a man who is the Son of God, who lived among us and taught and suffered and died and rose from the dead. He was born of the Jewish race and came and preached to Jews in the concrete language of the Semitic culture that was theirs and his. It is this culture and outlook and way of speech we must reckon with from the first book of the Bible to the last. If we persist in treating it as a twentieth century product of European thought we cannot fail to do it violence.

When we have once grasped this, our approach to the Bible will be along the right lines. If we do no more than realize that the mentality of the biblical writers is different from ours we can begin to understand many aspects of the Bible that had hitherto puzzled us. We should also remember that the latest part of Scripture was written almost two thousand years ago and that the earliest part of it took shape another thousand years or so before that. This is another obvious reason why the Bible can present difficulties; it is a product of its own time and we cannot hope to understand it as readily as we would a modern work. Besides, it has to be translated into our modern languages before we can even begin to read it, because very few can have an adequate knowledge of Hebrew and Greek.

All this is so, but most of all we should like to stress once again the fundamental truth that God has spoken to us *in human language*. The Bible is not only the Word of God, it is also the word of men, and the human aspect of it is something we may not ignore. Our only way of knowing what God had to tell us in his Scriptures is by knowing first of all what the human writer wishes to say. God has used him and moved him—in speaking to men he has spoken by the mouth of a man whom he has chosen for that purpose. It is only by listening carefully to that human voice that we can catch the accents of God himself.

4. THE BIBLE IN THE CHURCH

So far we have stressed the human aspect of the Bible. But we have never lost sight of the divine aspect of Scripture, for the fundamental fact of inspiration implies the divine authorship of Scripture. It is a factor that may not be overlooked if one is to understand Scripture. And while the Catholic exegete must employ the methods of rational interpretation, he must take the Bible too for what it really is, the Word of God. "An exegete who neglects the human author and the rational methods of procedure which are necessary to understand him, exposes himself to the danger of remaining on the outside of Scripture by introducing subtle and arbitrary interpretations which are not willed by God. One who rejects the divine author and the means necessary to approach him—faith and the Church —condemns himself to remain on the outer surface of the sacred book, and even to do violence to its meaning. The exegete who takes both authors into account and maintains an exact hierarchy between the directives of faith and the demands of reason is able to penetrate Scripture in a harmonious and truly comprehensive fashion. On the solid foundation of a *scientific and critical exegesis,* which takes into consideration every human quality of the book, he will be able to erect a *theological and spiritual exegesis* which will disclose the intentions and teachings of God with the firmest guarantees."[2] But in order to achieve this desired result it is necessary that the scholar should be guided not only by his scholarship, not only by his faith in the divine origin of Scripture, but also by the teaching office of the Church.

The Church is the authentic interpreter of Scripture, but this is a statement that must be correctly understood. It does not mean that the Church will pronounce, authoritatively and positively, on matters of criticism and on historical details, if these are unconnected with dogmatic or moral issues, for the Church is concerned with questions of faith and morals and matters directly connected with them. In fact, the Church has rarely solemnly and positively defined the sense of particular texts.[3] More frequently a text is indirectly interpreted—that is, by bringing forward a text as containing a defined doctrine or by rejecting an interpretation which implies formal error in Scripture; but in these cases care must be taken not to exaggerate the weight laid on a given text. Our assessment of the role of the teaching office is clarified by the discussion which led to the choice of a particular phrase in article 23 of the Constitution on Revelation: "Under the watchful eye of the sacred magisterium" (*sub vigilantia sacri magisterii*). In the course of the debates *vigilantia* was introduced to replace the previous term *sub ductu*, in order to make clear that the function of the teaching office is not to lead the way—progress is the concern of scholarship; the teaching office has the basically negative function of setting limits and of marking off impenetrable terrain.[4]

It follows that the Catholic exegete is not, or ought not to be, hampered by the teaching office of the Church. The Constitution text goes much further when it declares that the labors of exegetes will help to speed the surer judgment of the Church in scriptural matters. The truth of the statement is illustrated by official documents. Thus *Divino Afflante Spiritu*, rightly regarded as the "Magna Carta" of Catholic biblical scholarship, would have been impossible without the dedicated work of certain enlightened scholars from the turn of the century onwards. Even more strikingly, the 1964 *Instruction* of the Biblical Commission reflects the positive achievement of Catholic scholars since 1943 (the date of *Divino Afflante Spiritu*). Most remarkable of all is the consistent scriptural orientation and flavor of the decrees and constitutions of Vatican II. The teaching office of the Church has thus acknowledged its indebtedness to Scripture scholars and other theologians who are fully in touch with the revival of biblical studies. The hierarchy has indeed the role of guiding the Church, but bishops, individually and collectively—as the Second Vatican Council has dramatically shown—need to be informed if their guiding hand is to be a help. Besides, the Spirit, like the wind, blows where it wills. It is not too much to expect that those who study the inspired Scriptures with dedication, humility and in the service of the Church, may confidently hope to receive a measure of enlightenment from the Spirit, and so may contribute, in some degree, to the Church's ever-growing awareness and understanding of the Word of God.

---

[1] J. L. McKenzie, *Dictionary of the Bible* (Milwaukee: Bruce, 1965), 513.

[2] P. Benoit, *Prophecy and Inspiration* (New York: Desclée, 1961), 168.

[3] E.g. Mt. 16:16-19—the primacy of Peter (Denz. 1822 f); Mt. 26:26 f—the Eucharist (Denz. 974).

[4] See W. J. Harrington, *The Path of Biblical Theology* (Dublin: Gill and Macmillan, 1973), 384-91.

FOUR

THE CANON OF SCRIPTURE

CANON AND CANONICITY
DEUTEROCANONICAL AND APOCRYPHAL BOOKS
THE FORMATION OF THE CANON
THE NATURE OF CANONICITY

At the beginning of this study we listed the books of the Bible, now we have to examine the reason, or reasons, why we have accepted these books, and these only, as making up the body of inspired Scripture. We have to understand, too, why they are authoritative.

1. CANON AND CANONICITY

The Greek term *kanōn* meant originally a "measuring rod" and then, in a derived sense, a "rule" or "norm." The Fathers used the word "canon" for the "rule of faith," and the canon of Scripture was regarded as the written rule of faith. The idea which eventually prevailed was that of a determined collection of writings constituting a rule of faith. Ultimately the canon of Scripture came to mean what we understand by it today: the collection of divinely-inspired books received by the Church and recognized by her as the infallible rule of faith and morals in virtue of their divine origin. We may note that the designation "canonical," applied to Scripture, may be taken in an active or passive sense: (1) active—the Bible as the rule of faith and morals; (2) passive—the Bible as officially received by the Church.

Canonicity means that an inspired book, destined for the Church, has been received as such by her. Although all the canonical books are inspired, and no inspired book exists outside the canon, nevertheless the notions of canonicity and inspiration are not the same. The books are inspired because God is their author; they are canonical because the Church has recognized them and acknowledged them to be inspired. For, the Church alone, by means of revelation, can recognize the supernatural fact of inspiration. Recognition by the Church adds nothing to the inspiration of a book, but it does clothe the book with absolute authority from the point of view of faith, and at the same time it is the sign and guarantee of inspiration.

2. DEUTEROCANONICAL AND APOCRYPHAL BOOKS

When we compare Catholic and Protestant versions of the Old Testament, we find that the latter lists 39 books—as does the Hebrew Bible—whereas Catholics accept 45 books.[1] This discrepancy, obviously a major problem in its own right, has also given rise to a confusing terminology. The disputed books are the following: Tobit; Judith; Wisdom; Sirach; Baruch; 1,2 Maccabees; together with parts of Esther and Daniel (that is, Est. 10:4—16:24; Dn. 3:24-90; 13-14). Catholics call these the *deuterocanonical* books—an unfortunate designation since it seems to imply that they are not of the same authority as the other books. What is really meant is that there was a certain hesitation about having them universally accepted as canonical, that is, as Scripture. By contrast, the *protocanonical* books are those whose claims have never been doubted in the Church. The deuterocanonical books of the Old Testament, together with 3,4 Esdras and the Prayer of Manasseh, are called the *Apocrypha* by Protestants, that is, "books which are not held equal to the sacred Scriptures, and nevertheless are useful and good to read" (Luther). Certain books of the New Testament (that is, Hebrews; James; 2 Peter; 2,3 John; Jude; Apocalypse) which, in the early Christian centuries, raised doubts or hesitancy in some quarters, are also called deuterocanonical; but these are now accepted by all Christians.

The name *Apocrypha* is applied by Catholics to certain

Jewish and Christian writings which made some pretension to divine authority, but which, in fact, are not inspired Scripture. The Old Testament Apocrypha, the products of Judaism, are attributed to various patriarchs and prophets and reflect the religious and moral ideas of the Jewish world from the second century B.C. to the first century A.D. The New Testament Apocrypha are works of Christian origin. Attributed for the most part to apostles, they reflect the beliefs, doctrines, and traditions of certain circles, both orthodox and heretical, in the first centuries of the Church.

The confusion, mentioned above, is apparent: the term Apocrypha has one meaning for Catholics and an entirely different meaning for Protestants. The Apocrypha in the Catholic sense are designated *Pseudepigrapha* by Protestants.

3. THE FORMATION OF THE CANON

The one entirely sufficient criterion of the fact of inspiration is the testimony of the Church; and the Church, in the Council of Trent, formally defined the extent of the canon. Although the question, as a dogmatic issue, is thereby settled for Roman Catholics, the following sketch of the formation of the canon of both Testaments is of real historical interest.

1) History of the Canon of the Old Testament

In the first century A.D. the Jews possessed a collection of sacred books which they held to be inspired by God and in which they saw the expression of the divine will, a rule of faith and morals. The witness of Josephus (*Contra Apionem* 1:8), of 4 Esd. (14:37-48), and of the Talmud is decisive. These books, distributed among the three divisions of Law, Prophets, and Writings, include all our protocanonical books. The New Testament is also a valuable witness because it contains quotations or allusions from most of these books; its silence in regard to the others is not significant, since there is no reason why all the Old

Testament books should have been quoted. The threefold division is indicated: "Moses and the Prophets" (Lk. 24:27); "Moses, the Prophets, and the psalms" (Lk. 24:44).

The traditional division into Law, Prophets, and Writings—in that order—would seem to indicate, too, the chronological acceptance of each group of books. The *Pentateuch* took final shape in the fifth century, and from the time of Ezra the Jews accepted and officially recognized the collection of the Mosaic books as a sacred code. The majority of the books that make up the second division (the "Former Prophets": Jos.-Kgs.; and the "Latter Prophets": Is.; Jer.; Ezek. and the twelve minor prophets) would have been accepted at about the same time. However, the collection cannot have been finally closed until sometime after the last of the prophets (the author of Zeph. 9-14), sometime in the late fourth century. Sirach (46:1—49:10) testifies that the list was complete before 180. We may safely conclude that the collection of Prophets was fixed in the first half of the second century, and from that time took its place side-by-side with the Law of Moses. The third group is composite and seems to have grown up around the collection of Psalms. Five books, the *Megilloth* (rolls)—Ct.; Ru.; Lam.; Qoh.; Est.—were read in the liturgy of the great feasts. The Chronicler's work (Chr.-Ez.-Neh.) comes last in the list. The group took shape between the fourth century and the end of the second century (cf. 1 Mc. 1:59 f.; 2 Mc. 3:14).

It should be noted that none of the three collections was established by an official decision, that is, placed among the books that had, in practice, been accepted. It is not surprising, then, to find differences in outlook. The position that we have considered, one which limited the canon to older and traditional books, is that of Pharisaism. We know that the Sadducees regarded only the *Pentateuch* as canonical. On the other hand, in Alexandria and in Qumran it was felt that God had not yet spoken his last word and that an inspired message might still be accepted. Thus, in the Diaspora,[2] our deuterocanonical books were accorded a real authority and it seems that the community

at Qumran had attributed a similar authority to certain of
their sectarian writings.

At the time of Christ there was still some uncertainty
about the canon and the canonicity of certain books. It is
not until after the destruction of Jerusalem (70 A.D.) that
a group of Jewish doctors, seeking to preserve what remained of the past, met at Jamnia (= Yavne, 30 miles
west of Jerusalem) about 90 A.D. and formally accepted
the strict Pharisaic canon. On various grounds, including
the fact that the Greek Bible had been adopted by Christians, certain of the books that formed part of that Bible
(in effect, our deuterocanonical books) were rejected. The
ruling of the Synod of Jamnia was a decision for Jews
only—and they henceforth accepted the shorter list. It
could not be of universal import because the Church had
now replaced the synagogue. At the time of the Reforma-
tion, the Protestants, wishing to make translations directly
from the Hebrew, became keenly aware of this discrepancy; they ended by regarding the Jewish canon as the
authentic one.

The Christian Church developed in the milieu of the
Diaspora. In practice, the Bible of the Church was the
Greek Bible; hence we find that citations in the New Testament are regularly from the LXX (Septuagint)—and these
include explicit citations from at least three of the deuterocanonical books: Sir.; 2 Mc.; Wis. Most of the apostolic
Fathers accepted the Old Testament as they found it in the
LXX, or in the Old Latin versions based on the Greek. In
the East, however, the differences between the books accepted in Palestine and Alexandria was kept in mind; this
was an important factor in the controversy with Palestinian Jews. Hence Justin (second century), arguing with
Trypho; Melito, bishop of Sardis (second century), in a
list of accepted books; and Origen (third century) followed the Palestinian canon, as did Eusebius, Athanasius,
Cyril of Jerusalem, Epiphanius, and Gregory Nazianzen
(fourth century). So too did some of the Latin Fathers who
were influenced by the Greeks, notably Rufinus and Jerome (fifth century).

The sixtieth canon of the Council of Laodicea (c. 360)

supports the impression that the attitude of the East was, on the whole, unfavorable to the deuterocanonical books; for the Old Testament, it lists the books of the Hebrew Bible only. It is to be noted, however, that the Fathers admitted that these books could be read for the edification of the faithful and were useful for the instruction of catechumens. Besides, they often expressed great esteem for the books, admitting them for liturgical worship side-by-side with the others, and even cited them with the formulas: "It is written"; "God says in Scripture."

The attitude of the Eastern Fathers (together with Rufinus and Jerome) can be explained by two principal factors: 1) In controversy with the Jews, in order to have a common ground of argument, the Fathers confined themselves to the accepted Jewish canon. 2) Jewish apocrypha, making claims to canonicity, were in circulation; thus all books had to be carefully scrutinized, and the credentials of the deuterocanonical books did not seem to be quite as convincing as those of the others.

In the Western Church, however, no distinction was made between protocanonical and deuterocanonical books. Through the influence of St. Augustine, in reaction to St. Jerome and the Eastern attitude, the Councils of Hippo (393) and of Carthage (397 and 419) declared the disputed books to be canonical; Pope Innocent I did the same in a letter to Exsuperius of Toulouse (405). Therefore the complete canon as it was to be defined in the Council of Trent may be dated from St. Augustine. The Greeks later came around to the Western view, and at the Council "in Trullo" (692) accepted the entire canon.

2) *History of the Canon of the New Testament*

The Christian Church possessed, from the first day of its existence, a canon of inspired Scripture: the Old Testament. But for the early Church this Old Testament was, in its deepest sense, a prophecy of Christ—an acknowledgement that even here the ultimate authority was Christ himself. Christ had commissioned his Apostles to preach the Good News and to build up the Christian community, and had filled them with the power of the Holy Spirit. They had been eyewitnesses of his work and hearers of his words; and their importance was still greater in post-apostolic times. Therefore the early Church had three authorities: the Old Testament; the Lord; and the Apostles. But the ultimate, decisive authority was Christ the Lord, who spoke immediately in his words and works and mediately in the testimony of his witnesses.

In the beginning the words of the Lord and the account of his deeds were repeated and related by word of mouth, but soon they began to be written down. In their missionary work, the Apostles found it necessary to write to certain communities. Some, at least, of these writings were exchanged among the churches and soon gained the same authority as the writings of the Old Testament. It is understandable, however, that some time elapsed before the collection of these writings from the time of the Apostles had taken its place with unquestioned authority beside the books of the Old Testament, especially when it is taken into account that many were occasional writings addressed to individual churches.

The written words of the Lord, the Gospels, although they are not the earliest New Testament writings, were the first set on a par with the Old Testament and recognized as canonical. About 140, Papias, bishop of Hierapolis in Phrygia, knows Mark and Matthew. Justin (c. 150) cites the Gospels as an authority. Hegesippus (c. 180) speaks of the "Law and the Prophets and the Lord." The martyrs of Scili in Numidia (180) have as sacred writings "the books, and the epistles of Paul, a just man"; only the Old Testament and the Gospels were called "Books," that is, Scripture. The writings of the apostolic Fathers furnish certain proof that, from the first decades of the second century, the great churches possessed a book, or a group of books, which was commonly known as "Gospel" and to which reference was made as to a document that was authoritative and universally known.

It is likely that already towards the end of the first century, or in the beginning of the second century, thirteen Pauline epistles (excluding Heb.) were known in Greece,

Asia Minor, and Italy. All the manuscripts and text-forms of the Pauline epistles spring from one collection that agrees with our *Corpus Paulinum*. True, early collections show variations in the order of the epistles, but the number of writings remained the same. There is no quotation from Paul that is not taken from one of the canonical epistles, even though it is certain that the Apostle wrote other letters. Thus, about the year 125, there were two groups of writings which enjoyed the apostolic guarantee and whose authority was acknowledged by all the communities that possessed them. But there was no official pronouncement, and the collections varied from church to church.

We have little account of other apostolic writings in the first half of the second century. Clement knew Heb.; Polycarp knew 1 Pt. and 1 Jn.; Papias knew 1 Pt., 1 Jn., and Ap. In the second half of the century, Acts, Ap., and at least 1 Jn. and 1 Pt. were regarded as canonical; they took their place beside the Gospels and the Pauline epistles. We may note four factors which influenced the formation of the New Testament canon: (1) the many apocrypha which the Church rejected; (2) the heresy of Marcion who had set up his own canon, which consisted of an expurgated Lk. and ten epistles of Paul (excluding the pastorals and Heb.); (3) the Montanist heretics, who claimed further revelations from the Holy Spirit; (4) the great abundance of Gnostic writings.

It is generally admitted that, at the beginning of the third century, the New Testament canon comprised most, if not all, of the canonical books. The earliest list we have is that of the Muratorian fragment, a document discovered in the Ambrosian Library, Milan, in 1740; it gives the books which were accepted in Rome about the year 200. No mention is made of Heb., 1,2 Pt., 3 Jn., and Jas. The Chester Beatty papyri (P^{45}, P^{46}, P^{47})—first half of third century—contain all the New Testament writings except the Catholic Epistles. It may be seen that Jas., 2 Pt., 2,3 Jn., and Jude were not accepted immediately, while Heb. and Ap. encountered some opposition in the West and East respectively.

In fact we find that the attitude towards these books varied in the great churches: Greek, Latin, and Syriac. The Greeks tended to distinguish books which were "received by all" from books which were "questioned," the latter being Jas., Jude, 2 Pt., and 2,3 Jn. The Johannine authorship, and consequently the canonicity, of Ap. was frequently contested. However, in the second half of the fourth century, Cyril of Jerusalem, the Council of Laodicea, and Gregory Nazianzen testify to the full canon, minus Ap.; while Basil, Gregory of Nyssa, and Epiphanius include the latter also. Athanasius, in 367, enumerates all 27 books, and it may be said that, from this time, the canon was fixed. The canonicity of Ap., although discussed by some theologians in the fifth and sixth centuries, was eventually accepted without question, partly under the influence of the West where there was never any doubt about it.

The churches of the West were, on the whole, faithful in retaining the books which had been confided to them as coming from Apostles, but they made some difficulty about accepting as canonical those whose apostolic origin was not apparent. From Cyprian and Tertullian we learn that Heb., Jas., and 2 Pt. were not part of the collection of the African Church towards the middle of the third century. Furthermore our evidence supports the view that, at this time, the same was true throughout Latin Christendom. In the fourth century the evidence shows that the authority of Heb. and the Catholic Epistles was being more and more recognized in the West—at the very time that Ap. was a subject of discussion in the Greek Church. The Latin canon was, as we have seen, confirmed in Africa by the Councils of Hippo and Carthage, and in Italy by the letter of Innocent I to Exsuperius.

The Syrian Church of the first centuries was, in part, Greek-speaking, with its center at Antioch; and, in part, Syriac-speaking, with its center at Edessa; the attitude to the New Testament writings was not the same in each area. At Antioch, by the end of the second century, the collection of New Testament books included all except 2

Pt., 2,3 Jn., and Jude. A century later the authority of Ap. was contested; and 2 Pt., 2,3 Jn., and Ap. did not appear in the fifth-century canon of Antioch. In the sixth century there was a reaction in favor of Ap., and later the shorter epistles were accepted. St. John Damascene (d. 754) had the complete canon.

In Edessa the situation was different. Towards the end of the second century, Tatian, a disciple of Justin, made a harmony of the four Gospels in Greek, the Diatessaron— *to dia tessarōn* (*euaggelion*)—which he translated into Syriac about the year 172. It was adopted as the official text at Edessa, and remained the official text until it was supplanted by the Peshitto. At the beginning of the fifth century, the Peshitto became the official text; and Jas., 1 Pt., and 1 Jn. entered the Syriac canon. When, after the Councils of Ephesus (431) and Chalcedon (451), the Syrian Church divided into two heretical sects, the Nestorians remained faithful to the incomplete canon of the Peshitto, while the Monophysites also accepted 2 Pt., Jude, 2,3 Jn., and Ap.

Although the Latin Church canon was fixed in the fifth century, we find that doubts were raised in some quarters respecting the apostolic origin of many writings of the New Testament (Heb., Jas., 2 Pt., 2,3 Jn.). Discussions regarding Heb. persisted into the Middle Ages and final doubts were allayed only by the authority of Thomas Aquinas and Nicholas of Lyra who maintained that the epistle was Pauline. In the sixteenth century the question was raised once more. Erasmus (d. 1536) found himself censured by the theologians of the Sorbonne for querying the apostolic origin of Heb., Jas., 2 Pt., 2,3 Jn., and Ap. —although he did not deny their canonicity. Cardinal Cajetan (d. 1534) held much the same view. Today almost all scholars agree that Heb. and 2 Pt. were not written by Apostles and that the author of Jas. is not the Apostle of the same name; while the authenticity of Jn., Ap., and certain of the Pauline epistles is widely questioned. We must look at the criterion of canonicity.

4. THE NATURE OF CANONICITY

It follows from the history of the formation of the canon that the Church was guided in part by the practice and teaching of Christ and his apostles who certainly regarded the Old Testament as the word of God. And it was the Church that declared the Old Testament canonical once for all. But how can the Church have known which books of the New Testament are inspired? This cannot be established, it seems, for the individual books. It is not likely that writers, unaware of their own inspiration, could have revealed the inspiration of a particular book; and even if they were aware of their own inspiration it has to be shown that they have in fact revealed the inspiration of certain books. Yet, the inspiration of a group of writings is part of revealed truth which must date from the apostolic age, that is, from the first generation of the Church, the period of its coming into being. Historical research suggests that, in deciding which New Testament books are inspired, it is to the principle of apostolicity that the Church had recourse. But the criterion invoked by the Fathers is not always the apostolic origin of the books in a strict sense; they sometimes regard the apostles not as the authors of the books, but as the first link in the chain of tradition which finds its expression in the books.

It is arbitrary to assert that the apostles, or one apostle, "had left behind a formal and explicit revelation on the inspired nature of the New Testament writings *in individuo,* in some statement which directly expressed this revelation";[3] such a view is excluded by the complicated history of the canon and the long hesitation about certain books. It follows that "inspiration has to be conceived of in such a manner that it demonstrates by itself how the Church knows the inspiration of the books of the New Testament, without the necessity of having recourse to any statement about it in apostolic times that has no historical support."[4] It is true that ultimately the inspiration of a writing can be known only through revelation; the question is how this revelation is to be conceived. Since Scripture was born of and with the Church, the Church has no need of the explicit revelation of an apostle in order to be able to recognize the inspired books: it recognizes them connaturally. The required revelation is given by the fact that the relevant writing emerges as a genuine self-expression of the primitive Church. And there can be a time lag between the revelation of the inspired character of certain books and the clear expression of this fact. The Church, in practice, had a canon before there was any theory of canonicity or list of canonical books. This explains the hesitancy about the inspiration of certain writings.

Some New Testament scholars, mostly German and notably E. Käsemann, have argued for a "canon within the canon." They find "early Catholicism"—the initial stage of sacramentalism, hierarchy, ordination, dogma: the distinctive features of *Catholic* Christianity, in certain New Testament writings, particularly the Pastorals, Acts and 2 Peter. These—on the whole, later—writings should be regarded as secondary, while the writings such as Galatians and Romans, which form "the center of the New Testament," should be regarded as truly normative for Christians. This extreme and unacceptable position is, however, prompted by a real question. The fact is that Christians have been selective. Roman Catholics have chosen to accept and develop the "early Catholic" tendencies in the New Testament and have neglected the looser Church organization and the more charismatic atmosphere of the primitive period. The following observation is fully justified and is thought-provoking:

"The Church must certainly reassess her usage in light of those biblical theologies that she has *not* followed in order to be certain that what God meant to teach her through such theological views will not be lost. For example, if the Church has chosen to follow as normative the ecclesiastical structure attested in the Pastorals (bishop/ presbyters, deacons), she must ask herself does she continue to do proportionate justice to the charismatic and freer spirit of the earlier period. A choice between the two was necessary and this choice was guided by the Spirit of God; but the structure that was not chosen still has something to teach the Church and can serve as a modifying corrective on the choice that was made. Only thus is the Church faithful to the whole New Testament. In New Testament times the Church was ecumenical enough to embrace those who, while sharing the one faith, held very different theological views. The Church of today can be no less ecumenical."[5]

---

[1] This makes a difference of six books, whereas we go on to list seven. The explanation is that Lamentations, appended to Jeremiah in Catholic editions, is a separate book in Hebrew and Protestant Bibles.

[2] The Diaspora ("dispersion") was the ensemble of Jews who lived outside Palestine, "dispersed" throughout the civilized world.

[3] K. Rahner, *Inspiration in the Bible* (New York: Herder & Herder, 1961), 27.

[4] *Ibid.,* 29.

[5] R. E. Brown, "Canonicity," *The Jerome Biblical Commentary* II (Englewood Cliffs, N.J.: Prentice-Hall, 1968), 533.

FIVE

BIBLICAL CRITICISM

TEXTUAL CRITICISM
LITERARY CRITICISM
HISTORICAL CRITICISM

From the first we have stressed the human aspect of the Bible; and it is from the human standpoint that we have, in the main, considered it. Nevertheless we have not overlooked the divine aspect of Scripture. The fundamental fact of inspiration and the matter of secondary senses presuppose the divine authorship of Scripture; indeed these are realities only for one who acknowledges a divine Author. Thus it is that the Catholic scholar can never take an entirely detached view of the Bible. He may, and must, use the scientific methods at his disposal; but he is committed to a belief in the divine message of the human words he studies. This does not make his approach any less objective: as a scholar he must deal honestly and courageously with the facts; and for him, the divine authorship of Scripture—which he accepts on faith—is the basic fact. All things being equal, he is in a better position to understand the word of God than others. This does not mean, however, that writers who take an incomplete view of the Bible have not contributed mightily to our knowledge of Scripture. The Catholic exegete is not hampered by his faith: he is enlightened by it. And in this age of *Divino Afflante Spiritu* and Vatican II the Catholic scholar is certainly not hampered by the supreme teaching authority of the Church.

But he is faithful to the Church and to the confidence placed in him only if he sees the Bible for what it is: words of God *in words of men*. He must approach his task in a spirit of scientific freedom, applying to the Bible the principles of textual, literary, and historical criticism.

Rational interpretation applies to the Bible the rules of interpretation of any literary work; only the human aspect of Scripture is taken into account. Hence the Bible comes under a threefold criticism: textual, literary, and historical.

1. TEXTUAL CRITICISM

Textual criticism investigates the alterations which may have occurred in the text of a document with a view to restoring it to its original form. The directive principles of textual criticism are the same for all sorts of writing, although their application varies with the documents under consideration, especially with the number, the variety, and the quality of the texts to be examined. As applied to the books of the Bible, its object is to *classify* the numerous variants found in the manuscript tradition and to *choose* those that have the best chance of representing the original reading. Thus we must find out how the changes in the text may have come about (*verbal criticism*). Then we must consider the value of the witnesses of each variant (*external criticism*) and the intrinsic quality of each reading (*internal criticism*). In illustrating the principles of textual criticism, we shall confine ourselves to the New Testament.

1) Verbal Criticism

The New Testament has come to us in many shapes and via a multitude of scribes. From the beginning, until the invention of printing, it was copied and recopied from century to century. During this long process there was time and room for many alterations in the text.

INVOLUNTARY VARIANTS There is no such person as an infallible copyist; hence involuntary variants are to be found in the manuscripts of the books of the New Testament which have been copied over and over, often by amateur scribes. Involuntary variants come about through *dittography* (the faulty repetition of a letter, syllable, word, or group of words), and its opposite, *haplography* (the writing only once of letters, syllables, and words that ought to be written twice). Part of a text, even a whole paragraph, can be omitted through *homoioteleuton*, that is, through words, lines, or parts of a phrase having similar endings: the eye slips from one to the other. Letters that look alike or are sounded alike (in dictation), may be easily confused; and, because of poor penmanship, words may be mistakenly read or copied. Other changes are frequent, but less well defined.

INTENTIONAL Such variants, although deliberate, do not VARIANTS necessarily argue ill will on the part of a scribe. "When there was any doubt about the original text —since it was desired that the actual text to be read, studied, and taken as the rule of faith and life should be perfect —the copyist, convinced that he was doing a good work, was bold in his corrections, his additions, and suppressions; and he grew bolder as his intention became purer."[1]

A common tendency was to make corrections in spelling, grammar, and style; it was a temptation that copyists who prided themselves on their command of Greek found difficult to resist. Another widespread tendency was to achieve harmony and conformity by smoothing out discrepancies between parallel texts, between passages of the Synoptic Gospels, for instance. Exegetical and doctrinal corrections are not infrequent: difficulties were explained, or were avoided by suppressions. An example of explanation is "For the unbelieving husband is sanctified by the wife" (1 Cor. 7:14)—some add *"believing* wife." An example of suppression is: "There were also two other malefactors led with him" (Lk. 23:32)—"other" is sometimes dropped.

2) *External Criticism*

This branch of textual criticism is called *external* because it relies solely upon the authority of the documents containing the readings, rather than on the intrinsic quality of the readings. In determining the value of a variant, the age, number, and character of the manuscripts are to be given due weight, but they do not suffice to determine, beyond doubt, the original form of any reading. Eventually, we must look to the text itself.

3) *Internal Criticism*

Internal criticism is an estimation, according to the text and context, of the intrinsic value of variant readings. While numerous rules have been suggested, it seems that only two criteria are valid:[2]

1. *On examining the text* the critic will choose that variant which offers the best explanation of all the others and cannot itself be explained by the others. The variants must be compared one by one in detail; some will quickly appear secondary; from the rest, it will sometimes be possible to single out one reading that stands as the origin of the others. Admittedly, it is not easy to apply the principle; thus a decision is always a matter of delicate judgment.

2. *On examining the context* the critic will choose that reading which best accords with the writer's special tendencies. Not only the method of the writer, his vocabulary, his grammar, his style, and his manner of quoting must be considered, but also his purpose, his ideas, his temperament. This sense of "feeling" for a writing, although not easily defined, can be of great help to the critic in his search for the original reading. Parallel passages, and the variants of these passages, must be taken into account.

This hasty outline will, at least, have suggested that textual criticism is a highly specialized art, the art of bringing a balanced judgment to bear on a text in the light of the information furnished by the manuscript tradition. It is a dedicated task, for the textual critic should combine "a scrupulous observance of all the laws of criticism with the deepest reverence for the sacred text."[3]

2. LITERARY CRITICISM

Once the text has been established, its meaning must be studied and determined. This is the work of literary criticism which examines, first of all, the language and composition of the text, then investigates the literary character of a book to establish its literary form, and finally decides whether a book is authentic or whether it has been retouched.

1) The Language

The importance of philological study of the sacred text has been stressed in *Divino Afflante Spiritu*.

It follows that a knowledge of the biblical languages—Hebrew, Greek, and Aramaic—is essential. The exegete must study the vocabulary, grammar, and style of a writing; he should take note of technical terms and should not overlook the fact that words may change in use and meaning over the centuries. The context (the link and mutual relationship between any part of a writing and those parts which precede and follow it) must be kept in mind. Indeed, a text or passage should not be considered in isolation, for it can be fully understood only in its context. The study of parallel passages, too, where such exist, is often of great help in understanding a text.

2) The Composition

The next stage is to try to divine the author's plan, to identify his sources, if any, and to establish his literary form. This is difficult, because no biblical writing has a table of contents or even a division into chapters;[4] none is provided with a system of reference (although certain books do mention their sources), and the literary form is not always self-evident.

ANALYSIS OF THE CONTENTS OF A BOOK   This may enable us to discover the plan of the author and the unfolding of his thought or, at least, his method of procedure. There is danger here of subjectivity, of reading one's own ideas into the work that is being studied.

ONE MUST TRY TO TRACE THE AUTHOR'S SOURCES   While it is sometimes demonstrable that biblical writers

did use sources, and is highly probable in other cases, it is
always difficult to define the extent of a writer's debt to
others. Nor is it always possible to be sure that a writer
has followed a well-defined source, whether written or
oral. Nevertheless, this study has enormously helped our
understanding of many biblical books, for example, the
Pentateuch and the Synoptic Gospels.

THE LITERARY   We treated of this matter earlier; here it
FORM   will suffice to note that the encyclical
Divino Afflante Spiritu has stressed the importance of de-
termining the literary form of a biblical writing.

The point is this: the biblical writers adopted the literary
forms in use among their contemporaries; thus only when
we know what these literary forms were can we surely
interpret any given book. A further difficulty lies in prov-
ing that a biblical book, or part of a book, belongs to such
and such a literary form. Once the fact has been established, however, the interpretation of the book or passage
is easier and more assured. Conversely, failure to recognize
or to admit a given literary form will lead, inevitably, to
misinterpretation. Account must be taken, too, of the personal style of a writer, particularly when different writers
make use of the same literary form. For instance, the
cultivated style of Isaiah is not that of the shepherd Amos,
and St. Luke is far more literary than St. Mark.

3) *The Origin of a Writing*

We trace the origin of a book by getting back to its author
and to the circumstances in which it was written; the more
we know about the author the better. If possible, we must
fix the date and place of composition of the writing as well
as the purpose for which it was written, and we must discover to whom it was addressed. Normally we have two
kinds of evidence to go on: *external* and *intrinsic*.

EXTERNAL   Quotations in contemporary or later writings
EVIDENCE   may help us to identify the author of a biblical
book, or at least assure us of his existence at or before a
given date. In principle, external evidence carries more

weight than intrinsic evidence, but the testimony has to be carefully scrutinized, first concerning its genuineness and then to determine its exact sense. The various external witnesses, taken together, form a tradition; this tradition will be evaluated according to its early origin and its constancy.

INTRINSIC EVIDENCE This is based on an examination of the content and character of a work. It may confirm or weaken the testimony of tradition. We have, first of all, the express indications of the text; but here we must beware of pseudonymity, that is, the well-known device of attributing a book to a famous personage (for example, many of the wisdom books are, conventionally, attributed to Solomon). Then a study of language and style, of historical and geographical data, and of the doctrine will help us to determine the origin of a work. The result of such a study will often be negative, that is, we shall conclude that a given book cannot have been the work of the traditional author or cannot have been written in a particular epoch. Not infrequently, however, intrinsic evidence will confirm the authenticity of a book.

Here, *authenticity* is a technical term. A writing is *authentic* if it is shown that the person to whom it is traditionally ascribed did in fact write it; conversely it is called *inauthentic*. It should be clearly understood that *authenticity* and *inspiration* are distinct. Inspiration means that the author of a given writing was moved by the Holy Spirit—whether or not we can name that author is another matter. Thus, if it becomes clear that a writing is *inauthentic,* its inspiration is in no way affected: the eventual author, whoever he may have been, was inspired.

3. HISTORICAL CRITICISM

It is not sufficient to know the purpose and content of a scriptural book; it must be established as a trustworthy document. This is the work of historical criticism. But if a biblical writing is to be fairly judged, it must be seen in its true environment. What has been said in an earlier chapter about the background of the Bible is relevant here, for this is the first aspect that should be taken into account. A book must be set in its social milieu if it is to be understood and if its message is to be correctly read.

The historian will understand the data of the text only if he has a grasp of the laws that rule human society. History is not a collection of documents nor a catalogue of archaeological discoveries: it is a sharing in the life of men of a bygone age; and despite social, economic, and technical differences men of all ages are much alike. The good historian is aware of the enduring laws of human life and is able to conjure up the conditions of the epoch he is dealing with. Hence a proper appreciation of the past demands two things: (1) that one should have worked out, by study and experience, the unchanging laws which apply to past and present alike; (2) that one has enough imagination, guided by objective data, to reconstruct the situations and problems of another age.[5]

Clearly, the task of placing a Scripture text in its proper historical milieu is not always simple. The shorter the text, the more difficult this is; hence, for instance, the wide margin of disagreement in dating many of the psalms. In order to form a judgment we have to fall back on the results of literary criticism.

For a long time our knowledge of the biblical environment was derived exclusively from the Bible itself. Since the end of the last century, however, the situation has changed radically. The change is due to archaeological discoveries which have not only supplemented biblical data, but have brought to light whole civilizations that had disappeared, apparently without trace, and a rich and varied literature whose existence was not even suspected. Indeed today we are more accurately informed concerning certain periods of world history than of the corresponding period of Israelite history. Israel is no longer seen in isolation, but plays its part on a vast stage, a part that, humanly speaking, is scarcely more than that of an extra. The result is not only a better grasp of Israel's history, but a deeper appreciation of the mystery of God's choice. We see, as never before, how exact is Israel's awareness of her true dimension: "It was not because you were more in number than any other people that the Lord set his love upon you and chose you, for you were the fewest of all peoples" (Dt. 7:7).

Archaeology is concerned both with material remains and with inscriptions and texts. The former are indispensable for the reconstruction of Israelite history; the latter, however, have thrown more light on the text of the Bible, for "nothing can eliminate the stubborn fact that the Bible is a written document and will thus be illuminated more directly by written sources, especially when they belong to the same period."[6] This is why the Ugaritic texts (several thousand clay tablets and fragments unearthed during excavations at Ugarit—modern Ras Shamra on the Syrian coast—and dating from between 1400 and 1200 B.C.) have shed more light on the text of the Bible than all the non-epigraphic finds yet made in Palestine. Similarly the Qumran texts have notably illustrated the background of the New Testament.

The Catholic exegete is confident that the truth of the Bible will emerge triumphant from this comparison with human sources of information; evidently, an accurate notion of inerrancy is presupposed. Yet he is not preoccupied with apologetical considerations. He is aware that the surest, indeed the only way, to solve outstanding problems is to push ahead, without hesitation and boldly, the scientific criticism of the biblical text. Indeed, he must be prepared to make mistakes, to take wrong turnings, for it is only by following every line that our understanding of Scripture will deepen; and, after all, to map out and signpost a cul-de-sac is a positive achievement. All the while the scholar will be guided by his own critical faculty and by the searching scrutiny of his colleagues. Catholic biblical scholarship has come very far during the past fifty years. It is now serenely sure of itself and it seems certain that the next half-century must bring results that will dwarf the notable achievements of our own day.

---

[1] M.-J. Lagrange, "Project de critique textuelle rationnelle du N.T.," *Revue Biblique*, 42 (1933), 495.

[2] See L. Vaganay, *Introduction to the Textual Criticism of the New Testament,* trans. B. V. Miller (London: Sands, 1937), pp. 87-89.

[3] Pope Pius XII, *Divino Afflante Spiritu* (London: C.T.S.), n. 24.

[4] The division of the Bible into chapters dates from the thirteenth century. It is due to Stephen Langdon (d. 1228), archbishop of Canterbury, and was designed for facility of reference. The verse division was introduced in 1551 by the printer Robert Stephen (Estienne).

[5] See A. Robert and A. Feuillet, *Introduction à la Bible* (Tournai: Desclée, 1957), I, p. 161.

[6] W. F. Albright, *Peake's Commentary on the Bible* (London: Nelson, 1962²), n. 45 a.

SIX

AN OUTLINE HISTORY OF ISRAEL

THE WORLD OF ISRAEL'S ORIGINS

THE PATRIARCHS

EXODUS AND CONQUEST

THE PERIOD OF JUDGES

THE RISE OF THE MONARCHY

THE DIVIDED MONARCHY

THE KINGDOM OF ISRAEL

THE KINGDOM OF JUDAH

EXILE AND RESTORATION

THE WORK OF NEHEMIAH AND EZRA

FROM EZRA TO ANTIOCHUS IV

THE MACCABAEAN REVOLT AND THE HASMONAEAN
DYNASTY

Israel came face to face with her God at the moment of her emergence as a nation. Henceforth she was aware that God would constantly intervene in her history, and she came to know that he, the Creator, was active in all the events of history. Under his hand, nations came into being and passed away, and some of them, obeying his bidding though they did not know him, were instruments of punishment for his people or were its providential deliverers. The Bible, a faithful reflection of the life and faith of Israel, cannot be divorced from the history of Israel; indeed, it can be understood only in this context. To begin this study of the Old Testament, we shall set down, in sequence and as a whole, an outline of Israel's history. This provides the necessary setting and, as a conveniently built-in work of reference, will help our presentation of the wide and involved field of the Old Testament.

1. THE WORLD OF ISRAEL'S ORIGINS

Biblical history, in a strict sense, began with Abraham. He is a historical figure, a man of flesh and blood, even though we cannot establish when he was born or when he died; the best we can say is that he probably lived in the nineteenth or eighteenth century B.C. This means that Israel appeared late on the world stage, for great civilizations had already passed away. It will be helpful to sketch in lightly the distant and the immediate background of the patriarchal age.

1) The Ancient World in the Third Millennium B.C.

History, properly speaking, demands documentation by contemporary inscriptions that can be read by us. This condition is verified for the first time in the early third millennium B.C.

MESOPOTAMIA The creators of civilization in Lower Mesopotamia in the fourth millennium were the Sumerians, a people whose origin is still unknown. They invented cuneiform writing, made great progress in commerce, and developed a remarkably high culture. In the third millennium (c. 2800-2360 B.C.) we find them established in a system of city-states. Religion was highly organized and the temple scribes produced a vast body of literature; most of the epics and myths that are known to us in Assyrian and Babylonian versions were first given written form by the Sumerians.[1]

The Akkadians, a Semitic people, inhabited Mesopotamia at the same time as the Sumerians. They took over and adapted Sumerian culture and religion and, though their own language was entirely different, they borrowed the Sumerian cuneiform syllabic script. Eventually an Akkadian, Sargon, seized power and founded an empire which lasted for over a hundred years (c. 2360-2180 B.C.). The considerable literature of this period is in Akkadian.[2]

EGYPT In the early third millennium Egypt emerged into history as a unified nation; the kings of Upper Egypt had gained ascendancy over the whole land and the Old Kingdom (twenty-ninth to the twenty-third century B.C.) was founded. Egypt's classical age began with the rise of the Third Dynasty (c. 2600 B.C.). This was the period of the earliest pyramids, though the great pyramids were built in the Fourth Dynasty (twenty-sixth to the twenty-fifth century B.C.). Egyptian religion, like that of Mesopotamia, was a highly-developed polytheism; the texts of this period are almost entirely religious.

PALESTINE The early third millennium in Palestine was a time of great urban development and the towns, though small, were well built and strongly fortified, as excavations at Jericho, Megiddo, and elsewhere show. The population was predominantly Canaanite (a Semitic people). It is likely that Canaanite religion was already established as we know it from the Bible and from the fourteenth-century Ras Shamra texts. There are no Palestinian inscriptions from this millennium.

2) *The Eve of the Patriarchal Age*

MESOPOTAMIA The Akkadian Empire was brought to an end about 2180 B.C. by a barbarian people called the Guti. About a hundred years later the power of these invaders was broken by the Sumerians; here we witness a rebirth of Sumerian culture under the kings of the Third Dynasty of Ur (c. 2060-1950 B.C.). The founder of the dynasty, Ur-nammu, is known especially for his law code, the oldest we possess. However, the Akkadian language had entrenched itself during the ascendancy of Akkad, and by the eighteenth century Sumerian was no longer spoken, though it continued as a written language for centuries.

EGYPT The Old Empire came to an end in the twenty-third century B.C. and was followed by a period of disorder known as the First Intermediate (twenty-second to the twenty-first century B.C.). Internal disunity, with rival pharaohs claiming the throne, produced social chaos and

economic depression. The literature of the period[3] reflects
the prevalent spirit of dejection. About the middle of the
twenty-first century—roughly contemporaneous with the
Sumerian renaissance—the land was reunited by the first
kings of the Eleventh Dynasty. The beginning of the second millennium marked the start of another period of
stability, the Middle Kingdom.

PALESTINE Late in the third millennium Palestine suffered the shock of invasion by seminomadic peoples, during which most of the Canaanite towns were destroyed;
the twentieth century was the period of greatest disruption.
Though the newcomers settled in Palestine, the country
was not fully occupied, while in southern Transjordan
sedentary occupation ceased altogether. These newcomers
were part of a Semitic people called the Amorites.

We have seen that, long before Abraham was born,
great civilizations had not only existed but had waxed
strong and then waned, sometimes to waken again to a
fresh flowering. World history did not begin with Israel.
And yet, when the Lord called Abraham from his country
and his kindred and his father's house (Gn. 12:1) a history did begin—the *Heilsgeschichte,* God's saving history.
And though Israel, as a nation, emerged in the thirteenth
century, her roots are firmly fixed in the earlier centuries;
Abraham is indeed the father of this nation. Once again
we shall look at the contemporary scene in order to see
more clearly, silhouetted against that backdrop, the ancestors of the Chosen People.

3) The Patriarchal Age

MESOPOTAMIA The Third Dynasty of Ur came to an end
about 1950 B.C. A contributory factor in its fall was the
incursion of the Amorites; by the eighteenth century almost every state in Mesopotamia was ruled by Amorite
kings. They had adopted Sumerian and Akkadian culture
and wrote in Akkadian. Until the middle of that century
there was rivalry between the city-states of Lower Mesopotamia: Isin, Larsa, Mari, Babylon, and Elam. Two

newly-discovered law codes come from this period (both nineteenth century B.C.): one, in Akkadian, from Eshnunna; the other, in Sumerian, promulgated by Lipit-Ishtar of Isin.[4] Both show striking similarities with the Covenant Code (Ex. 21-23).

Mari and Assyria were the rival contenders in Upper Mesopotamia. Eventually Mari emerged as the dominant city-state in that region, and for half a century (c. 1750-1700 B.C.) it stood as one of the major powers of the day. Excavations have brought to light a city of great size and wealth, and an abundance of tablets and fragments (over 20,000) in old Akkadian (official correspondence and business documents). Its people were Northwest Semites who had adopted Akkadian culture and who spoke a language akin to that of Israel's ancestors.

In the keen Mesopotamian rivalry one power eventually emerged triumphant: Babylon; and the man who engineered the triumph was Hammurabi (1728-1686 B.C.). He had control of most of the great valley of the Tigris and Euphrates. The cultural flowering of Babylon at this time has left us a wealth of texts. Most remarkable for our purpose are the Babylonian accounts of the Creation and the Flood, which are copies of ancient Sumerian epics.[5] Hammurabi is best known for his famous law code, based on a long legal tradition already represented by the codes of Ur-nammu, Lipit-Ishtar, and Eshnunna.[6] It has numerous and striking parallels with the laws of the Pentateuch.

The empire of Hammurabi practically ended with him. In the seventeenth and sixteenth centuries B.C. a new people, the Hurrians, pressed down from the north; by the middle of the second millennium they had won control of Upper Mesopotamia and Northern Syria, while Babylon itself was split internally. One of the cities with a predominantly Hurrian population was Nuzi, and the fifteenth-century Nuzi texts, which reflect Hurrian laws, are important for an understanding of patriarchal customs.[7] It was not the Hurrians, however, but a Hittite king, in a bold expedition from Asia Minor, who (c. 1530 B.C.) sacked Babylon and brought the First Dynasty to a close. For some time to come the kingdom of Mitanni, with a predominantly Hurrian population, maintained the leading position in Upper Mesopotamia. It survived a collision with Egypt in the early fifteenth century, but was finally overcome by the Hittites in the fourteenth century. Assyria, which had been a vassal of Mitanni, now, under Ashuruballit I, became the dominant power in Upper Mesopotamia.

EGYPT In contrast to the confusion in Mesopotamia, Egypt, in the early patriarchal age, was remarkably stable: the First Intermediate was over and the Middle Kingdom had been founded. The Twelfth Dynasty, with its capital at Memphis, maintained itself in power for over two hundred years (1991-1786 B.C.). This was a period of great prosperity and a golden age of Egyptian culture. Wisdom literature abounded; from this time, too, comes the delightful *Tale of Sinuhe*.[8] A loose Egyptian control extended over most of Palestine and Phoenicia, while Byblos was an Egyptian colony. The Execration Texts give us an impression of the extent of Egyptian control in Asia.

These consist of two series of inscriptions from the twentieth and nineteenth centuries which illustrate how Pharaoh sought to bring magical powers to bear on his enemies, actual or potential. In the first series, imprecations against various foes were inscribed on jars or bowls, which were then smashed—thus making the imprecation effective. In the other, the imprecations were written on clay figures representing bound captives. The places mentioned indicate that the Egyptian sphere included western Palestine, Phoenicia to a point north of Byblos, and southern Syria.[9]

In the eighteenth century the power of the Middle Kingdom declined; before the end of the century rival dynasties (the Thirteenth and Fourteenth) contended for power, thus leaving the way open to an invasion of a foreign people called the Hyksos. The name means "rulers of foreign peoples" or "foreign chiefs." It seems probable that most of the Hyksos rulers were Canaanite or Amorite princes from Palestine and southern Syria; they were certainly Semites. The Hyksos won control of the whole of Egypt and placed their capital at Avaris (Tanis); they ruled Egypt from about 1700 B.C. to 1560 B.C. It is not unlikely that the ancestors of Israel entered Egypt during this time.

A movement against the conquerors began in Upper Egypt. Amosis, the founder of the Eighteenth Dynasty, took Avaris and expelled the Hyksos from Egypt (c. 1560 B.C.); he even pursued them into Palestine. This marked the beginning of the New Empire (1560-715 B.C.) and the hour of Egypt's greatest glory. For the moment, however, we are concerned only with the Eighteenth Dynasty (1560-1345 B.C.). Under Thutmosis III (c. 1500-1450 B.C.), Egypt reached the zenith of its power: the empire extended to the Euphrates. This expansion brought Egypt into conflict with the kingdom of Mitanni in Upper Mesopotamia, a conflict which ended in a treaty; relations between the countries remained peaceful.

In the fourteenth century the young Pharaoh Amenophis IV (1377-1358 B.C.) brought about a strange revolution. A devotee of Aten (the Solar Disk), he promoted the cult of this, the sole god (for it does seem that the Aten cult, if not a strict monotheism, was something approaching it), and changed his own name to Akhenaten (the Splendor of Aten). This brought him into conflict with the priests of Amun; hence he left Thebes and built his new capital, named Akhetaten, at modern Tell el-Amarna. This period, then, is known as the Amarna Age.

Due to the internal dissension, Egyptian power waned, a fact that is illustrated by the Amarna letters: clay tablets discovered in the excavation of Tell el-Amarna.[10] Written in Akkadian, the diplomatic language, they are, for the most part, frantic appeals for help by Pharaoh's vassals in Palestine and Phoenicia: many towns are in open rebellion against Egypt; trouble is everywhere fomented by an element called the Habiru. To make matters worse, this eclipse of Egypt coincided with the rise of the Hittite Empire under Shuppiluliuma (c. 1370-1345 B.C.). Most of Syria and northern Phoenicia came under Hittite control and the kingdom of Mitanni was conquered. In Egypt the situation was saved by Horemheb (c. 1350-1315 B.C.). He managed to put the country back on a sound footing and ruthlessly removed all vestiges of the Aten cult. With him the Eighteenth Dynasty came to an end.

The real founder of the Nineteenth Dynasty was Seti I (1315-1301 B.C.), who soon regained possession of Palestine, thus coming into direct conflict with the Hittites. Under his successor Rameses II (1301-1234 B.C.) there was full-scale war, which dragged on until about 1271 B.C. when a treaty was signed by the two countries; copies of this treaty have been found in Egypt and in the Hittite capital.[11] Henceforth the long reign of Rameses II was peaceful and marked a period of prosperity for Egypt. But this brings us to the time of the Exodus and is best considered in the context of that event.

THE HITTITES   The Hittites were an Indo-European people who, by the mid-sixteenth century, had established a strong kingdom in eastern and central Asia Minor, with its capital at Hattusas (Bogazköy). We have noted that a Hittite king, Mursilis I, brought the First Babylonian Dynasty to an end about 1530 B.C. The expedition had no lasting effect; it was more than a century before Hittite influence was again felt outside Asia Minor.

Under Shuppiluliuma (c. 1370-1345 B.C.) the Hittite kingdom became an empire extending over Syria and Phoenicia, with Mitanni as a vassal state. Soon the Hittites clashed with a renascent Egypt, but under Hattusilis III (c. 1270-1250 B.C.) hostilities came to an end. (A copy of the treaty with Rameses II has been found at Bogazköy.) But if there was peace in the west, the Hittites were being harassed in the east by the Assyrians under the energetic successors of Ashur-uballit I—Adad-nirari I (c. 1298-1266 B.C.) and Shalmaneser I (1266-1236 B.C.)—and the Assyrians gained control of Mitanni. Indeed, the Hittite Empire was doomed, but at the hands of another enemy; its fall may be mentioned here though it forms part of the background to the Exodus and Conquest. By the middle of the thirteenth century the Hittites had increasing difficulty in maintaining their position against coalitions of Aegean peoples in western Asia Minor. Finally the empire was engulfed by these groups whom the Egyptians named the Peoples of the Sea.

THE HABIRU   Groups known as Habiru were found over all western Asia from the third millennium to about the eleventh century B.C. The name does not have an ethnic connotation; it is a social designation (or so it would appear).

> The term apparently denoted a class of people without citizenship, without fixed place in the existing social structure. At times pursuing a seminomadic existence, living either peacefully or by raiding, as occasion offered they settled in the towns. They might, in disturbed times, hire themselves (so in the Amarna letters) as irregular troops for whatever advantage they could gain. Or they might, when driven by need, dispose of themselves as clients to men of station, or even sell themselves as slaves (as at Nuzi); in Egypt, numbers of them were impressed as labourers on various royal projects. On occasion, however, some of them—like Joseph—rose to high position.[12]

For, as we shall see, it is reasonable to suppose that the Hebrew ancestors belonged to this class.

PALESTINE   In the period from 2000 B.C. to 1750 B.C. Palestine was infiltrated by seminomadic groups, who began to settle down in western Palestine and in northern Transjordan; the Execration Texts and archaeological data are proof of this. However, the central mountain range was thinly populated. It seems certain that the newcomers were Amorites, of the same Northwest-Semitic stock as the Canaanites; hence the two peoples speedily merged. It appears, too, that some of the Hurrians (in the Bible called Horites) had spilled into the land from northern Mesopotamia. In the seventeenth and sixteenth centuries B.C. Palestine was part of the Hyksos Empire and the city-state system developed—the same political system that obtained at the time of the Israelite conquest.

2. THE PATRIARCHS

Our sketch of the world of Israel's origins has had the
purpose not only of underlining the comparative moder-
nity of biblical history but also, and more immediately, of
setting the biblical story in its proper framework right from
the beginning. Besides, our knowledge of that other world
has wonderfully illuminated the world of the Bible. At the
same time, it has assured us that the traditions which have
preserved the memory of the patriarchs must indeed stem
from patriarchal times. For, when the traditions are examined in the light of the evidence, the stories of the patriarchs fit authentically into the milieu of the early second
millennium.

It must be noted, however, that the narrative of the patriarchal age is at once historical and popular. Passed on
for centuries by oral tradition, it accurately describes the
essentials but freely develops and amplifies the story according to the character of the various personages. It is a
family history which takes no account of general history
or of political events. (Gn. 14 is an exception.) It is religious history since it not only sees the divine Providence
in everything but also presents and explains events in a
religious light in order to demonstrate a definite thesis: the
one, only God has chosen one people to dwell in one land:
Canaan. Hence the promises of God and the relations of
the patriarchs with the land of Canaan.

Contemporary evidence shows that the traditions relating to Abraham, Isaac, and Jacob are not only probable
but well-grounded. In a popular, distinctive form they preserve the memory of the origin of the people of Israel.
Thus, what is said of the patriarchs regarding their seminomadic way of life agrees with the history of Palestine
and adjacent countries in the nineteenth and eighteenth
centuries as we know it from archaeology.[13] They are por-
trayed as seminomads living in tents; partly nomad, going
from place to place in search of pasture, even as far as
Egypt in times of drought; partly sedentary since they remained for long periods at Shechem, Hebron-Mambre,

Beer-sheba, and Bethel. Their wanderings in Palestine fit perfectly into the situation of the Execration Texts. As nomads they had a profound sense of family or clan and hence of collective responsibility and of the necessity for preserving purity of blood. Then, too, their juridical and social customs agree with the juridical and social customs of the same period throughout the East. Thus the rite of making a treaty (Gn. 15:7-11), the contract for the purchase of the cave of Machpelah (Gn. 23:17 f.), the adoption of a servant in lieu of a son (Gn. 15:1-3), the custom by which a sterile wife permits her husband to have intercourse with her handmaid, with the child born of the union not being the heir without special adoption (Gn. 16:1 f.; 30:1-6, 39-13), the right of the first born (Gn. 25:29-34), the practice of levirate (Gn. 38)—and many others—are paralleled in the Nuzi texts, the Hittite laws, and later Assyrian laws (which reflect earlier legislation). But this is a general background and all we can say with confidence is that the customs and laws—and the events—reflected in Gn. 12-50 fit best between the twentieth and seventeenth centuries B.C.

We can be a little more precise about the geographical background of the patriarchal narratives. The biblical tradition mentions Haran as the starting-point of Abraham's journey (Gn. 11:32; 12:5; cf. Jos. 24:2 f.); and a further tradition (Gn. 11:28, 31; 15:7) specifies that Abraham's father, Terah, had earlier migrated to Haran from Ur. The home of Laban, Abraham's kinsman, is placed in Paddan-Aram (Gn. 27:43; 28:10; 29:4) and, more precisely, in the city of Nahor in Aram-naharaim (Mesopotamia) (Gn. 24:10); and Laban is repeatedly called an Aramean (Gn. 25:20; 28:1-7; 31:20, 24). An early cultic credo began: "A wandering Aramean was my father" (Dt. 26:5). It seems that the name, originally designating the Aramaic-speaking people of Upper Mesopotamia, was gradually extended to neighboring seminomadic peoples who adopted the same language.

There appears to be a relationship, too, between the patriarchs and the Habiru mentioned above. Undoubtedly, there is a similarity between the name "Hebrew" (*'ibri*) and *Habiru*. It is surely significant that the name "Hebrew," in the Old Testament, is practically confined to narratives of the earliest period and occurs chiefly in the mouth of a foreigner speaking to the Israelites (e.g., Gn. 39:14, 17; Ex. 2:6; 1 Sm. 4:6, 9) or of an Israelite identifying himself to foreigners (e.g., Gn. 40:15; Ex. 3:18; 5:3). It is reasonable to think that the patriarchs would have belonged, or were regarded as belonging, to the social class of Habiru.

Finally, the Hyksos must be considered. These Semitic princes ruled Egypt for almost a century and a half (c. 1700-1560 B.C.). It is entirely credible that this period is the setting of Joseph's career and marks the beginning of the Hebrew sojourn in Egypt. The Hyksos would have welcomed fellow Semites and would have permitted one of them to attain high office.

It appears, then, that the patriarchs were a part of that migration of seminomadic groups which brought a new population into Palestine in the early centuries of the second millennium B.C.

We may tentatively suggest the following dates:

c. 1850 B.C.: Arrival of Abraham in Canaan.

c. 1850-1700 B.C.: The patriarchs in Palestine.

c. 1700-1250 B.C.: The Hebrews in Egypt.

3. EXODUS AND CONQUEST

1) *The Background*

EGYPT The long reign of Rameses II (1301-1234 B.C.), especially after the treaty with the Hittites (c. 1271 B.C.), was one of prosperity and of great building activity. The rebuilding of the capital Avaris, started by Sethi I (1317-1301 B.C.) was completed by Rameses and the new city named "The House of Rameses." The reign of the next pharaoh, Merneptah (1234-1225 B.C.) ended in a period of weakness and anarchy that saw the end of the Nineteenth Dynasty. We know from a stele of his fifth year (c. 1230 B.C.) that Merneptah campaigned in Palestine.[14] Among foes defeated there he lists the people of Israel—

the earliest reference to Israel in a contemporary inscription. Significantly, Israel is listed as a people, not a territory, so it is not yet sedentary. Indeed, it is not clear what the stele reference implies, perhaps no more than a clash with some of the Israelites of the Exodus. About this same time Merneptah had to face an invasion of Libyans and the Peoples of the Sea who moved on Egypt along the African coast. The raiders were repelled but Egyptian power was weakened; during the subsequent period of anarchy Egyptian control of Palestine ceased—a circumstance favorable to the Israelite conquest and consolidation.

With Rameses III (1197-1165 B.C.) a new era seemed to be about to dawn for Egypt: this was the beginning of the Twentieth Dynasty (1200-1085 B.C.). But almost at once, Rameses had to face successive waves of the Peoples of the Sea, who came this time from the east, along the Mediterranean coast, and beat on the gate of Egypt. Each invasion was staved off but Egypt was terribly weakened. The days of her greatness were over.

THE PEOPLES These peoples came from the Aegeo-
OF THE SEA Cretan world and had been on the move
since the mid-thirteenth century. They had overthrown the Hittite Empire and Merneptah had to repel an invasion from the west. Later, in the reign of Rameses III, from the Asia Minor they had overrun, they pushed by land and sea, in wave after wave, against Egypt; the Egyptian fleet and army just managed to keep them at bay. The change wrought in Palestine by their appearance is important. In the first place it meant that the attempt to re-establish Egyptian control there was effectively stifled; secondly, some of these people, notably the Philistines—who were to give their name to the whole country—settled on the Palestinian coast. Thus the nation that was to come within an ace of destroying Israel arrived in Palestine at approximately the same time as Israel.

CANAAN In the thirteenth century the two chief ethnic groups in Palestine were the Canaanites, a Northwest Semitic people, already in Palestine and Syria in the third millennium, and the Amorites, also Northwest Semites who had come into the land in the early second millennium; among them were the ancestors of Israel. For the most part the Bible does not distinguish sharply between these peoples for, by the time of the conquest, the Amorites had adopted the language and culture of Canaan. Other elements were Hurrians (Horites) from the Hyksos period. By "Hittites" are meant elements who had come from the parts of northern Syria once under Hittite control (most likely they were Hurrians). Other inhabitants of the land (Hivites, Jebusites, Girgashites, Perizzites) are of unknown origin. But all had become essentially Canaanite in culture.

Politically, Canaan was a patchwork of small city-states without a central authority. During the period of Egyptian dominance these cities were vassals of Egypt; when Egyptian control declined they were at the mercy of invaders. Culturally, the Canaanites were advanced; more remarkable is the development of writing among them. By the end of the third millennium a syllabic script had been developed at Byblos, and it was the Canaanites, too, who invented the linear alphabet that is the ancestor of our own. The fourteenth-century Ras Shamra (Ugarit) texts, which preserve, in a poetic style akin to early Hebrew verse, the myth and epic of Canaan, are of great value and interest.[15] "It must be stressed, and stressed again, that the age of Israel's origins was one of widespread literacy."[16]

Canaanite religion was essentially a fertility cult. Head of the Canaanite pantheon was El, but the chief active deity was Ba'al (Lord). Female deities, variously named Asherah, Astarte, Anat, represented the female principle in the fertility cult. A central element of Canaanite myth was the death and resurrection of Ba'al, corresponding to the annual death and resurrection of nature. In this context such rites as sacred prostitution become understandable: by sexual union at the shrine, the union of god and goddess was re-enacted, and by a sort of sympathetic magic the desired fertility in soil, beast, and man was secured. Though the Bible vehemently condemns it, the Canaanite religion continued to have a powerful fascination for the Hebrews, especially when they had settled down to agricultural life.

2) The Exodus

It may seem strange that, after a relatively full presentation of the historical background, we shall go on to treat of the Exodus itself in a few lines. The truth is that, when we get down to details, the situation is seen to be extremely complicated; and this outline is obviously not the place for a thorough review of all the evidence.

We have suggested that the Hebrews settled in Egypt during the Hyksos period. It is understandable that, after the expulsion of the hated invaders, the Egyptians should have looked with no friendly eye on the Semitic elements in their midst: "There arose a new king over Egypt, who did not know Joseph" (Ex. 1:8). In any case we know that the Hebrews had become slaves, forced to labor at the building of Pithom and Raamses (Ex. 1:11). The latter is the ancient Hyksos capital of Avaris, rebuilt by Pharaohs Sethi I and Rameses II and named by the latter "House of Rameses"; the reference seems to demand the presence of the Hebrews in Egypt during at least part of the reign of Rameses II. On the other hand, the stele of Merneptah seems to demand the presence of Israel in Palestine by 1230 B.C. (or, perhaps, 1220). At any rate, a thirteenth-century date for the Exodus seems assured.

If we wish to be more precise, we must consider two alternatives:

1. Pharaoh of the oppression: Sethi I (1317-1301 B.C.)
   Pharaoh of the Exodus: Rameses II (1301-1234 B.C.)
2. Pharaoh of the oppression: Rameses II
   Pharaoh of the Exodus: Merneptah (1234-1225 B.C.)

In conclusion the best we can say is that the Exodus is most likely to have taken place between 1250 B.C. and 1230 B.C. To this uncertainty of date we might add that the exact route of the Israelites is uncertain. The truth is that the relevant Pentateuch passages are liturgical texts which celebrate the saving event, the mighty intervention of Yahweh; in the liturgy the event of the past became a saving event of the present. But this could be only because God really had intervened to save his people. So, if we are sure neither of exact date nor of exact location, we are certain that the Exodus itself was, and remained, the central *fact* in Israel's history.

The traditional site of Sinai is not unchallenged, though a reasonable case can be made for it. But, again, it is what happened at Sinai that is important: there Israel received the Law and Covenant which made her a people. Nor are we very clear about Israel's subsequent wanderings. All we can say is that the headquarters of the desert sojourn was Kadesh, an oasis fifty miles south of Beersheba.

A final point concerns the number of the Israelites who took part in the Exodus. Here the biblical numbers cannot be taken at their face value: over 600,000 fighting men (Ex. 12:37; 38:26; Nm. 1:46; 2:32; etc.)—which would give a total population of two to three millions. Such a throng would require a month to cross the Red Sea and, stretched out in a column, would reach over one hundred miles! Besides, the Sinai peninsula today supports at most 10,000 inhabitants, and at a low living standard. If we are to avoid geographical and historical absurdities we must say that the total population, including the elements that had joined after the liberation, was not likely to be more than 20,000 people or, at the most, 30,000.[17]

3) *The Conquest*

Chapters ten and eleven of Joshua link the conquest of the whole of the south and the conquest of the whole of the north of Palestine with two expeditions of Canaanite kings and with two battles, at Gibeon and "by the waters of Merom." The countercampaigns against these kings are depicted as having been carried out with the participation of all the tribes and under the leadership of Joshua. But it is clear from several references in Jos. and from the first chapter of Jgs. that this is an idealized picture: to Joshua, the conqueror, are attributed the successes won by others in later times; for the essential fact is that these successes were due ultimately to God—"The Lord God of Israel fought for Israel" (Jos. 10:42).

But if we are certain that the Conquest was a more complicated and a far slower affair than Jos. 10-11 would suggest, we may not deny the essential historical fact of a conquest under Joshua. The archaeological evidence, while providing some major problems, on the whole confirms the biblical presentation. It is true that Jericho, long thought to offer the decisive proof, is now seen to be no help in this matter. It is true that Ai, said to have been captured by Joshua (Jos. 8:1-23) is now known to have been destroyed about 2200 B.C. and to have remained unoccupied until the twelfth century B.C. (It may be that the story of Jos. 8 originally referred to the taking of Bethel, little more than a mile away, which was violently destroyed in the second half of the thirteenth century B.C.) But it is also true that, on the positive side, a number of places in Southern Palestine, said to have been taken by Israel, appear to have been destroyed in the latter half of the thirteenth century—for example, Debir (Jos. 10:38 f.), Lachish (10:31 f.), Eglon (10:34 f.), and, in the north, Hazor (11:10).

We may conclude, with J. Bright:

> The evidence is really very impressive, and it is not sound method to brush it aside. It does not, to be sure, substantiate the biblical narrative in detail; nor does it allow us to suppress evidence that the conquest was also an involved process. We have two pictures of the conquest to keep in mind. If they are not to be artificially harmonized, neither is one or the other to be ruled out. However complicated the Israelite occupation of Palestine may have been, and however schematized the narrative of Joshua, it may be regarded as certain that a violent irruption into the land took place late in the thirteenth century.[18]

The precise date of the conquest depends, of course, on the date adopted for the Exodus—here, about 1250-1230 B.C. We may take it that the "forty years" of wandering need not be interpreted too literally; it was probably much shorter. Thus the conquest would have taken place between 1220 B.C. and 1200 B.C.

Without going into detail we might add that there is evidence to suggest that components of Israel had been in Palestine before the conquest under Joshua. A large element of the Palestinian population was of the same Amorite stock as Israel and would have joined forces with the incoming Israelites. In support of this view we have the impression that much of the land, especially in central Palestine, did not have to be conquered. And the Covenant ceremony (Jos. 24) could well mark the formal incorporation of these other elements into the tribal structure of Israel.

4. THE PERIOD OF JUDGES

1) The Background

The world situation favored the invasion of the Israelites and their settlement in Canaan. Though Egypt still maintained her claims on the Syrian coast, she was unable to do anything at all to implement them; eventually even the claims ceased. In Asia Minor the Hittite Empire had disappeared. Assyria had been a force in the thirteenth century, but her power had waned. Under Tiglath-pileser I (c. 1114-1076 B.C.), she knew a brief resurgence, but soon sank into a slumber that lasted for two centuries. In Upper Mesopotamia and Syria small Aramean states sprang up. Until the middle of the ninth century Israel could be free of serious interference on the part of great powers. The first threat came from a people no greater than herself and, like herself, a recent invader: the Philistines.

2) The Amphictyony

Early Israel was a confederation of twelve tribes united in Covenant with Yahweh. There was no central government and the various tribes enjoyed complete independence, while tribal society was on a patriarchal basis. The rallying point of the confederation was the shrine which housed the Ark of the Covenant; during most of the early period it was located at Shiloh. This system resembles the religious league of a somewhat later period in Greece, which was called an "amphictyony." The Delphic League, for instance, had twelve members; the number probably points to a monthly maintenance of the central shrine.

The Covenant assembly at Shechem (Jos. 24) suggests that the amphictyony was already in existence. It seems that a league of clans must have existed before the conquest—a campaign that demanded concerted action. It is reasonable to look for the origin of the amphictyonic system at Sinai (though we may not doubt that it took on its final and classical form only after the settlement) and to see it as a concrete expression of the Covenant of Yahweh with his people. Indeed, the tent that housed the Ark was "the Tent of Meeting"—the place of tribal assembly presided over by Yahweh. Later on, in Palestine, the shrine of the Ark still remained the meeting-point and the heart of the confederacy; Shiloh quickly became the center of assembly (Jos. 18:1; Jgs. 18:31).

3) *The Period of Judges*[19]

The Judges (*shophetim*), like the *suffetes* of Tyre and Carthage, were "tyrants" who led the people in war and who saved them from danger. The "Judge" essentially was a man chosen by God to free the oppressed people; his mission was therefore charismatic. He was not a saint, but a hero in the service of the community, and was invested with moral and physical strength sufficient to assert his authority over his fellow citizens and to bring about the downfall of his enemies. The mission of the Judge varied according to the circumstances, and, generally, he acted on behalf of a particular tribe. There is no question of a "government" of Judges, nor is it possible to establish their chronological order with exactitude, since some may have been contemporaries.

The chronology of Jgs., which appears to give 410 years for the period of Judges, is evidently artificial; this is indicated by the recurrence of 40 years (= a generation) and of 80 and 20. The total is arrived at by adding the years of the Judges, but some may have overlapped. From extrabiblical data we know that the conquest took place at the end of the thirteenth century and that the reign of David began before 1000 B.C. The period of Judges, then, is not more than one and one-half centuries (the middle of it is marked by the victory of Taanach under Deborah and Barak [c. 1125 B.C.]). This victory was earlier than the Midianite invasion (Gideon) and the Philistine expansion (Samson).

POLITICAL SITUATION AT THE BEGINNING OF THE PERIOD OF JUDGES 1. *The Israelites.* At the death of Joshua the Promised Land was far from being conquered. The elders, who succeeded Joshua, were unable to maintain the unity of the people and there was a manifest lack of central authority: "In those days there was no king in Israel; every man did what was right in his own eyes" (Jgs. 17:6). The Canaanites still held out at important points, while the constant contact with this people had grave effects on the religion of Yahweh. The Israelites, in fact, held only the mountain regions; the Canaanites and Philistines, with their chariot forces, held the plains. Judah and Simeon, aided by the Calebites, gained the territory of Hebron and the Negeb. The "House of Joseph" (Ephraim and Manasseh) got control of the central region north of Jerusalem; the Ark of the Covenant was established in the sanctuary of Shiloh in Ephraim. None of the tribes won all of the territory allotted to them by Joshua; hence there was rivalry among the tribes and migration of discontented clans. Ephraim gained territory at the expense of Manasseh—which in its turn pushed north into Issachar and Asher—while Dan emigrated to the sources of the Jordan, under pressure of Amorites who took Aijalon and Bethshemesh. Judah and Simeon alone attained a measure of stability, though they soon became isolated from the northern tribes; this is the germ of the future political schism.

It is remarkable, for instance, that they are not mentioned in the canticle of Deborah (Jgs. 5).

2. *The Canaanites* and the division of Israel. The Canaanites were established in Accho, Harosheth, Megiddo, Taanach, and Bethshan, thus separating Ephraim from the northern tribes. The southern tribes, Judah and Simeon, were cut off from Benjamin and the "House of Joseph" by Jerusalem and Gezer and the cities of the Gibeonite confederacy: Gibeon, Chephirah, Beeroth, and Kiriathjearim. The tribes of Transjordan were cut off from the rest by the Jordan valley, and they had to be on the defensive against Ammon and Moab.

3. *The Philistines.* One of the most important changes wrought in Palestine by the invasion of the "Peoples of the Sea" was the installation along the littoral south of Carmel of peoples from the Aegeo-Cretan world, notably the Philistines. They established themselves in the Shephelah (the hill country west of the mountain region of Judah) and the corresponding coast, southward from Jaffa. Their allies, the Tsikal pirates, had their center further north at Dor and had control of the plain of Sharon. The Philistines had a colony at Aphek which controlled the route to Jezreel (Esdraelon). Politically they formed five toparchies with capitals at Gaza, Ashkelon, Ashdod, Ekron, and Gath. Each toparchy was ruled by a *seren*, the five forming a Supreme Council of the nation. They had a well-equipped army and a strong force of chariotry, and with their unity and military strength the Philistines were a great danger to the Israelites during the period of Judges (and after). At first, however, it was the unconquered cities in their midst that caused trouble.

4. *Transjordan.* From about the twentieth century B.C. until the thirteenth, central and southern Transjordan had remained without settled population. In the thirteenth century, however, new Semitic peoples settled there: the Edomites and the Moabites. The former settled in the highlands east of the Arabah (continuation of the Jordan valley) between the southern end of the Dead Sea and the Gulf of Aqabah, while the latter established themselves north of Edom, east of the Dead Sea. When we first came

to know of them they were already set up as kingdoms
(Gn. 36:31-39; Nm. 20:14; 22:4). A third people, the
Ammonites, settled northeast of Moab. Farther north were
the Amorite states of Heshbon and Bashan which were
conquered by the Israelites.

THE JUDGES 1. *Othniel.* Judah and Simeon were menaced by Edomite incursions (Edom, not *Aram* [= Meso-
potamia]) (Jgs. 3:8, 10). Yahweh raised up Othniel, the
Calebite who defeated the Edomites. He was the only
Judge of Judah.

2. *Ehud.* The Moabites subdued Reuben and, crossing
the Jordan, established themselves in the plain of Jericho.
They compelled the Benjaminites to pay tribute. Ehud
brought the tribute to Eglon, the king, in his dwelling beyond the Jordan, and assassinated him. He then declared
a "holy war" and drove the Moabites across the river.

3. *The Canaanite reaction.* The Canaanites, with fortresses from Accho to Bethshan, held the valley of Jezreel,
and began to molest the northern tribes. The prophetess
Deborah, in her contact with the tribes, stirred them to
revolt. When she thought they were emotionally prepared,
she declared the "holy war" and set up as leader *Barak*
of Naphtali. Issachar, Ephraim, Benjamin, Zebulun, and
Naphtali answered the call. Barak took counsel with Zebulun and Naphtali at Kedesh of Galilee and led 10,000
men to Tabor, the place indicated by Deborah.

The Canaanites assembled a large force, with 900 chariots, under Sisera of Harosheth, and camped south of
Megiddo; the battle was fought between Megiddo and
Taanach. Heavy rain had made the Kishon overflow and
the chariots were bogged down. Barak attacked the Canaanites in front, while others, coming from the south by
Taanach, took them on the flank. The Canaanites fled and
Sisera was killed by the woman Jael. In the canticle of
Deborah, Reuben, Gad, Dan, and Asher were blamed for
failing to join Barak. The victory of Taanach, "by the waters of Megiddo," had lasting effects. The Canaanites, de-
prived of their chariots, never recovered. They still held

the cities, but excavations at Megiddo point to a decline which set in at this time.

4. *The Midianites.* After the victory of Taanach the Israelites had possession of the fertile plain of Jezreel and were engaged in agriculture. The way was open to two quite different dangers: the temptation of the fertility cult and nomad incursions. The Midianites came from the south along the confines of Moab and Ammon, then up the Jordan valley and into the plain of Jezreel at Bethshan. The domestic camel was now extensively used and they were able to carry out lightning raids. Eventually a savior appeared: Yahweh raised up *Gideon,* a young man of Ophrah. He destroyed the altar of Baal on the high place of Ophrah and built one to Yahweh in its place. For this he was named Jerubbaal—"that Baal may defend himself (from him)." His war against the Midianites had, probably, different phases which are difficult to distinguish.

He assembled the people of Manasseh and neighboring tribes. With a chosen band (300) he surprised the Midianites camped at the foot of Moreh and put them to flight. Gideon pursued them beyond Bethshan and across the Jordan, because the law of blood compelled him to avenge his two brothers slain at Tabor by the Midianite chiefs Zebah and Zalmunna. At a place called Karkor, deep in Transjordan, he caught up with the Midianites and seized their chiefs, who were later put to death. But the Midianites would have raided again the following year. This time Gideon had the fords of the Jordan watched. When the raiders went to flee across the river as before they were intercepted by the Ephraimites; their leaders, Oreb and Zeeb, were captured and killed. The Ephraimites, who arrogated to themselves a certain hegemony among the tribes, tried to pick a quarrel with Gideon, but he spoke diplomatically and was able to pacify them. The grateful people offered Gideon a hereditary princedom; he refused the title but accepted the substance.

Gideon was succeeded by his son Abimelech whose mother was a woman of Shechem. Supported by the Canaanite clan of Shechem he massacred his brothers and declared himself king. He reigned for three years, and not

THE JUDGES		
GREATER JUDGES	TRIBE	OPPRESSOR
Othniel	Judah	Edomites
Ehud	Benjamin	Moabites
Barak (Deborah)	Naphtali	Canaanites
Gideon	Manasseh	Midianites
Jephthah	Gad	Ammonites
Samson	Dan	Philistines
LESSER JUDGES		
Shamgar	Simeon?	Philistines
Tola	Issachar	
Jair	Manasseh (territory of Gilead)	
Ibzan	Asher?	
Elon	Zebulun	
Abdon	Ephraim?	

●　●　●　●　●　●　●　●　●　●　●

CHRONOLOGICAL SEQUENCE OF JUDGES

1. Oppression of Cushan-rishathaim and the Edomites: *Othniel.*

2. Oppression of Eglon, king of Moab: *Ehud.*

3. Oppression of the Canaanites—Sisera: *Deborah* and *Barak* (c. 1130 B.C.).

4. Midianite oppression: *Gideon;* kingship of Abimelech; Tola; Jair.

5. Ammonite (and Philistine) oppression: *Jephthah;* Ibzan; Elon; Abdon.

6. Philistine oppression (c. 1100 B.C.): Shamgar; *Samson;* Eli;

7. Samuel (c. 1050 B.C.).

peacefully. In striving to put down a revolt he destroyed
Shechem. Finally he was killed at the siege of Thebez—
by a millstone thrown from a tower by a woman.

5. *Transjordan*. In Transjordan, Gad, Reuben, and the
half-tribe of Manasseh were in difficulties. The Ammonites
were established at the upper courses of the Jabbok and
wanted to push into the fertile lower reaches and to get as
far as the Jordan. The Palestinian tribes, owing to pressure from the Philistines, were unable to help. This was
towards the close of the period of Judges (c. 1050 B.C.).

The chieftains of Gilead gathered at Mizpah could find
no military leader. Finally they appealed to an outlaw
who had been driven from his clan and was now a high-
wayman in the region of Tob (north Transjordan).
Jephthah agreed to lead them, on condition of receiving
the title of prince (*rosh*). In order to gain time he entered
into negotiations with the Ammonites, and all the while
was building up an army. Eventually, he turned on the
Ammonites and defeated them; in fulfillment of his rash
vow, he sacrificed his only daughter (Jgs. 11:31-39). The
Ephraimites, who had turned against Jephthah, were driven
back across the Jordan.

6. *The Philistine peril*. The Philistines, already strongly
established in the Shephelah, had been slowly and me-
thodically expanding. From Ekron and Gath they were
spreading into Dan and Judah, while the weakening of
Canaanite power had opened up the coastal plains to them.
It appears that this expansion did not alarm Judah, Simeon,
and Dan at first, and there were only a few isolated in-
stances of resistance. One such who resisted was Shamgar.
Another was the last of the "great Judges," *Samson*, the
very type of the popular hero.

From Aphek the Philistines began to molest Ephraim
and Benjamin. Eli, the priest, exercised a sort of judgeship
at Shiloh. The Philistines wanted to get control of Shiloh
and Bethel—the religious and political centers—and defeated the Israelites at Ebenezer. Now they had control
of the whole mountain region. *Samuel* organized a national
resistance, but not with any great measure of success.

5. THE RISE OF THE MONARCHY

1) *The Institution of the Monarchy*

The authority of Samuel was more religious than political. Besides, his sons were unworthy to succeed him and the people did not want them. The Philistine danger was pressing; they were established in the mountains of Ephraim, while the Ammonites had resumed their raids on Gilead. It was felt that a king was needed to unite the people against their enemies. 1 Sm., however, gives two very different traditions of the institution of the monarchy.

THE TRADITIONS 1. *The antimonarchist tradition* (1 Sm. 8; 10:17-24; 12). Samuel was old and his sons did not walk in his footsteps; the people demanded a king so that they could be like other nations. Yahweh assured Samuel that the people rejected not him but Yahweh. In the name of Yahweh Samuel warned the people of the price they would have to pay for a king. The people still persisted, so Yahweh told Samuel to accede to their request. He assembled the people at Mizpah and proceeded to choose a king by lot. The lot fell on Saul, son of Kish, of the tribe of Benjamin. Samuel then made profession of his fidelity as Judge. He showed how God had always taken care of his people. The demand of the monarchy was a grave fault; as a sign, Yahweh sent thunder and heavy rain—in the harvest time! However, Yahweh would not reject his people despite their fault, if they remained faithful. Samuel retired from public life after the election of Saul.

2. *The monarchist tradition* (1 Sm. 9; 10:1-16; 11). This time the narrative is centered on Saul. Samuel is presented as a prophet (seer) rather than as a Judge, and Saul meets him by chance. Saul sets out in search of the asses of his father Kish. His servant advises him to consult the "seer" at Ramah. On the previous day Yahweh had warned Samuel of Saul's imminent arrival and had designated him as king. Saul was anointed secretly by Samuel.

The antimonarchist narrative is late; it presupposes sad

experience of the failure of the monarchy. The monarchist tradition, on the other hand, is near the events; its popular style is a gauge of authenticity. In fact, the monarchy is the natural fruit of the unity that was being achieved towards the close of the period of Judges, for unity was imperative in face of the growing Philistine peril.

The last Judge anointed the first king, and this first king has many of the traits of a Judge. The charismatic nature of this kingship is marked: the king is chosen by God, possessed by his Spirit; it is this Spirit that moves him to great exploits. A new element is the recognition by all the tribes of a permanent authority conferred on the chosen king. Thus appears for the first time the concept of a national monarchy. This notion was not borrowed from the Canaanites—a multitude of city-states; nor from the Philistines—a league of "tyrannies." The kingship of Israel was modeled on those of Ammon, Moab, and Edom, set up shortly before the conquest, and on those of the Aramean kingdoms of Syria. Rather than imitation, it is parallel development among peoples akin in race and but recently sedentarized.

THE REIGN   Saul was proclaimed king by the people of
OF SAUL   Gilgal about 1030 B.C. and made his headquarters at Gibeah, four miles north of Jerusalem, where he built a fortress. The Philistines had, apparently, not given much weight to the institution of the monarchy and Saul did not provoke them. Eventually Jonathan, as a token of revolt, overturned a Philistine stele at Gibeah (LXX). The Philistine reaction was immediate: they invaded Benjamin and set up their camp at Michmash. The Israelites hid or fled to Transjordan, while, in Gilgal, Saul tried to collect an army around him. With his troops he went up and camped at Geba, opposite Michmash. After a sortie by Jonathan, panic was sown in the Philistine ranks and they gave way before an Israelite attack.

After the victory of Michmash, Saul took action against the peoples along his frontiers: the Ammonites, Moabites, Edomites, and the Arameans of the north, and built up a standing army. A special action was his campaign against

the Amalekites in order to preserve the southern tribes
from the raids of these nomads of the Negeb. Saul diso-
beyed the command of Yahweh conveyed to him by Samuel and was rejected for his disobedience. Separate traditions (1 Sm. 13:8-15; 15:1-31) of Saul's rejection reflect
speculation on the problem of how and why the Lord's
anointed could be set aside. The tragedy of Saul is that
he was unable to choose between obedience to Yahweh,
who had chosen him, and the wishes of the people, who
had acclaimed him. He sought a compromise. The Prophet
intervened to protect the absolute rights of Yahweh against
the people and the king. The opposition, inherent in the
monarchy, between profane policy and the interests of
Yahweh, is already stressed. This strife of king and prophet
will occur over and over in the history of the monarchy.

For the appearance of David at the court of Saul we
again have two traditions:

1. David is called as a minstrel to the court of Saul
and becomes his armor-bearer. As such he accompanies
the king to the war against the Philistines and thus is able
to meet the challenge of the Philistine champion (1 Sm.
16:14-23; 17:1-11; 17:32-53).

2. David is a young shepherd unknown to Saul. He
comes to visit his brothers in the army just as Goliath is
making his challenge (1 Sm. 17:12-30; 17:32-53; 17:55–
18:2).

Both traditions merge in the narrative of the single combat; this victory was the beginning of David's rise to fame.

After his rejection Saul was seized by an "evil spirit"
(it is obvious, from now on, that Saul is neurotic) and
David became his minstrel and *aide-de-camp*. David's successes convinced Saul that this was his rival, and he was
moved by an insane desire to destroy him. David was
hounded through the wilderness of Judah, until, in des-
peration, he placed himself beyond Saul's clutches by becoming a vassal of a Philistine prince, Akish, *seren* of
Gath, who ceded to him the territory of Ziklag. This gave
him the opportunity, by a dangerous double game, of in-
gratiating himself both with his overlord and the princes
of Judah.

Meanwhile, the Philistines decided to move against Saul. They mustered their troops at Aphek. David had deceived Akish so effectively that the suspicions alone of the other Philistine leaders saved him from the decidedly awkward situation of having to take the field against his own people. The Israelites were disastrously defeated at Mt. Gilboa and Saul and his sons were killed. We should not think of Saul as a bad man—rather, he was a sick man, and unfortunate; he is a tragic figure, not without considerable nobility.

Despite the failure of Saul and his defeat it was felt that a king was still the only hope. The men of Judah anointed David king of Hebron (c. 1010 B.C.). The northerners went their own way. Abner, general of Saul, collected the remnants of the broken army in Transjordan and proclaimed Ishbaal (Ishbosheth), son of Saul, king in Mahanaim. There was civil war. Eventually Abner, breaking with Ishbaal, came over to David, but was murdered by Joab, David's right-hand man, who saw that his own position was threatened. Soon Ishbaal too was assassinated and David was left with no rival. He had already been king of Judah for seven years when, at Hebron, he was anointed king of Israel by the elders of Israel. Thus, about the year 1000 B.C., David became king of Judah *and* Israel.

2) *The Reign of David (c. 1010-970 B.C.)*

By the anointing at Hebron, David became king of Judah and Israel, that is, king of a united kingdom. We do not know very much about his reign even though 2 Sm. is entirely dedicated to it. But this history is more concerned with showing the fate of Jerusalem, which was to become the sanctuary of the Ark of the Covenant, and to fix the succession to the throne of David. (It is really a family history.) Still, we can distinguish the salient points of his reign.

WAR OF   Apparently the Philistines had ignored
INDEPENDENCE the king of Judah; but when David was proclaimed king of Judah and Israel they realized the danger and reacted at once. Taking the offensive they occu-

pied Bethlehem and camped in the valley of Rephaim,
west of Jerusalem. David organized the resistance from
the fortress of Adullam. The war was long, but David
eventually drove the invaders back and, pursuing them
into their own country, captured Gath. The Philistine
power was broken forever, and Philistine mercenaries
served in David's royal bodyguard.

Next it was necessary to absorb the foreign islands
within the national territory. From the situation under
Solomon we gather that David had won possession of
Megiddo, Taanach, Bethshan, and the other Canaanite
towns. He won over the Gibeonites by delivering up to
them the descendants of Saul (the latter had treated them
harshly). Then he turned to the Jebusite stronghold of
Jerusalem. The capture of Jerusalem was of considerable
historical importance: David had won a residence, situated
more or less in the center of his kingdom, which was his
own personal property; this freed him from the undue
influence of any tribe. It was his royal residence and became the religious capital too by the transference of the
Ark there.

THE EMPIRE   Once the Philistines had been defeated and
OF DAVID   the Canaanite cities occupied, the power
and importance of David's kingdom had already out-
stripped that of neighboring states; it became a danger to
them. The Ammonites were the first to react, and they
found ready allies in the small Aramean states to the north.
War was declared. In the first campaign, David's general,
Joab, was able to prevent the joining of the Ammonites
with the forces of their allies, the Arameans of Beth-rehob,
Zobah, and Maacah. The latter retreated at the first onset,
and the Ammonites withdrew to their capital of Rabbath-
ammon; Joab, who was not prepared for a siege, retired
to Jerusalem. Next year the war was resumed. Hadadezer
of Zobah had formed an Aramean league which, under
the general Shobach, invaded Transjordan. David went
against him in person and inflicted a severe defeat on him
at Helam; the Ammonites were now isolated. In the third
campaign, commanded by Joab, Rabbath-ammon was be-

sieged and taken. (It was during this siege that David was guilty of adultery with Bathsheba and of the murder of her husband.)

It is very difficult to fix the chronology of the other campaigns of David. Edom was annexed to the kingdom, giving Israel access to the Gulf of Aqabah and control of the great caravan route. Moab was subdued, as well as Damascus, and David made an alliance with the king of Hamath. He entered into commercial relations with Hiram I of Tyre. The empire of David included all Palestine (the Philistines, as vassals, held a narrow coastal strip); and in Transjordan: Edom, Moab, and Ammon, and northwards as far as Kadesh on the Orontes, that is, including Damascus and Aram Zobah and terminating on the confines of the allied kingdom of Hamath.

DOMESTIC TROUBLES The realization of national unity, the creation of a centralized and personal power, the considerable extension of his possessions, the introduction of new customs into public life—and all this in a few decades —could not but come into conflict with the old spirit of liberty of the tribes. The national unity was based solely on the personality of the king. And David could never really free himself from the influence of the tribes of the south, and especially from that of the great families of Hebron.

But there was tension within the royal family, now grown large through diplomatic marriages. David's own crime of adultery and murder was the beginning of ills, as foretold by the Prophet Nathan. Amnon's rape of his half-sister Tamar was avenged, in blood, by her full-brother Absalom. Some years later Absalom staged a revolt that came within an ace of overthrowing David. The king had to flee to Transjordan, but there the well-tried and faithful personal troops of David defeated the rebel army. Joab killed Absalom, despite the orders of the king, and then succeeded in stopping the conflict.

David, in coming to terms with the rebels, had appointed Amasa, Absalom's commander, as his own commander-in-chief, entrusting him with the subduing of another, and less serious, revolt that broke out among the Northerners. Again Joab assassinated his rival, and then went on to crush the revolt himself; David accepted the *fait accompli* and Joab remained as general.

THE   At the death of Absalom, Adonijah became
SUCCESSION   heir apparent. He was supported by the representatives of the Hebron tradition: Joab, Abiathar, and the princes of Judah. An opposing party led by Nathan, Zadok (the new priest of Jerusalem), and the royal guard supported Solomon, son of Bathsheba. Adonijah gathered his supporters for a banquet at En-rogel; this was interpreted by the others as a token of revolt. Through the intervention of Bathsheba, David was induced to designate Solomon as his successor. Solomon was taken, with royal pomp, to the spring of Gihon and there anointed and proclaimed king. Adonijah and his party submitted.

3) *The Reign of Solomon* (*c. 970-931* B.C.)

Solomon soon got an opportunity of getting rid of his rival Adonijah and quickly disposed of Joab too; the priest Abiathar was banished. He organized a great religious festival at the old sanctuary of Gibeon, in the midst of which he had a prophetic dream and received magnificent promises; the ceremony ended in Jerusalem.

THE EMPIRE   The death of David had awakened hopes
OF SOLOMON[20] of independence in some of the conquered territory. The Edomite prince Hadad, who had found refuge in Egypt, returned to Edom where he established an independent principality. Solomon still retained control of the mines and of the caravan route. Among the Arameans a certain Rezon won possession of Damascus and founded a dynasty that was to become the great enemy of Israel. Apart from these losses, however, the empire of David was maintained. The territory properly Israelite was protected by a series of fortresses provided with garrisons, including the new chariot divisions.

ADMINISTRATION   For internal administration Solomon
OF THE KINGDOM   divided the kingdom into twelve pre-
fectures (plus Judah which had a special administration).
The districts did not correspond to the area of the twelve
tribes, but to the months of the year: each had to supply
all that was necessary to support the royal household for
one month. Labor was also recruited according to the districts. The army was reorganized and modernized and
Jerusalem was refortified. The fortresses of Hazor, Megiddo, Beth-horon, and Gezer dominated the traditional
route between Syria and Egypt. Baalath and Tamar, southwest of the Dead Sea, guarded the "copper route." We
have a good idea of these Solomonic constructions from
the walls and the remains of the great stables uncovered
at Megiddo.

Solomon did not use his military force to make war;
rather, he used it to bolster up his diplomacy. Egypt's support of Hadad was disturbing, so the king sought an alliance with Egypt and married the daughter of Pharaoh
(commonly believed to be Psusennes II). Solomon entered
into commercial relations with Hiram of Tyre, who had
already established friendly relations with David. Solomon
imported horses from Cilicia and sold them in Egypt and
in return traded Egyptian chariots with Syria. The mineral
resources of the Arabah were exploited and a great foundry
has been excavated at Ezion geber on the Gulf of Aqabah.
Here, too, with Hiram, he had built a trading fleet; perhaps
it was the appearance of these ships along the Arabian
coasts that moved the queen of Saba (Sheba), on the southwest of the Arabian peninsula, to visit Solomon. All this
trade provided riches that were to become proverbial in
the country and also won Solomon renown among the
neighboring princes.

THE GREAT   David had hoped to build a temple to
CONSTRUCTIONS   Yahweh; now Solomon was ready to do
so. His difficulty was lack of architects and skilled workmen,
which were supplied by Hiram. He also provided the timber
from the forests of Lebanon (cut by Solomon's men). The

logs were floated along the coast, probably to Tell Qasileh
on the right bank of the Yarkon (near modern Tel Aviv).
The foundation of the Temple was laid in 969 B.C. and the
building was completed seven years later. South of the sacred enclosure Solomon built the royal palace, which included the "house of the forest of Lebanon," the throne
room, and a special apartment for the daughter of Pharaoh.
These great constructions at Jerusalem gave to the kingdom
of Solomon a splendor never before achieved in Israel,
but the exactions they entailed in taxes and labor weighed
heavily on his subjects and boded ill for the stability and
permanence of his kingdom.

THE REVERSE   Solomon's constructions and his love of
OF THE COIN   ostentation were a heavy burden on the
kingdom; he was even obliged to cede part of his territory
in payment to Hiram. For a king of the Chosen People,
Solomon was too immersed in worldly affairs. His vaunted
wisdom was mainly profane and his religious sentiment
went much less deeply than that of David. The popular
prophets who had at first acclaimed him now turned against
him, and he was condemned by the Prophet Ahijah of
Shiloh.

In internal policy Solomon made no advance in the uni-
fication of the kingdom. In fact his favoritism, shown in
the special administration of Judah, fomented the existing
tension and sowed the seeds of the schism. It is not surprising that there should have been a movement of revolt
during his lifetime, nor that it should have come from the
house of Ephraim, nor that its leader should be involved
in the forced-labor policy, nor that it should have the support of a prophet. The leader of the revolt was the
Ephraimite Jeroboam, an organizer of labor, and he was
supported by Ahijah. The rebellion was premature; Jeroboam, forced to flee, found refuge with Shishak (Shoshenq) of Egypt, founder of the Twenty-second Dynasty.
This reception of the rebel was a bad augury for the kingdom of Israel. Solomon died about 931 B.C.

6. THE DIVIDED MONARCHY

1) The Schism (1 Kgs. 12; 2 Chr. 10)

Rehoboam, son of Solomon, was at once accepted as king by the Judeans. It was necessary, because of the dual monarchy, that he should be accepted by the Israelites too. These held for the primitive concept of royalty: the king, chosen by Yahweh, is acknowledged by his subjects and enters into a pact with them. That is why Rehoboam went to Shechem, the meeting-place of the tribes of the north. These had no objection, in principle, to the king, but they asked that he should lighten the burden of taxes and of work levies imposed by his father. The intransigent arrogance of Rehoboam provoked the rupture and the situation worsened when he got Adoram, the hated master of works, to intervene; the latter was promptly lynched and the king had to flee to Jerusalem. Rehoboam, with his well-organized army, might yet have put down the revolt, but the Prophet Shemaiah dissuaded him from civil war. The schism was a *fait accompli*.

But it is not altogether correct to term the disintegration of the dual monarchy a "schism." Such a separation is rather a return to the situation that had prevailed since the conquest and it is the union, incomplete and unsteady, achieved under David and Solomon, that is revealed as the exceptional situation in the history of the Chosen People. But there followed a religious schism in the strict sense, and this was the graver aspect. Jerusalem had become the religious capital—with its Temple enshrining the Ark of the Covenant—of the kingdom of David and Solomon, and this religious center insured a certain political unity.

Jeroboam knew this and saw that his people must be won away from allegiance to Jerusalem. This was all the more necessary since the Temple cult was a constant reminder of Yahweh's eternal Covenant with David—and the North had broken with the house of David. Hence Jeroboam set up two official shrines, with an organized cult and priesthood, at opposite ends of his kingdom: Bethel

and Dan. Bethel had been a holy place in the time of the
patriarchs and Dan was a shrine in the period of Judges.
The golden bulls (in 2 Kgs. 12:28 contemptuously called
"calves") set in these shrines were not idols; we know
from Semitic iconography that these were pedestals upon
which the invisible Yahweh was conceived as standing or
enthroned—in much the same way that Yahweh was enthroned upon the cherubim in the Temple. Certainly
Jeroboam did not wish to change the essential nature of
Yahwism, but the bull symbol was too evocative of the
fertility cult to be safe, and a breach was open to the
infiltration of Canaanite religious practices. This religious
schism was the sin of Jeroboam so stigmatized by the orthodox tradition, the "original sin" of Israel.[21]

The period of the divided monarchy is covered by the
Books of Kings (from 1 Kgs. 12 onwards) and also, for
Judah, by Chronicles (from 2 Chr. 10 onwards). In Kgs.
the presentation of the history of the kingdoms is syn-
chronized: a king of Israel is dated in terms of the contemporary king of Judah, and the next Judean king is
dated by cross reference to the reigning king of Israel.
This can be confusing and it has seemed better, in this
outline, to take the kingdoms separately. It should also be
noted that Kgs. reflects the outlook of the deuteronomical
editors of the book,[22] especially with regard to the centralization of the worship in Jerusalem and the removal of
local shrines (the "high places"). Hence all the kings of
Israel are condemned because of the "original sin" of
Jeroboam I; while the religious conduct of the kings of
Judah is either condemned outright or praised, with the
qualification that "the high places were not removed."
Hezekiah and Josiah alone merit unreserved approval. But
before going on to treat of the two kingdoms it will be
helpful to sketch in the historical background of the divided monarchy.

2) The Background of the Divided Monarchy

ASSYRIA   Just at the turn of the eleventh century, under
Tiglath-pileser I (c. 1114-1076 B.C.), Assyria was on the

verge of becoming a dominant force in Mesopotamia, but circumstances checked her rise to power. The Assyrian resurgence began under Ashur-dan II (934-912 B.C.) and his successors. Ashur-nasir-pal II (883-859 B.C.) overran Upper Mesopotamia and campaigned in northern Syria. He was succeeded by Shalmaneser III (859-824 B.C.) who undertook to complete the work of his father by opening up the commercial routes to the west. In 858 B.C. northern Syria was invaded and devastated and the Phoenicians sent gifts to the conqueror. The states of central Syria were fully alive to the danger that threatened. Hamath and Damascus united and persuaded the neighboring states to join an anti-Assyrian league. Ahab made an important contribution: 2,000 chariots and 10,000 infantry.[23] When Shalmaneser returned in 853 B.C. he was met at Qarqar on the Orontes by a confederacy of eleven kings. The Assyrian king claimed a great victory but, significantly, he did not advance on Hamath and Damascus and it was several years before he was ready to try again. In 841 B.C. Shalmaneser invaded Aramean territory and laid siege to Damascus. Failing to capture the city, he devastated the country and took tribute from Tyre, Sidon, and Jehu of Israel; the latter is depicted on the black stele of Shalmaneser.[24] Internal troubles, coupled with the pressure of neighboring states, prevented the Assyrians from maintaining control of the west; this situation persisted under the next king, Shamshi-adad V (824-811 B.C.) and under Queen Semiramis who was regent during the minority of Adad-nirari III (811-783 B.C.). The latter resumed the campaigns against the Aramean states and about the year 802 B.C. Benhadad II of Damascus and Jehoahaz of Israel had to pay tribute. Once again, however, the Assyrians were unable to consolidate their gains. The kings Shalmaneser IV (783-773 B.C.), Ashur-dan III (773-754 B.C.), and Ashur-nirari V (754-745 B.C.) were scarcely able to maintain a foothold west of the Euphrates, for Assyria was not only weakened by internal dissensions but also was menaced by the kingdom of Urartu, in the Armenian mountains, which was expanding to the west and east.

Succeeding to the weak kings who had been unable to

prevent the expansion of Urartu, and who had lost control of Syria, Tiglath-pileser III (745-727 B.C.) is the real founder of the Assyrian empire. He defeated the Chaldeans (Babylonians) in the south and broke the power of Urartu in the north. In a series of campaigns, begun in 738 B.C., he gained dominion over Syria: "Menahem of Samaria" paid tribute. Later, Rezin of Damascus and Pekah of Israel joined in a league against Assyria; in 734 B.C. Tiglath-pileser attacked. First he moved along the coast and subdued the Philistine cities; then turning against Israel he devastated Galilee and Gilead and deported their inhabitants. This deportation of peoples was calculated policy: patriotic sentiment and a spirit of rebellion would be dulled in a population that had been uprooted from its homeland. In 732 B.C. Damascus fell; Rezin was executed and many of his people were deported. Israel too would have been destroyed altogether had not the pro-Assyrian party got rid of Pekah and put Hoshea on the throne. Judah became a vassal of Assyria.

Shortly after Shalmaneser V (727-722 B.C.) had succeeded to the throne, Hoshea got involved in another intrigue against Assyria; the Assyrian king acted at once. In 724 B.C. Hoshea was arrested and Samaria was besieged; it held out for three years, but fell to Sargon II (722-705 B.C.) in 721 B.C. After this Sargon was fully occupied in the east, particularly against Marduk-apal-iddina (Merodach-baladan) who had won control of Babylon in 721 B.C. and was not finally driven out of it by Sargon until 710 B.C. In the previous year (711 B.C.) the Assyrian king had put down a revolt in the west and had taken Ashdod.

Sargon was succeeded by his son Sennacherib (705-681 B.C.) who was at once faced with rebellion at both extremities of his empire. Marduk-apal-iddina had again taken possession of Babylon and had set himself up as king (703 B.C.). While Sennacherib was trying to dislodge him, the western provinces, supported by Egypt, rose in revolt—Hezekiah of Judah played a prominent part. Sennacherib defeated Marduk-apal-iddina in 703 B.C. and devastated the Chaldean region. Then, in 701 B.C., he was free to move into Syria. His own account of the campaign[25] tells how he was called into Palestine by a revolt. The ringleaders were the king of Sidon, the king of Ashkelon, the inhabitants of Ekron, and Hezekiah of Judah. In four operations Sennacherib proceeded first against the cities of the North and subdued Tyre; then he moved against Ashkelon; next he dealt with Ekron whose king Padi had been handed over by his subjects to Hezekiah and was kept prisoner in Jerusalem; lastly came the turn of the king of Judah. The country was overrun, forty-six fortified towns were taken and Hezekiah was shut up in Jerusalem "like a bird in a cage." Sennacherib did not take the city but imposed a heavy tribute and had the king of Ekron restored to his throne.

After this Sennacherib was fully occupied for some time in the east where Babylon was in open rebellion; the rebellion was put down in 689 B.C. It seems that about this time Hezekiah, with promise of support from Egypt, had again rebelled. The Assyrian king moved to the west about 688 B.C.; at this time Lachish was taken and Jerusalem was besieged.[26] Tirhakah of Egypt came to Hezekiah's aid and Sennacherib intercepted him. The outcome of the encounter is unknown. But Jerusalem was not taken because the Assyrian army was decimated by an epidemic (2 Kgs. 19:35), and also because Sennacherib's presence was required in Assyria (2 Kgs. 19:7).

Sennacherib was assassinated in 681 B.C. and was succeeded by his son Esarhaddon (681-669 B.C.). He campaigned in Egypt where he defeated Tirhakah and captured Memphis (671 B.C.). Soon Tirhakah rebelled and Esarhaddon's son and successor, Ashurbanipal (669-632 B.C.), crushed the rebellion (c. 667 B.C.). In 663 B.C. the Assyrians came again and destroyed the ancient capital of Thebes.

The Assyrian Empire had reached its apogee under Ashurbanipal, but its decline was extremely rapid. Egypt was too far away to be effectively controlled and in 650 B.C. the Assyrian garrisons were evacuated. The reason is that Assyria herself was menaced by a formidable invasion of Indo-European peoples: Medes, Cimmerians, and Scythians. There was internal strife also. In 652 B.C. the king's brother, Shamash-shum-ukin, led a revolt in Babylon and won the support of the Elamites; Babylon was taken in 648 B.C. by Ashurbanipal who then turned on Elam. The date of Ashurbanipal's death is uncertain, but 632 B.C. is probable. The greatest of the Assyrian kings, and almost the last of them, he is particularly remembered for his great library, discovered in excavations at Nineveh, which sheltered, among other copies of ancient Babylonian myths and epics, the famous creation and flood stories.[27]

Ashur-etil-ilani (632-629 B.C.) had a short reign and was succeeded by Sin-shar-ishkun (629-612 B.C.). In 626 B.C. the Chaldean prince Nabopolassar took possession of Babylon. This was the beginning of the Neo-Babylonian Empire. Soon Assyria was fighting for her life against the Babylonians and Medes. Until 614 B.C. the struggle was indecisive, but in that year the Medes took Ashur, the ancient Assyrian capital. In 612 B.C. Nineveh itself fell to Nabopolassar and the Medes and Sin-shar-ishkun perished in the utter destruction of his city. This was the decisive stroke. The Assyrians, under Ashur-uballit II (612-606 B.C.) made a last stand at Haran, but in 610 B.C. they were driven out and the king fled, with the remnant of his forces, west of the Euphrates.

Meanwhile, Egypt had taken a hand. Psammetichus I thought it politic to maintain two rival powers in Mesopotamia, and intervened on the side of Assyria; some Egyptian forces were dispatched in 616 B.C. In 609 B.C. the next pharaoh, Neco II, arrived at Carchemish with a large force. He and Ashur-uballit attempted to retake Haran, but failed. Neco retired west of the Euphrates and set up his headquarters at Riblah. By 606 B.C. the Assyrian Empire was definitely at an end, and in 605 B.C. Nebuchadnezzar crossed the river and crushingly defeated the Egyptians at Carchemish; news of the death of his father prevented him from exploiting his success to the full.

EGYPT   In Egypt the Twenty-first Dynasty was overthrown (c. 945 B.C.) by a Libyan named Shishak (Shoshenq) who founded the Twenty-second Dynasty (945-725 B.C.) and made Bubastis his capital. Shishak (945-925 B.C.) had granted Jeroboam political asylum; but then, after the political schisms, he had invaded and devastated Palestine. He had hopes of re-establishing the Egyptian Empire in Asia, but internal weakness prevented him even from maintaining control in Palestine. It was centuries before Egypt would again intervene.

The Twenty-fifth Dynasty was founded (c. 715 B.C.) by Piankhi, an Ethiopian king. Egypt was keenly aware of the strength and threat of Assyria and was anxious that the Assyrian advance should not reach her own borders. Consequently it became deliberate Egyptian policy to undermine Assyrian authority in Palestine; and Egyptian help, or promise of help, stands behind the anti-Assyrian leagues of the future. But Egypt was never again more than a broken reed.

The Pharaoh Shabako (710-696 B.C.) supported the revolt that led to the Assyrian invasion of 701 B.C.; an Egyptian army went to the relief of Ekron but was defeated. The next king was Shebteko (696-695 B.C.), but his brother Tirhakah became coregent and effective ruler in 690 B.C.; the latter fomented another rebellion in Palestine, but when he marched to Hezekiah's aid (c. 688 B.C.) he was checked, and probably defeated, by Sennacherib. In 671 B.C. Esarhaddon invaded Egypt and occupied Memphis. Tirhakah escaped and began an attempt to regain his throne. He was once more defeated in another Assyrian campaign under Ashurbanipal (c. 667 B.C.). This time a prince called Neco was set in his place by the Assyrians. But Tirhakah's successor, Tanutamun, continued the resistance, and in a third Assyrian campaign (663 B.C.) Thebes, the ancient capital, was destroyed. This was the end of the Twenty-fifth Dynasty.

Neco was succeeded by his son Psammetichus I (663-609 B.C.) who, during the period of Assyria's final decline, became independent and founded the Twenty-sixth Dynasty. When he realized that the Medes and Babylonians were threatening to destroy Assyria, he decided to intervene on the side of the latter; his policy was the shrewd one of maintaining rival powers in Mesopotamia. He sent troops to the east in 616 B.C., but it was too late to save Assyria. His son Neco II (609-593 B.C.) marched with a large army to Carchemish on the Euphrates in 609 B.C. and supported Ashur-uballit in an attempt to retake Haran. (At Megiddo, Josiah, who had intercepted Neco, was defeated and killed.) The assault on Haran failed and Neco set up his headquarters at Riblah in Syria; the Egyptian army remained stationed west of the Euphrates. In 605 B.C. Nebuchadnezzar, prince-royal, defeated the Egyptians at Carchemish and then, following their retreat, struck again at Hamath. In 601 B.C. Nebuchadnezzar (now king) moved on Egypt and was met at the frontier by Neco; a fierce pitched battle was fought and the Babylonians, if not defeated, at least were forced to retire.

The next pharaohs, Psammetichus II (593-588 B.C.) and his son Apries (Hophra) (588-566 B.C.), resumed the policy of stirring up and supporting revolt in Palestine. In 690 B.C. Psammetichus appeared in Palestine and, later, Apries prevailed on Tyre and Sidon to join a league against Babylon. During the siege of Jerusalem in 587 B.C., Pharaoh appeared in the Shephelah with an Egyptian army, but was quickly forced to retire. All that the Egyptians could now do was to grant shelter to refugees from a devastated Judah. In 569 B.C. Amasis succeeded Apries, and in 568 B.C. Nebuchadnezzar invaded Egypt. The details of this campaign are obscure, but it marked the end of conflict between Babylon and Egypt.

DAMASCUS   Already during the reign of Solomon an Aramean named Rezon seized Damascus and made himself king. With the breakup of the empire of Solomon, the position of Damascus became much stronger. Soon we find Baasha of Israel making a treaty with Ben-hadad I of Damascus; then we see the same Ben-hadad harass northern Galilee at the request of Asa of Judah. During the reign of Ahab, Ben-hadad II first invaded Israel and then suffered a shattering defeat. Thereupon the two erstwhile foes became allies against a common Assyrian peril. They formed part of a coalition which met, and checked, Shalmaneser III at Qarqar on the Orontes in 853 B.C. But once the immediate danger was over, war between Damascus and Israel was resumed and dragged on.

Ben-hadad II was assassinated (c. 842 B.C.) by Hazael. In 841 B.C. Shalmaneser III laid siege to Damascus, but when the Assyrian army had retired Hazael turned on Jehu who had paid tribute to Shalmaneser. Jehu lost the whole of Transjordan, and his son Jehoahaz became a vassal of Hazael's successor, Ben-hadad III. Aramean forces pushed along the coast as far as Philistia. However, Damascus was crushed by Adad-nirari III (c. 802 B.C.); its grip on Israel was broken, and Jeroboam turned the tables by annexing some Aramean territory.

The last king of Damascus was Rezin (c. 740-732 B.C.). He and Pekah of Israel became leaders of a coalition against Assyria. In an attempt to force the hand of Ahaz they invaded Judah; their intention was to place an Aramean, the "son of Tabeel" (Is. 7:6) on the throne of Judah. Tiglath-pileser moved quickly against the coalition. In 732 B.C. Damascus was taken and destroyed, Rezin was executed, and a large part of the population was deported. It was the end—as it soon would be the end for Israel.

BABYLON During the reign of Sin-shar-ishkun, the Chaldean prince Nabopolassar defeated the Assyrians at Babylon and made himself king there in 626 B.C.; this was the foundation of the Neo-Dabylonian Empire. Nabopolassar (626-605 B.C.), with Cyaxares, king of the Medes, utterly destroyed the Assyrian Empire. He was succeeded by his capable son Nebuchadnezzar (605-562 B.C.) who had already defeated Assyria's Egyptian allies. In 604 B.C. Nebuchadnezzar was in the Philistine plain and destroyed Ashkelon. It was probably at this time that Jehoiakim became a vassal of the Babylonian king (2 Kgs. 24:1). In 601 B.C. Nebuchadnezzar moved on Egypt and was met by Neco in a pitched battle; the Babylonians were obliged to retire. Jehoiakim promptly rebelled, but Nebuchadnezzar was not ready to take decisive action until 598 B.C. Jehoiakim had been succeeded by his son Jehoiachin, who surrendered after a siege of three months. The king and the leading citizens were deported to Babylon, and the king's uncle, Mattaniah (Zedekiah), was installed in his place. The Babylonians were back again in 588 B.C. to quell a revolt in which Zedekiah was implicated. Jerusalem was besieged—a siege that was momentarily raised when the Babylonians went to intercept the Egyptian army of Apries —and fell in 587 B.C. The city was destroyed and a group of the population was deported to Babylon; this was the end of the Davidic monarchy. The assassination of Gedaliah, the governor appointed by the Babylonians, seems to have been the occasion of another deportation in 582 B.C.

Nebuchadnezzar was able to maintain his position of successor to Assyria despite the challenge of his former ally, the Median King Cyaxares, who built up a powerful state with its capital at Ecbatana. Nebuchadnezzar campaigned in the west in 585 B.C. when he laid siege to Tyre (which did not fall); in 582 B.C., when he deported some of the inhabitants of Judah; and in 568 B.C. when he invaded Egypt. With his death, Babylonian power declined rapidly. This later phase of Babylonian history forms the background of the Exile.

Throughout the whole of the monarchy, the history, first of the united kingdom, and then of Israel and of Judah, reflects the decline and rise of the great powers. David achieved his remarkable success and Solomon was able to maintain his position because no foreign influence bore on Palestine. This situation came to an end soon after the death of Solomon and aggravated the weakness of the divided monarchy. Assyria began to harass and hamper the two small kingdoms, and destroyed Israel at last. Assyria and Babylon dominated the last century of Judah and the latter brought it, too, to an end. Any measure of prosperity or success in Israel and Judah was gleaned during brief moments of decline in the East, and the great armies were back again, without fail, to snatch away whatever little had been gained. Assyria and Babylon were the scourges of God, to punish his ungrateful and stubborn people; but

God would also raise up another nation to be the instrument of his mercy.

7. THE KINGDOM OF ISRAEL

A feature of the monarchy in Israel is lack of stability: no royal family remains in power for long, and a change of ruler usually comes as a result of an army revolt. To indicate this lack of continuity we speak of different "dynasties."

1) Dynasty of Jeroboam I

JEROBOAM I (931-910 B.C.):
1 KGS. 12:20–14:20;
CF. 2 CHR. 13

The Northern tribes gathered at Shechem proclaimed Jeroboam, who had returned from his refuge in Egypt, king of Israel. He set up his capital at Tirzah (Tell el-Far'ah, northeast of Shechem). To counteract the unifying influence of Jerusalem he set up national shrines at Bethel and Dan and organized his own cult and priesthood. Israel comprised, in principle, the ten Northern tribes but, in fact, Benjamin was divided between the two kingdoms. We know scarcely anything of the reign of Jeroboam except that there was continual friction between himself and Rehoboam of Judah and that Abijah inflicted a heavy defeat on Jeroboam near Bethel.

NADAB (910-909 B.C.):
1 KGS. 15:25-32

Son of Jeroboam, Nadab was the victim of a conspiracy. Thus ended the First Dynasty.

2) Dynasty of Baasha

BAASHA (909-886 B.C.):
1 KGS. 15:33–16:7

Baasha, head of the conspiracy against Nadab, became king, and, to remove possible rivals, exterminated the family of Jeroboam. He was an energetic leader who drove Asa of Judah back within the limits of his own kingdom, and took and fortified Ramah, six miles north of Jerusalem. Asa ap-

pealed to Ben-hadad I of Damascus who attacked northern
Israel and won some territory there. This led to the downfall of the Dynasty of Baasha.

ELAH (886-885 B.C.):   Elah, son of Baasha, reigned for
1 KGS. 16:8-14   less than two years; he was assassinated by Zimri, officer of a chariot division.

ZIMRI (885 B.C.—SEVEN DAYS):   This was a period of
1 KGS. 16:15-22   anarchy. Zimri exterminated the family of Baasha. The army did not accept the
coup d'état, and Omri, commander of the army, was declared king and besieged Zimri in Tirzah; Zimri died in
the royal palace which he had set on fire. Omri was opposed by another competitor, Tibni, and there was civil
war for four years. Omri triumphed in the end.

3) *Dynasty of Omri*

OMRI (885-874 B.C.):   The reign of Omri includes the
1 KGS. 16:23-28   four years of struggle with Tibni.
After this he set about repairing the damage caused by
the civil war. He changed his capital from Tirzah to Samaria, which remained the capital of Israel until the destruction of the kingdom. The change was a significant
one, comparable to the selection of Jerusalem by David.
Though the Bible tells us little about him, Omri was regarded by the Assyrians as the founder of the Northern
Kingdom which they continued to name *bit Humri*, the
"house of Omri." We learn, incidentally, of an unfortunate war with Damascus in which Omri lost some territory;
apart from this his reign was crowned with success. He
put an end to strife with Judah, where Asa was reigning,
and was able to re-establish his dominion over Moab. He
entered into a commercial alliance with the Phoenicians,
and his son Ahab married Jezebel, daughter of Ethbaal,
king of Tyre.

An important factor of this period is the rebirth of Assyrian power under Ashur-nasir-pal II.

AHAB (874-853 B.C.):   Ahab succeeded his father and
1 KGS. 16:29—22:40   had a brilliant reign. His alliance
with Tyre proved advantageous, and the wealth of his
kingdom is manifested by the great constructions at Samaria, Megiddo, and Jericho. The army was reorganized
and a powerful chariot division was stationed at Megiddo.
Unfortunately, this material prosperity was accompanied
by religious decadence, chiefly due to the influence of
Jezebel who was fanatically attached to the Phoenician
cult. The worship of Baal was introduced into Samaria
and the faithful of Yahweh were persecuted. The Yahwistic reaction was represented by the extraordinary figure
of Elijah the Tishbite (from Tishbe in Gilead).

Ahab concluded a treaty with Jehoshaphat of Judah,
which was sealed by the marriage of Athaliah (daughter
or sister of Ahab) with Jehoram, son of Jehoshaphat.
The alliance of Israel with Phoenicia affected the commercial interests of the Arameans, and the king of Damascus, Ben-hadad II, tried to destroy the growing power
of Israel. He invaded Israel and besieged Samaria, but
was driven back with losses. The following year he tried
again and this time was disastrously defeated at Aphek,
east of Lake Tiberias. Ben-hadad was captured and Ahab
concluded a treaty with him.

This accord between the two states was dictated by a
common danger: Assyrian expansion under Shalmaneser
III. An anti-Assyrian league was formed to which Ahab
made an important contribution: 2,000 chariots and 10,-
000 infantry. Shalmaneser was met in 853 B.C. at Qarqar
on the Orontes by the confederacy of eleven kings, and
though he claimed a great victory he did not press his
alleged advantage. Once the immediate danger was past
the league broke up. Ben-hadad infringed the treaty of
Aphek, and Ahab declared war; with Jehoshaphat of Judah
he moved against the frontier town of Ramoth-gilead. Ahab
was mortally wounded in the engagement. Despite this
reverse the reign of Ahab had been very successful, at
least materially. The old religion was saved only by the
efforts of Elijah and Elisha.

AHAZIAH (853-852 B.C.):   Ahab was succeeded by his
1 KGS. 22:52—2 KGS. 1:18   son Ahaziah who reigned
one year only. Mesha of Moab rebelled during this reign.
(The mission of Elijah was undertaken under Ahab and
Ahaziah.)

JEHORAM (852-841 B.C.):   Ahaziah was succeeded by
2 KGS. 3:1—10:17   his brother Jehoram. He attacked Moab from the south with the aid of the king of
Judah (probably Jehoram) and the king of Edom. The
expedition was at first successful, but was later checked at
Kir-hareseth, the Moabite capital. Mesha, in his stele,
claims a victory.[28] This reverse led to the defection of
Edom; and, in Judah, Libnah was lost to the Philistines.
In Damascus Ben-hadad II was assassinated by Hazael who
seized power. Jehoram profited from the disturbances at
Damascus to take Ramoth-gilead and war broke out between himself and Hazael. In an encounter at Ramoth-
gilead, Jehoram was wounded and retired to Jezreel where
his cousin Ahaziah of Judah came to visit him. This was
the moment that Elisha chose to bring the dynasty of Omri
to an end.

Jehu was commander of the army at Ramoth-gilead;
there he was anointed by a disciple of Elisha and was
proclaimed king by the army. He set out in haste for
Jezreel and killed Jehoram, who had come out to meet
him; Ahaziah fled, but was overtaken and wounded at
Ibleam and died at Megiddo. Jehu entered Jezreel and
had Jezebel, the queen-mother, thrown from a window.
He seemed mad with blood and massacred all about him:
many functionaries of the king of Judah, who were in
Jezreel, were killed; the family of Omri was wiped out;
the prophets and worshipers of Baal were massacred and
the temple of Baal at Samaria was destroyed. Thus Jehu
exterminated the dynasty of Omri and destroyed too the
religion of Baal that was the sad fruit of that dynasty.

4) *Dynasty of Jehu*

JEHU (841-814 B.C.):   We know that Jehu was king in
2 KGS. 10:28-36   or before 841 B.C., because he

figures on the black stele of Shalmaneser III, dated 841 B.C. When in that year Damascus was attacked by Shalmaneser III, Jehu inaugurated his new policy by not only not helping Hazael but by sending tribute to the invader. In 839 B.C. Shalmaneser returned, but Damascus still held out; the Assyrian king retired and domestic troubles held his attention. Hazael then turned on Israel. He won possession of Transjordan as far as the Arnon. Phoenicia and Judah had already broken with Jehu. At his death the kingdom of Israel had dwindled to a third of its size.

JEHOAHAZ (814-798 B.C.):   Son of Jehu, Jehoahaz found
2 KGS. 13:1-9   himself in difficulties with
Hazael. Elisha remained faithful to the Dynasty of Jehu and his influence at court was great; he foresaw the difficulties and encouraged king and people. About the year 802 B.C. Adad-nirari III intervened in Syria; Damascus was devastated and Israel had to pay tribute. But the Assyrians had to retire owing to troubles in the east.

JEHOASH (798-783 B.C.):   Jehoash was the son of Jeho-
2 KGS. 13:10-13   ahaz. Damascus had been
weakened by the Assyrian invasion. Jehoash defeated the Arameans in three battles and won back the lost territory. Under his reign Israel slowly returned to its old prosperity, and there was a parallel renaissance in Judah. Jehoash had a clash with Amaziah of Judah at Bethshemesh and went on to take Jerusalem. (The mission of Elisha was undertaken under Jehoram and Jehoash.)

JEROBOAM II (783-743 B.C.):   The long reign of this
2 KGS. 14:23-29   able prince gave Israel the
illusion of a return to Solomonic times. The Bible has not much to say of him; it is certain, however, that his reign marked the apogee of Israel. Excavations at Samaria and Megiddo, as well as the Books of Amos and Hosea, illustrate the prosperity of the kingdom. All the territory of Israel was free from foreign influence and Judah was an ally, if not indeed a tributary state; trade and commerce flourished in both kingdoms. For the first time, however, the "social question" emerged: the wealth

was in the hands of a few and the mass of the people lived in misery. Amos paints a vivid picture of the state of affairs. (The Prophets Amos and Hosea; the latter continued his mission under the successors of Jeroboam.)

ZECHARIAH (743 B.C.):   The reign of Jeroboam II was
2 KGS. 15:8-12   followed by a period of anarchy.
His son Zechariah remained on the throne for six months only; he was assassinated by Shallum. This is the end of the Dynasty of Jehu. A period of anarchy followed.

SHALLUM (743 B.C.):   Shallum reigned for one month
2 KGS. 15:13-16   only. His rival, Menahem of
Tirzah—a representative of the pro-Assyrian party—disposed of him and seized power.

5) *Dynasty of Menahem*

MENAHEM (743-738 B.C.):   Menahem displayed all the
2 KGS. 15:17-22   cruelty of the Assyrians towards his rivals. He submitted to Tiglath-pileser III, paying him a rich tribute, and was recognized by him.

The development of history is now dominated by the reawakening of Assyria: Tiglath-pileser III (745-727 B.C.) is the real founder of the Assyrian Empire. In the Bible he is called Pul; from Assyro-Babylonian documents we know that he took the Babylonian throne and ruled there under the name Pulu. In 738 B.C. he gained control over Syria; in that year "Menahem of Samaria," with a number of other kings, paid tribute. In order to pay this tribute Menahem had heavily taxed his nobles and as a pro-Assyrian he had lost the support of the people. On the testimony of the Prophet Hosea it seems that his reign was marked by the strife of pro-Assyrian and pro-Egyptian parties.

PEKAHIAH (738-737 B.C.):   Menahem was succeeded by
2 KGS. 15:23-26   his son Pekahiah who reigned only two years. He was assassinated by Pekah. This ended the Dynasty of Menahem.

PEKAH (737-732 B.C.):   Pekah was the son of Remaliah,
2 KGS. 15:27-31   general of Pekahiah; he was an
anti-Assyrian. His first act was to enter into alliance with
Damascus, for Rezin of Damascus had seen the need for
an anti-Assyrian league. The two kings tried to win over
Jotham of Judah, but without success. Alliance with Judah
was important because it would place the league in immediate contact with Egypt. Thus Rezin and Pekah decided to attack Judah; they would overthrow the reigning
dynasty and put on the throne a certain "son of Tabeel,"
an Aramean. Jotham died and his son, Ahaz, had to bear
the brunt of this, the Syro-Ephraimite war. Meanwhile,
support for the league had been growing. It now included
Tyre, Sidon, Gaza, Philistia, Edom, and the queen of the
Arabs. Ahaz was defeated by the Syro-Ephraimites and was
besieged in Jerusalem; he appealed to Tiglath-pileser III.
The year was 734 B.C. and the Assyrian king was probably
already on the march against the league. Aram and Israel
formed the heart of the league, and so the Assyrian king
decided to isolate them from actual and potential supporters. To prevent any interference from Egypt he subdued
Philistia; he took Gaza, whose king, Hanun, fled to Egypt.
Tiglath-pileser then turned on Israel; he devastated Galilee
and Gilead and deported the inhabitants. In 733 B.C. he
campaigned against Rezin who put up a fierce resistance;
but in 732 B.C. Damascus fell: Rezin was executed and
his people deported. Israel too would have been destroyed
altogether, but the pro-Assyrian party overthrew Pekah and
placed Hoshea on the throne.

HOSHEA (732-724 B.C.):   Israel was now reduced to Sa-
2 KGS. 17:1-4   maria. The conquered territory,
whose inhabitants had been deported, was divided into
three Assyrian provinces: Megiddo, Dor, and Gilead.

In 727 B.C. Tiglath-pileser III died; when his son
Shalmaneser, governor of Phoenicia, went to take possession of the throne, the anti-Assyrian party was given
a new lease of life. But Shalmaneser V (726-722 B.C.)
was recognized as king throughout the empire. The Phoenician cities, however, had rebelled. Shalmaneser be-

sieged Tyre but could not take it; during the siege (c. 725 B.C.), Hoshea of Samaria paid the annual tribute. Soon, however, the king came to hear that Hoshea was conspiring with Egypt; he acted at once. In 724 B.C. Hoshea was arrested and Samaria was besieged; Samaria held out for nearly three years. In 722 B.C. Shalmaneser V died and was succeeded by Sargon II (722-705 B.C.). In 721 B.C. Samaria fell to Sargon. The population was deported, in stages, beginning with the ruling class. The mass of the people, some 27,290 according to Sargon,[29] was deported to Upper Mesopotamia and there lost their identity. Peoples from other regions were brought in and settled in their place and the colonization of Samaria continued during the reign of Sargon and his successors. These colonists brought their own religions, but accepted Yahweh as a local deity; the Israelites who were left became lost in the midst of this pagan syncretism. After the fall of Samaria the destiny of Yahwism was centered on Judah alone.

8. THE KINGDOM OF JUDAH

In sharp contrast to Israel, the principle of Davidic succession was rigidly adhered to in Judah. While kings of Judah were sometimes assassinated, the rightful heir automatically came to the throne; there was no question of overthrowing the line of David.

REHOBOAM (931-913 B.C.): On the death of Solo-
1 KGS. 14:21-31; 2 CHR. 10-12 mon, his son Reho-
boam was at once recognized as king of Judah. He failed to be proclaimed king of Israel; in fact he precipitated the schism. Just at this time Palestine became a target for Egyptian expansion. Shishak (Shoshenq), founder of the Twenty-second Dynasty—who had granted asylum to Jeroboam—invaded Judah; Rehoboam had to surrender the treasure of his capital. It appears that the Egyptian expedition traversed the whole country, because a stele with the name of this Pharaoh was found in Megiddo. The Egyptians did not retain control over Palestine. Rehoboam built a line of fortresses along his frontiers. Apart from the

Egyptian exaction his reign seems to have been prosperous. His religious conduct is condemned.

ABIJAM (913-911 B.C.):   Abijam succeeded his father.
1 KGS. 15:1-8; 2 CHR. 13   The enmity between the two kingdoms broke out in open hostility. Abijam inflicted a crushing defeat on Jeroboam I at Zemaraim near Bethel and Judah won control of all the territory of Benjamin. His religious conduct is condemned.

ASA (911-870 B.C.):   Asa lost to Baasha the
1 KGS. 15:9-24; 2 CHR. 14-16   territory that Abijam had won. He had to face a serious incursion of nomads from the Negeb, but he defeated them. When Baasha had taken and fortified Ramah, six miles north of Jerusalem, Asa appealed to Ben-hadad I of Damascus and persuaded him to break his alliance with Baasha. The latter had to abandon his conflict with Asa who promptly took Ramah and fortified Geba and Mizpah. This recourse to foreigners was a grave error; yet the religious conduct of Asa is praised—though he did not remove the "high places." He became ill towards the end of his reign.

JEHOSHAPHAT (870-848 B.C.):   Jehoshaphat was al-
1 KGS. 22:41-51; 2 CHR. 17-20   ready coregent during the illness of his father. He had friendly relations with Ahab of Israel, and his son, Jehoram, married Athaliah, the daughter (or sister) of Ahab. Kgs. and Chr. each shows the reign of Jehoshaphat in a different light, though both present him as a sincere Yahwist who continued the tradition of Asa; but the "high places" were not removed.

1. Kgs. presents his reign as unfortunate. He took part in the expedition against Ramoth-gilead in which Ahab was killed. Even before this he may have been one of the league of kings which met the Assyrians at Qarqar. He had control of Edom and Eziongeber, but his fleet, which he had built for trade with Ophir, was destroyed in port. If the "king of Judah" who took part in the expedition against Mesha is Jehoshaphat, and not his son Jehoram, we have another unfortunate episode.

2. Chr. on the other hand, gives more space to the

Yahwism of the king and also paints his reign as prosperous and fortunate. He won control over Edom and victoriously countered an invasion of Maonites supported by Moabites and Edomites; he won tribute from the Philistines and the Arabs. In internal administration he organized the kingdom militarily and established a judiciary. He set up a commission, composed of officials and Levites, to instruct the people in the Torah.

It seems we can reconcile these accounts by supposing that, if Jehoshaphat shared in the misfortune of Israel in joint ventures, he met with success when acting on his own. His gravest error was the introduction of an Omrite princess into the dynasty of David; this was to have serious consequences in the dynastic, religious, and political fields.

JEHORAM (848-841 B.C.):   The son of Jehoshaphat,
2 KGS. 8:16-24; 2 CHR. 21   who had married Athaliah,
Jehoram was an anti-Yahwist and permitted the cult of Baal. He took part with Joram of Israel in an unsuccessful expedition against Mesha of Moab. As a result Edom became independent and Libnah was lost to the Philistines. His religious conduct is condemned.

AHAZIAH (841 B.C.):   Ahaziah was the son of Jehoram.
2 KGS. 8:25—9:29;   He joined Joram of Israel in an
2 CHR. 22:1-9   expedition against Ramoth-gilead
and was killed by order of Jehu. His religious conduct is condemned.

ATHALIAH (841-835 B.C.):   On the death of Ahaziah,
2 KGS. 11;   his mother Athaliah seized
2 CHR. 22:10—23:21   power. She was able to do
this in virtue of her official position as *gebirah* or "Grand Lady"—a position held by the queen-mother. She began her reign by massacring all the royal family, a necessary measure if she was to keep the throne. Fortunately for Judah, the sister of Ahaziah, wife of the high priest Jehoiada, was able to rescue her little nephew, Joash, the infant son of Ahaziah.

It was a disastrous reign for the religion of Yahweh. The worshipers of Baal who had escaped the suppression of Jehu found refuge at the court of Judah, and Baal had his temple in Jerusalem, served by the priest Mattan. The Temple of Yahweh was allowed to stand, more or less without interference. Both religious and national sentiment was opposed to Athaliah but, in view of the principle of Davidic succession, there seemed to be no way out of the impasse—there was no heir of David. However, unknown to the people, the young Joash was growing up in the shelter of the Temple.

At last Jehoiada, the high priest, organized the revolt. He won over the Temple and palace guards, and on a sabbath, when the three corps of guards were on duty, he received their oath of allegiance and entrusted the young descendant of David to their protection. Joash, then seven years old, was proclaimed king in the Temple. Athaliah, roused by the clamor, came to the Temple; she was dragged outside the sacred precincts and killed.

JOASH (835-796 B.C.):   During his minority Joash was
2 KGS. 12; 2 CHR. 24   under the guardianship of Jehoiada who brought him up a sincere Yahwist. He restored the cult and repaired the Temple. At this time Hazael of Damascus, who was harassing Israel, made his presence felt even in Judah, and Joash was constrained to pay a heavy tribute. Perhaps it was as a result of this indignity that he fell victim to a palace plot. His religious conduct is praised; but the "high places" were not removed.

AMAZIAH (796-781 B.C.):   Damascus had been weak-
2 KGS. 14:1-22; 2 CHR. 25   ened by the Assyrians, and Jehoash of Israel had brought back prosperity to his kingdom; there was a parallel improvement in Judah. Amaziah avenged the death of his father. He moved against the Edomites and took their stronghold, Sela (Petra), and he rebuilt Elath on the Gulf of Aqabah. Carried away by these successes, he challenged Jehoash of Israel. He was defeated at Beth-shemesh and Jehoash went on to take Jerusalem. At the occasion of this national disaster, Amaziah had to flee from Jerusalem; he sought refuge at Lachish, but was put to death. His religious conduct is praised—except for the "high places."

UZZIAH (AZARIAH) (781-740 B.C.):   The reign of Uz-
2 KGS. 15:1-6; 2 CHR. 26   ziah, son of Amaziah, contemporary with that of Jeroboam II, marks a
period of stability, with both kingdoms availing of the
weakness of Damascus and the eclipse of Assyrian power.
It was a period of expansion, with increase in trade and
material prosperity.

Uzziah exploited the success of Amaziah against the
Edomites and developed Elath. In an expedition against
the Arabs he insured the passage to the south; he also
gained advantages over the Philistines and Ammonites.
Internally, his reign was marked by the strengthening of
the defenses of Jerusalem, by a reorganization of the army,
and by the development of agriculture. He became leprous
towards the end of his life and handed over the administration to his son Jotham. According to Chr. the leprosy was
a punishment for his usurpation of certain priestly preroga-
tives; this would appear to hint at a tension between the
priesthood, grown strong under Jehoiada, and the monarchy.

JOTHAM (740-736 B.C.):   Uzziah was succeeded by
2 KGS. 15:32-38; 2 CHR. 27   his son Jotham who had
already been coregent. We know nothing of his short
reign except that he continued the policy of his father and
saw the beginning of the Syro-Ephraimite war. His religious
conduct is praised—with the usual reservation.

AHAZ (736-716 B.C.):   Pekah of Israel and Rezin of Da-
2 KGS. 16; 2 CHR. 28   mascus, who had formed a league
against Assyria, invited Jotham to join them, but he refused to be drawn into the league. The allies declared war,
meaning to overthrow the dynasty and place on the throne
a creature of their own, a certain "son of Tabeel." This
was the situation Ahaz inherited from his father. Meanwhile, many other states had joined the league, and these
took action. Edom gained possession of the port of Elath,
the Ammonites freed themselves from the tribute imposed
by Jotham, the Philistines attacked the towns of the
Shephelah, and the Syro-Ephraimites invaded Judah. Ahaz
moved against them, but was defeated; he retired to Jeru-

salem where he was besieged. Isaiah tried to persuade the
king that he needed only to have trust in Yahweh and all
would be well: this is the purpose of the Immanuel prophecy and its background. But Ahaz rejected the counsel of
Isaiah and turned for help to the king of Assyria, and
despoiled the Temple treasury in order to send rich gifts.
Thus Ahaz freed himself from a difficult situation by taking upon himself the yoke of Ashur. It was 734 B.C. when
Tiglath-pileser III moved against the league,[30] and in 732
B.C., with all resistance broken, in the Damascus that had
fallen to him, the Assyrian king held a great assembly to
receive the homage and tribute of his vassals.

Ahaz had chosen to become the vassal of Assyria, while
Isaiah had strenuously counseled strict neutrality. At first
sight it would seem that the king was right. Submission to
the might of Assyria was inevitable and it was politically a
shrewd move to anticipate it. But it was not the appeal of
Ahaz that had moved Tiglath-pileser to take action against
the league—he would certainly have done so in any case.
The kingdom of Judah was of no importance to Assyria
since it lay beyond the great roads of Syria and Egypt. The
king would have been satisfied with a strict neutrality on
Judah's part, and neutrality would have safeguarded the
national and religious independence of the country. But
by declaring himself a vassal, Ahaz had invited Assyrian
interference in Judah, with all its political and religious
consequences. In the political field it entailed absolute submission;[31] any gesture of independent action would be
regarded as an act of rebellion. The way was open to
cultic and religious influences. Thus when Ahaz was in
Damascus in 732 B.C. he sent back to Jerusalem the model
of an altar he had seen there and ordered the immediate
construction of a similar altar. On his return he inaugurated it himself and installed it in place of the bronze altar
which Solomon had set before the entrance to the Temple.
These and other cultic changes are modifications, inspired
by Assyrian cult, and partly by Syrian cult, introduced into
the cult of Yahweh; they were bound to have repercussions
on the religion of Yahweh.

During the reign of Ahaz the kingdom of Israel fell

(721 B.C.). The king was dissuaded by Isaiah from joining another anti-Assyrian league; Sargon II easily crushed
this revolt in 720 B.C. The Assyrian danger was more and
more pressing: the Assyrian province of Samaria ran along
the northern frontier of Judah and the provinces of Gaza
and Ascalon lay to the west. Judah was in a sad state:
the country was a vassal of Assyria, foreign influence had
weakened national sentiment and religious syncretism had
weakened Yahwistic sentiment. The religious conduct of
Ahaz is roundly condemned.

HEZEKIAH (716-687 B.C.):   The great glory of the son
2 KGS. 18-20; 2 CHR. 29-32   of Ahaz is the restoration
of pure Yahwism. This was due to the personal activity of
the young and energetic king, but it was also due in great
measure to the support of the Prophets, Micah, who exercised his ministry during this reign, and Isaiah, whose
mission, held in check by Ahaz, developed effectively under Hezekiah.

Religious reform, even from a political point of view,
was the first essential task. The chief aims of the reform
were: the extirpation of idolatrous practices; the re-
establishment of pure Yahwism (involving the purification
of the Temple); and the centralization of the cult, that is,
the suppression of the "high places." The role of the
Prophets in these reforms is obscure; they were, it seems,
not particularly interested in the cultic reforms, but demanded interior, spiritual reform. The preaching of these
Prophets, however, must have aided a reform that was,
at least in part, the practical realization of that return to
Yahweh which was the burden of their preaching. Jeremiah testifies that the preaching of Micah was efficacious
(Jer. 26:18 f.).

The religious reform was accompanied by a national
restoration. Judah seems to have been left unmolested by
the Assyrians until 701 B.C.; the expedition of 711 B.C.
was not aimed at Hezekiah, who had remained neutral.
Besides, during this time Sargon and Sennacherib were
fully occupied in the east. There was a return of prosperity to the kingdom. It must have been during this period

that the great tunneled canal from Gihon to Siloam was cut; it was too difficult a job to have been carried through in the stress of a siege.

In 703 B.C. Marduk-apal-iddina (Merodach-baladan) had taken Babylon for the second time and had installed himself as king. From there he sent an embassy to Hezekiah during the latter's illness; undoubtedly his real motive was to stir up a diversion in the west while he sought to consolidate his position. Sennacherib defeated Marduk-apal-iddina in 703 B.C. and devastated the region around Babylon. During this campaign Phoenicia and the Palestinian states as well as Edom and Moab had rebelled (with Egyptian encouragement and support). Sennacherib moved into Syria in 701 B.C.; we have two accounts of this campaign:

1. *Assyrian account.*[32] The Assyrian king was called into Palestine by a revolt. The principal leaders were: the king of Sidon; the king of Ashkelon; the inhabitants of Ekron; and Hezekiah of Judah. There were four operations: against the Phoenician cities, Sidon and Accho; against Ashkelon; against Ekron; and against Jerusalem. Sennacherib did not take Jerusalem, but accepted tribute.

2. *Biblical account.* Hezekiah rebelled by refusing to pay tribute. Sennacherib suddenly appeared against him. All the fortified cities of Judah were taken; Hezekiah submitted and paid tribute. Sennacherib, from Lachish, sent an army against Jerusalem and demanded the surrender of the city; this force retired to meet the Egyptian army of Tirhakah. From Libnah another demand for surrender was sent to Hezekiah. The Assyrian army was decimated by "the angel of the Lord."

While it is not surprising that the Assyrian Annals say nothing of the disaster which befell the king's army in Palestine, it is surprising that the capture of Lachish is not mentioned, especially since this event was depicted in bas-relief in Nineveh.[33] The most satisfactory explanation is to suppose that the biblical account has conflated two campaigns. The first, in 701 B.C., ended with the payment of tribute by Hezekiah. Then, in 690 B.C., Tirhakah became coregent in Egypt and fomented rebellion in Palestine (Hezekiah was implicated). Sennacherib was engaged in the east where Babylon was in open rebellion but, in 688 B.C., he moved to the west. Lachish was taken and Jerusalem was besieged; Tirhakah's relief army was driven back. Nevertheless the city was not taken because the Assyrian army was struck by an epidemic (2 Kgs. 19:35) and also because Sennacherib's presence was required at home (2 Kgs. 19:7).

The rebellion of Hezekiah ended in the reduction of Judah to the mountain district around Jerusalem. The king dedicated the last years of his life to the restoration of the public life of his gravely-stricken people. His religious conduct is praised without reserve. (The mission of Isaiah and Micah was undertaken under Jotham, Ahaz, and Hezekiah.)

MANASSEH (687-642 B.C.):   The long reign of Ma-
2 KGS. 21:1-18; 2 CHR. 33:1-20   nasseh was disastrous for the religion of Yahweh. The reforms of Hezekiah had not been popular because they had been aimed at inveterate habits; now there was a strong reaction. Besides, under Ashurbanipal, Assyria was at the height of its power and its influence was felt in the cultic and religious field; as a faithful vassal, Manasseh sought to please his masters by yielding to this influence. However, there was resistance, particularly in the circle of those who were faithful to the teaching of Isaiah; the suppression of this resistance was cruel and effective.

Nevertheless, Manasseh's loyalty seemed suspect and he was sent in chains to Babylon; this probably happened after 648 B.C. when Ashurbanipal, having taken Babylon, reasserted his authority in Palestine. The king was released after a few years. On his return he tried to do something about restoring the religion of Yahweh. He also set about strengthening the defenses of his capital and kingdom, but death cut short his work. His religious conduct is condemned.

AMON (642-640 B.C.):   Manasseh was suc-
2 KGS. 21:19-26; 2 CHR. 21-25   ceeded by his son Amon who belonged to the antireform, pro-Assyrian party.

He reigned only two years before being assassinated by a palace conspiracy. His religious conduct is condemned.

JOSIAH (640-609 B.C.): The assassination of Amon dis-
2 KGS. 22:1–23:30; pleased the "people of the land"
2 CHR. 34-35 (that is, the citizens who en-
joyed full civil rights), who were faithful to the Davidic line; they rose against the conspirators and placed on the throne the son of Amon, Josiah, a child of eight.

The reign of Josiah coincided with the sudden collapse and fall of Assyria; it is this factor that enabled the young king to push through his reform and permitted him to re-organize his kingdom. Though the Bible is silent about the internal profane policy of Josiah, it is certain that there must have been a national renaissance which went hand-in-hand with the religious reform and policy of independ-ence. There were territorial gains, too, but we cannot de-termine them. The Megiddo incident points to a reorgani-zation of the army.

Josiah began his reform in his twelfth year (628 B.C.). This reform attacked primarily the Assyrian cult, and was therefore also a rejection of foreign domination. In his eighteenth year, when the secretary Shaphan was sent to see about the collection for the restoration of the Temple, the priest Hilkiah gave him "the book of the law" which had been found in the Temple; this providential dis-covery gave a fresh impetus to the reform. It is generally agreed that the "book of the law" is the deuteronomical code (Dt. 12-26), the legal tradition of the Northern King-dom, which was brought to Jerusalem by Levite refugees about the time of the fall of Samaria in 721 B.C.; it was deposited in the Temple to be neglected and, eventually, forgotten.

The hopes raised by the national restoration under Jo-siah were rudely dashed. In 609 B.C. Neco, seeking to maintain the balance of power in Mesopotamia, went to the aid of the stricken Assyrians. He followed the normal route of Egyptian armies going into Syria—along the coast road towards Carmel, then inland at Megiddo. Josiah in-tercepted him at Megiddo and was defeated and killed.

It seems that Josiah was striving to uphold his policy of independence. The Egyptians were a threat whether they were to re-establish Assyria or to profit from the situation by seizing Palestine. The tragic death of the king meant the end of the reform and the beginning of the end of Judah. The reform had come too late; the Exile was needed for a thorough purification of Yahwism. The religious conduct of Josiah is praised without reserve. (Zephaniah and Nahum undertook their mission during the reign of Josiah.)

JEHOAHAZ (609 B.C.): After the death of Josiah the 2 KGS. 23:31-35; "people of the land" proclaimed 2 CHR. 36:1-4 Jehoahaz, his son, king. Three months later Neco summoned Jehoahaz to his headquarters in Riblah, deposed him, and deported him to Egypt. He placed his brother Eliakim on the throne, changing his name to Jehoiakim.

JEHOIAKIM (609-587 B.C.): Jehoiakim was a vassal of 2 KGS. 23:36—24:6; Neco and paid tribute to 2 CHR. 36:5-8 Egypt; to do this he oppressed the people. The tragic death of Josiah had been a scandal for Judah; Yahweh had not saved the pious king and the promises of the prophets were misleading. There was a violent anti-Assyrian reaction, headed by the king and court, and all the old syncretism invaded the Temple.

Meanwhile, Nebuchadnezzar, as general of his father Nabopolassar, had defeated Neco at Carchemish and had driven him back to Egypt. In 604 B.C., now king, he was in Palestine and destroyed Ashkelon; it was probably at this time that Jehoiakim changed allegiance and became a vassal of Babylon. In 601 B.C. Nebuchadnezzar moved on Egypt, but had to retire without gaining his objective. At this time Judah was split by factions; the pro-Egyptian party gained the upper hand and Jehoiakim rebelled. Nebuchadnezzar was not free to take personal action immediately, but he dispatched local Babylonian forces, together with bands of Edomites, Ammonites, and Moabites to harass the country. In 598 B.C. the Babylonian king moved. Before he arrived in Palestine Jehoiakim had died, under obscure circumstances, and had been replaced by his son Jehoiachin. The religious conduct of the last four kings of Judah is condemned.

JEHOIACHIN (597 B.C.): Jerusalem was besieged and
2 KGS. 24:8-17; Jehoiachin surrendered after
2 CHR. 36:9-10 three months. The king and the
queen-mother, together with the leading citizens, were taken to Babylon. This is the first deportation.

ZEDEKIAH (597-587 B.C.): Nebuchadnezzar installed as
2 KGS. 24:18—25:7; king the uncle of Jehoiachin,
2 CHR. 36:11-13 the twenty-one year old Mat-
taniah, to whom he gave the name of Zedekiah. (As in the case of Jehoiakim, this is a Yahwistic name, and would scarcely have been imposed by a Babylonian; perhaps, in both cases, it is a question of a coronation name.) Due to the deportation of the leading citizens the kingdom was almost in a state of anarchy. Zedekiah was weak and quite unable to control the rival parties: one, represented by Jeremiah, counseled submission to the Babylonians; the other and stronger party sought the support of Egypt and had the favor of the people. In 590 B.C. Psammetichus II appeared in Palestine; after this, Zedekiah, whose conduct was suspect, went to Babylon to clear himself. All this time Jeremiah preached against alliance with Egypt and had to contend with false prophets; and Ezekiel, who had been deported with Jehoiachin, foretold the fall of Jerusalem.

Zedekiah finally yielded to the Egyptian party. A league was formed with Ammon; and Apries (who had succeeded Psammetichus) persuaded Tyre and Sidon to join. Nebuchadnezzar acted at once: he subdued Phoenicia and blockaded Tyre and then sent his main force against Judah. In 588 B.C. Jerusalem was besieged. All the fortresses of the kingdom were taken; only Lachish and Azekah held out for some time.[34] The siege was lifted when Apries appeared in the Shephelah with an Egyptian

THE KINGS OF JUDAH AND ISRAEL

| David | | c. 1010-970 |
| Solomon | | c. 970-931 |

JUDAH		ISRAEL		ASSYRIA	
Rehoboam	931-913	Jeroboam I	931-910	Ashur-dan II	934-912
Abijah	913-911			Adad-nirari II	912-890
		Nadab	910-909		
Asa	911-870	Baasha	909-886		
		Elah	886-885		
		Zimri	885		
		Omri	885-874	Ashur-nasir-pal II	883-859
Jehoshaphat	870-848	Ahab	874-853		
		Ahaziah	853-852	Shalmaneser III	859-824
Jehoram	848-841	Jehoram	853-841		
Ahaziah	841				
Athaliah	841-835	Jehu	841-814		
Joash	835-796				
		Jehoahaz	814-798	Shamshi-adad V	824-811
Amaziah	796-781	Jehoash	798-783	Adad-nirari III	811-783
Uzziah	781-740	Jeroboam II	783-743	Shalmaneser IV	783-773
				Ashur-dan III	773-754
				Ashur-nirari V	754-745
				Tiglath-pileser III	745-727
		Zechariah	743		
		Shallum	743		
Jotham	740-736	Menahem	743-738		
		Pekahiah	738-737		
Ahaz	736-716	Pekah	737-732		
		Hoshea	732-724	Shalmaneser V	727-722
				Sargon II	722-705
		721—Fall of Samaria			

		EGYPT			
Hezekiah	716-687	Piankhi	c. 715		
		Shabako	710-696	Sennacherib	705-681
		Shebteko	696-685		
Manasseh	687-642	Tirhakah	690-667	Esarhaddon	681-669
		Neco I	667-663	Ashurbanipal	669-632
Amon	642-640	Psammetichus I	663-609		
Josiah	640-609			Ashur-etil-ilani	632-629
				Sinsariskun	629-612
		Neco II	609-593	Ashur-uballit II	612-606

				NEO-BABYLONIAN EMPIRE	
				Nabopolassar	626-605
Jehoahaz	609				
Jehoiakim	609-597			Nebuchadnezzar	605-562
Jehoiachin	597				
Zedekiah	597-587	Psammetichus II	593-588		
		Apries	588-566		
587—Fall of Jerusalem					

army, but he was quickly driven back and the siege was resumed. The city held out stubbornly despite terrible famine conditions. In July, 587 B.C., the wall was breached. Zedekiah, with some of his officers, escaped by night and fled towards Jericho, but they were captured and taken before Nebuchadnezzar at his headquarters in Riblah. The sons of Zedekiah were executed in his presence, then he was blinded and sent to die in a Babylonian prison. The walls of the city were levelled, the Temple and buildings were burned, and the sacred vessels were carried off. Part of the population was deported to Babylon. The kingdom of Judah had come to an end.

After the fall of Jerusalem. Judah had become a Babylonian province. Before he left Syria, Nebuchadnezzar appointed as governor a certain Gedaliah, a man of noble family who, as a seal found at Lachish bearing his name indicates, had been a chief minister of Zedekiah. He settled at Mizpah, apparently because Jerusalem was uninhabitable, was supported by a small Babylonian garrison, and had the moral support of Jeremiah. Gedaliah sought to conciliate the people, but he fell victim to a plot hatched by one Ishmael, a member of the royal house; the Babylonian garrison and some Jews faithful to Gedaliah were massacred. Ishmael escaped to Ammon, while many Jews, fearing Babylonian vengeance, fled to Egypt, taking with them an unwilling Jeremiah. In fact, Nebuchadnezzar did not at once chastise the Jews. Jer. 52:30 speaks of a third deportation in 582 B.C.; this would have been about five years after the murder of Gedaliah. (Jeremiah carried on his mission from the reign of Josiah until after the fall of Jerusalem.)

There were three deportations (in 597 B.C., 587 B.C., and 582 B.C.), but it is difficult to arrive at a definite figure. In Jer. 52:28-30 precise totals for the three deportations are given and the sum for all is only 4,600. This seems a reasonable figure for, though it probably counts only adult males, the grand total would probably not be more than four times that many—perhaps, at most, 20,000 people.

9. EXILE AND RESTORATION

1) *The Background*

LAST YEARS OF THE   With the death of Nebuchadnezzar
BABYLONIAN EMPIRE   in 562 B.C. Babylonian power declined rapidly; the situation was aggravated by lack of internal stability. The son of Nebuchadnezzar, Avil-marduk
(562-560 B.C.)—the Evil-merodach who released Jehoiachin (2 Kgs. 25:27-30)—reigned only two years; it is likely
that his brother-in-law, Neriglissar (560-556 B.C.), came
to the throne as a usurper. His son and successor, Labashi-
marduk (556 B.C.), was a minor and was soon removed
by Nabonidus (556-539 B.C.) who seized the throne. This
king seems to have been more of an archaeologist than
a ruler: he excavated temple sites in Babylonia and had
ancient inscriptions deciphered. For reasons that are not
clear he resided for eight years (c. 552-545 B.C.) at the
oasis of Teima in the Arabian desert[35] and left the affairs
of the empire in the hands of his son Belshazzar.

The Medes, under Cyaxares, had been a potential danger to Babylon and the same threat persisted under
Astyages (585-550 B.C.). Thus when Cyrus, a Persian
prince, rebelled against his Median overlord, he was supported by Nabonidus. But Cyrus soon proved a greater
menace than Media had ever been and Nabonidus quickly
entered into a defensive alliance with Amasis of Egypt
(569-525 B.C.) and Croesus of Lydia (c. 560-546 B.C.).
In 546 B.C. Lydia was defeated; though Cyrus did not
move at once, his rapidly-growing power made the fate
of Babylon inevitable. In 539 B.C. Cyrus attacked and
Nabonidus was defeated at Opis on the Tigris and subsequently taken prisoner. Cyrus' general, Gobryas, took
Babylon without striking a blow; Belshazzar was killed,
apparently assassinated. The short-lived Neo-Babylonian
Empire was at an end.

THE RISE   Cyrus, a Persian, was ruler of the small king-
OF PERSIA   dom of Anshan in southern Iran and was a
vassal of Astyages, king of the Medes. In 555 B.C. he

rebelled; by 550 B.C. he had seized Ecbatana, the capital of Astyages, and had taken over the Median Empire. In 546 B.C. he invaded Lydia (in western Asia Minor), now allied with Babylon and Egypt, and took the capital Sardis. Lydia was incorporated into his realm and, apparently, he had control of Upper Mesopotamia. The Egyptian alliance was now of no avail and Babylonia was isolated. But Cyrus was in no hurry; he campaigned in the East and extended his dominion almost as far as India. Then in 539 B.C. he won Babylon at the price of a single battle.[36] Cyrus was master of the greatest empire the world had known.

Cyrus was an enlightened ruler who sought to win the respect and loyalty of his subject peoples. It is clear that the Babylonians themselves, aware of his magnanimous character, had gladly changed masters; no doubt this helps to explain the astounding ease of his conquest. He was particularly careful to respect the religious susceptibilities of his subjects and he allowed them cultic autonomy; he even permitted peoples who had been deported by the Babylonians to return to their homelands. All this meant no weakening of political power. The Persian army was maintained at full strength and a complex governmental system was set up to control the vast empire, which was divided into provinces and satrapies. But Cyrus' general policy sets his benevolent treatment of the Jews in a clearer light. For in 538 B.C., the first year of his reign in Babylon, Cyrus published an edict authorizing the return of the Jewish captives to Judah and providing funds for the re-building of the Temple (Ez. 1:2-4; 6:3-5). It is no wonder that Second Isaiah (the unknown author of Is. 40-55) has painted, in glowing colors, the career of this liberator, the Lord's Anointed (Is. 45:1; cf. 44:28—45:13; 41:2 f., 25).

There was peace throughout the Persian Empire, but Cyrus was killed in a campaign against nomadic peoples beyond his eastern frontier. He was succeeded by his son Cambyses (530-522 B.C.), who conquered Egypt—which remained under Persian control until 401 B.C. In 522 B.C., while Cambyses was absent, Gaumata usurped the throne. Cambyses died—apparently he committed suicide—and an officer, Darius, accepted and supported by the army, overthrew Gaumata. Darius I (522-486 B.C.), during his first two years, had to cope with rebellion on all sides; the Persian Empire seemed about to break in pieces. But when he had passed through the crisis, Darius not only consolidated his position but further extended the boundaries of his realm so that, under him, Persia reached her zenith. His one failure was in Greece where the battle of Marathon (490 B.C.) checked his bid to take that country.

Darius was succeeded by his son Xerxes I (486-465 B.C.). Babylon rebelled and was destroyed. In 480 B.C. Xerxes invaded Greece, overwhelmed the Spartans at Thermopylae, and captured Athens. However, the decisive naval battle of Salamis, and subsequent military reverses, forced the Persians from Europe. Xerxes was ultimately assassinated and replaced by a younger son, Artaxerxes I Longimanus (465-424 B.C.). This takes us to the age of Nehemiah, the subject of the following section.

2) *Judah after 587* B.C.

In the campaign of 588-587 B.C. Judah was utterly devastated; not only Jerusalem but all the towns of the Shephelah and mountain country were razed. Apart from the deportees, thousands must have died by the sword or of starvation and disease, and thousands must have fled the country, finding refuge especially in Egypt. The political situation is difficult to ascertain. However, the country was not repopulated with other peoples as had happened in Samaria; though the neighboring Edomites, Ammonites, and Arabs did settle in parts of it. The remainder of the land, where a very poor people dwelt (considerably less than 20,000), was annexed to the administration of Samaria. It was a limited territory; for one thing, the Edomites had advanced half-way between Hebron and Bethlehem. Yet, despite its complete destruction, Jerusalem still attracted spirits attached to Yahwism and in the ruins of the Temple people came to pray (see Lam.). But hope for the future rested, not on this pitiful debris, but, as Jeremiah and Ezekiel had promised, with the exiles in Babylon.

3) *The Exiles in Babylon*

It should be kept in mind that the Jews exiled in Babylon were the cream of the country: its political, ecclesiastical, and intellectual leaders. This explains why the total (4,600 adult males) given by Jeremiah is so restricted. They lived in special settlements near Babylon and their lot was not unduly hard. Indeed there was the opportunity of economic advancement and many of them did so well that they elected to remain on in Babylon after Cyrus had opened the way for a return to Palestine.

It was inevitable that many Jews, their faith shaken by the terrible disaster that had befallen their nation, were won over by Babylonian culture. But others only clung more closely to their past. In God's inscrutable plan, the Exile was one of the most fruitful moments in the history of Israel. The people learned to know their God as never before, and, encouraged first by Ezekiel and then by the great Second Isaiah, they were buoyed up by a new and unquenchable hope. Most important of all, from our point of view, the Bible as we know it began to take definite shape. The Temple was gone with its elaborate cult; hence the faithful of Yahweh fell back on their traditions. This was the time when the Deuteronomic history was given its final form, when the sayings of the prophets were compiled, and when the priestly tradition was fixed. A new community was being forged for the final stage of God's preparatory plan.

4) *The Restoration*

In the first year of his reign in Babylon (538 B.C.) Cyrus issued a decree which authorized the restoration of the Jewish community and the cult of Yahweh in Palestine (Ez. 1:1-4; 6:25). The decree covered not only the return of the sacred vessels which Nebuchadnezzar had carried off, it also directed that the cost of rebuilding the Temple should be met out of imperial funds. The Jews in Babylon were encouraged to support the whole venture financially and all who wished to do so were free to return to Judah. Shesh-bazzar, "prince of Judah," that is, a member of the royal family and, seemingly, a son of Jehoiachin, was put in charge of the project. A small group set out under his leadership. One of the first tasks of the returned exiles was to restore the altar of holocausts. In the midst of the Temple ruins a regular cult was re-established—the first, essential thread of the past had been picked up again. In the spring of 537 B.C. the foundation of the Second Temple was laid.

But this seems to have been the extent of the first attempt at restoration. Only a handful had returned: Jews who had done well in Babylon were content to remain there, while a whole generation had grown up to whom Palestine was a foreign land. The Jews who had been left in Judah, and those who had taken over Jewish lands, were not pleased to see the exiles coming back. Furthermore the returned Jews themselves refused proffered Samaritan help in rebuilding the Temple. Because of this the first friendly advances hardened into opposition and the work had to cease altogether. The people grew despondent and the venture was in imminent danger of fading out. But a further group of exiles returned, sometime between 538 B.C. and 522 B.C., under the leadership of Zerubbabel and the high priest Joshua. Zerubbabel, a descendant of Jehoiachin, succeeded his uncle Shesh-bazzar as *pekah* (governor). Yet, by the end of the reign of Cambyses, the total population (including both returned exiles and Jews already in the land) of the tiny territory of Judah cannot have been much more than 20,000.

Discouragement was aggravated by tensions within the community. Not all who had returned, and still fewer of those who had never left, were imbued with the highest motives. Some were quick to profit from the misfortunes of others (Is. 58:1-12; 59:1-8) and certain syncretistic religious practices still prevailed—apparently among the people who had remained in the land (Is. 57:3-10; 65:1-7, 11; 66:3 f., 7). The bitter reality seemed to mock the words of Second Isaiah. But the Prophets Haggai and Zechariah countered the despondency and in 520 B.C. Zerubbabel began, in earnest, the rebuilding of the Second Temple. There was an anxious moment when Tattanai, satrap of Abar-nahara ("Beyond the River"—the trans-Euphrates satrapy, which included Syria and Palestine), questioned Zerubbabel's authorization. He decided to inquire into the authenticity of the decree of Cyrus; in the meantime, he did not hold up the work. The decree of Cyrus was found in the royal archives of Ecbatana, the summer capital. Darius I published a new decree in favor of the construction of the Temple, with precise indications of cult provision and expenses and with sanctions against any who might oppose the decree (Ez. 6:1-12). During the Pasch of 515 B.C. the Second Temple was dedicated.

We know nothing of the situation in Judah during the next half-century and more. Zerubbabel is not mentioned again. It is possible that, as a descendant of David and the center of messianic hope (see Hag. 2:23; Zech. 6:9-14), he was removed by the Persian authorities.[37] Some time during this period the province of *Yehud* (Judah) was set up; in extent it was roughly the same as the territory entrusted to Gedaliah in 587 B.C. Its northern limit was Bethel; to the south it reached a little beyond Bethlehem; in the west it was limited by the province of Ashdod. Though the Temple had been restored, all attempts to rebuild the walls of Jerusalem were opposed by the Samaritans. It was left to Nehemiah and Ezra to bring about the full restoration of the Jewish community.

10. THE WORK OF NEHEMIAH AND EZRA

1) *The Background*

Judah had become a Persian province and, until the rise of Alexander the Great, the fortunes of the Jewish community were inseparable from the history of the Persian Empire. The long reign of Artaxerxes I Longimanus (465-424 B.C.) was beset with difficulties. In 460 B.C. the king faced a rebellion in Egypt, which had been stirred up by a Libyan named Inaros. Megabyzus, satrap of Abarnahara, led the campaign against Egypt; it dragged on until 454 B.C. when Inaros was taken prisoner. Subsequently (449-448 B.C.) Megabyzus himself rebelled, but ended by being confirmed in his office. After this it was in the king's interest to look to the stability of Abar-nahara, and he showed a concern for Palestinian affairs. In 449 B.C. Artaxerxes agreed to the peace of Callias whose terms required that the Greek cities of Asia Minor be granted independence and that the Persian fleet be excluded from the Aegean. However, the Peloponnesian War (431-403 B.C.) enabled Persia to regain control of the Greek cities.

Xerxes II, who succeeded his father, was assassinated after little more than a month on the throne. Following further disorders, another son of Artaxerxes, Darius II Nothus (423-404 B.C.), became king. He was succeeded by Artaxerxes II Mnemon (404-358 B.C.). In 401 B.C. Egypt became independent; in the same year Artaxerxes had to face a revolt led by his brother, Cyrus the Younger. At Cumaxa in Babylonia, Cyrus was defeated and killed; the campaign, and especially the subsequent retreat of 10,000 Greek survivors of Cyrus' army, has been immortalized by Xenophon in his *Anabasis*. Shortly after this the Western satraps rebelled and won Egyptian support, but about the year 360 B.C. the revolt collapsed.

2) *Chronology of Ezra-Nehemiah*

We have no direct evidence of the situation in Judah between 515 and 445 B.C., but it is clear enough from the following period that there was an air of disillusionment in the tiny province. The Davidic monarchy had not been restored and the drab reality reflected nothing of the glowing colors of Second Isaiah. A political reorganization and spiritual renewal of the community were urgently needed and, happily, the men who would accomplish both were soon to appear. Yet surprisingly enough, since they are the architects of Judaism, the relationship of the careers of Ezra and Nehemiah remains a perplexing problem.

The real difficulty is to determine the date of Ezra's arrival in Jerusalem; the date of Nehemiah's career is certain, being independently confirmed by evidence from the Elephantine texts.[38] There are three main positions: some accept the order apparently adopted in Ezra-Nehemiah; others argue that the solution lies in taking Artaxerxes II into consideration; still others claim that the "seventh year" (Ez. 7:7) is a scribal error for the thirty-seventh year of Artaxerxes I. We shall set these positions out more clearly as follows:

1. According to the order of Ezra-Nehemiah:[39]

a) Ezra arrived in Jerusalem in 459 B.C.: the seventh year of Artaxerxes I (Ez. 7:8).

b) Nehemiah arrived in Jerusalem in 445 B.C.: the twentieth year of Artaxerxes I (Neh. 2:1).

c) Nehemiah remained twelve years (Neh. 13:6), that is, until 433 B.C.

d) He came to Jerusalem a second time, still under Artaxerxes I (465-424 B.C.).

2. Many authors invert the order of the texts—the object of the Chronicler (the author of 1,2 Chr.-Ez.-Neh.) was to place the *religious* work of Ezra before the political restoration of Nehemiah.[40]

a) Nehemiah arrived in 445 B.C.: the twentieth year of Artaxerxes I.

b) He remained twelve years—until 433 B.C.

c) He made a brief return to Jerusalem after 433 B.C.

d) Ezra came to Jerusalem in 398 B.C.: the seventh year of Artaxerxes II (404-358 B.C.).

3. The visit of Ezra may be placed between the two missions of Nehemiah.[41] This is achieved by a textual correction of Ez. 7:8. Ezra arrived not in the seventh but in the thirty-seventh year of Artaxerxes I: in 428 B.C.

a) Nehemiah arrived in 445 B.C.: the twentieth year of Artaxerxes I.

b) He remained from 445 B.C. to 433 B.C.

c) Ezra arrived in 428 B.C.: the thirty-seventh year of Artaxerxes I.

d) Nehemiah returned between 433 B.C. and 424 B.C. Therefore Ezra and Nehemiah were contemporaries.

None of these views can claim to solve all the problems. Since the third seems the most satisfactory, however, it is followed in our presentation of the work of Nehemiah and Ezra.

3) Nehemiah

After the disappearance of Zerubbabel the district of Judah seems to have been administered from Samaria. There was constant friction with the Samaritan officials; attempts to build the walls of Jerusalem were frustrated. In 445 B.C. a delegation from Jerusalem, led by Hanani (brother of Nehemiah) came to Susa, the Persian capital. Nehemiah, cupbearer (a position of high rank) to Artaxerxes I, was informed of the deplorable conditions in Judah. Taking advantage of his access to the king he had himself invested with full powers to restore the fortifications of Jerusalem; he may have been immediately appointed governor of Judah. Although armed with letters to the officials of Abar-nahara, he met with opposition from Sanballat (governor of Samaria), Tobiah (governor of Ammon in Transjordan), and Geshem "the Arab" (a sheik of northwestern Arabia). Yet despite all opposition, Nehemiah built the walls of Jerusalem in fifty-two days, and he arranged for the repopulation of the city. The whole province could have numbered no more than 50,000 inhabitants.

Though Nehemiah was governor of Judah until 433 B.C. we know little of his administration; what evidence there is, however, supports the view that he was a just and able ruler. Nevertheless, the opposition against him continued and he was also aware that a religious reform was called for. He returned to Susa in 433 B.C., and though his absence was a short one, many abuses arose while he was away. Through the complacency of the high priest Eliashib, Tobiah, the Ammonite governor and enemy of Nehemiah, obtained quarters in the Temple itself; and a grandson of Eliashib married the daughter of Sanballat, another bitter opponent of Nehemiah.

Nehemiah returned to Judah, certainly before the death of Artaxerxes I, and, most probably, within a year or two of his return to Susa. At once and with energy he attacked the abuses: he took over the quarters that had been allotted to Tobiah and expelled the grandson of Eliashib. Ac-

cording to Josephus this marked a definite break with the
Samaritans and the beginning of a religious schism: Sanballat built a temple on Mt. Gerizim after his son-in-law
had been banished from Jerusalem. However, it seems
more probable that the temple came later. In general, Nehemiah attacked mixed marriages, the violation of the
sabbath observance, and the rapacity of the upper classes.
We do not know how long this second term of office lasted;
all we can say is that by 410 B.C. a Persian named Bagoas
was governor.[42]

4) *Ezra*

During Nehemiah's second term as governor the man who
was to push through the much-needed religious reform arrived on the scene. The measures taken by Nehemiah
in this field had been *ad hoc* solutions; there was need for
something more radical and better organized. Ezra was
of a priestly family and was learned in the Law; he was
a "scribe." His commission (see Ez. 7:12-26) was quite
different from that of Nehemiah, and concerned religious
matters only. He carried with him a copy of the Law of
Moses together with a rescript from the king which, in
effect, made that Law the state law of the Jewish community. His authority extended over all Jews living in Abar-
nahara.

> Ezra's status is concealed in the title "scribe of the
> law of the God of heaven" (Ez. 7:12). This does not
> denote a doctor of the law in the later sense—though
> tradition with some justice (see v. 6) came to con-
> sider Ezra as such—but was Ezra's official title as
> a commissioner of the government. He was "Royal
> Secretary of the Law of the God of Heaven" (that
> is, the God of Israel) or, to modernize somewhat,
> "Minister of State for Jewish Affairs," with specific
> authority in the territory of Abar-nahara.[43]

In 428 B.C. Ezra came to Jerusalem from Babylon at the
head of a large company. Two months after his arrival,

on the Feast of Tabernacles, he initiated his reform, which had the support of the high priest Johanan. He read the Law to the people, and the people swore to uphold it. On the whole the demands of the Law, especially in the matter of cult, caused no difficulty, but the question of mixed marriages did prove to be a real crux. Some two months later, at an extraordinary assembly of the people, Ezra set up a commission to deal with the problem. Early in the following year the matter was radically dealt with: foreign wives and their children were sent away. However, we are not sure that these sweeping measures were conscientiously implemented, because the memoirs of Ezra finish abruptly at this point. At any rate such legislation did assure the separate identity of the Jewish people and, inevitably, did bring about their isolation.

The religious reform of Ezra certainly presupposed the political stability achieved by Nehemiah, but the latter was a reformer also. Though the canonical books of Ezra-Nehemiah give no clear-cut evidence that Nehemiah and Ezra were contemporaries, that assumption is not unreasonable. We depend almost exclusively on the memoirs of Ezra and Nehemiah and on the Chronicler's presentation of them; hence we have to take different viewpoints into account. The Chronicler himself, whose interests were primarily ecclesiastical, is understandably more interested in Ezra; while Nehemiah's memoirs are largely a personal apologia. Nehemiah is content to describe the part he played in the religious reform, while the Chronicler gives all the credit to Ezra.

At any rate, Nehemiah and Ezra, between them, had established a theocracy and founded Judaism. The Jews were politically subject to Persia, but they formed a recognized community and were authorized to regulate internal affairs in accordance with the Law of their God. And the Law which Ezra had brought with him, and around which he had reorganized the Jewish community, is, plausibly, the complete Torah, the *Pentateuch*. What is certain is that henceforth the distinguishing mark of a Jew would be adherence to the Law of Moses.

5) *The Elephantine Colony*

We learn from documents[44] (papyri and *ostraca* dated 498-399 B.C.) found on the island of Elephantine, just north of the first cataract of the Nile and opposite Aswan, that a Jewish military colony was established on the island, with a temple to Yahweh. It was there when the Persians conquered Egypt in 525 B.C. It was probably set up by Apries (588-569 B.C.) and was composed largely of refugees from Judah after 587 B.C. A study of the names shows that there were Arameans among the Jews; the nature of the syncretistic cult suggests that the colonists had originated among the mixed population around Bethel.[45] Besides Yahweh other divinities were worshiped: Eshembethel, Herem-bethel, Anath-bethel. It may be, however, that these names represent hypostatizations (personifications) of certain aspects of Yahweh (thus, for example, Eshem-bethel = "Name of the House of God"). While their Yahwism was obviously far from orthodox, these Jews of Elephantine still looked to Jerusalem as spiritual center.

The Jewish colony was favorably regarded by the Persians, since it was in the interest of the colonists to uphold Persian authority. But when the power of the Great King waned, the Jews became the object of national resentment. Aswan was the sacred city of the ram-headed god Khnum; a temple dedicated to him stood on the island of Elephantine. The Jewish animal sacrifices, and especially the immolation of a great number of lambs at the Pasch, were offensive to the worshipers of Khnum. When in 410 B.C. the satrap of Egypt, Arsames, was absent, the temple of Yahweh was destroyed in the course of a riot. Yadoniah, priest of the Elephantine community, wrote to Johanan, the high priest at Jerusalem, requesting him to use his good offices on their behalf to enable them to rebuild their temple. He received no reply, which is not surprising since the Jerusalem religious authorities must have been scandalized at the very idea of a temple of Yahweh anywhere else except in the holy city. Three years later (407 B.C.) the

Elephantine Jews wrote again, but this time to Bagoas, governor of Judah, and also to Delaiah and Shelemiah, sons of Sanballat, governor of Samaria. Bagoas and Delaiah did intervene on their behalf and the temple was rebuilt; animal sacrifices, however, were henceforth excluded. This temple did not stand for long. Egypt became independent of Persian rule in 401 B.C. and the last document from Elephantine is dated 399 B.C.—the colony must have disappeared about this time. Apart from their intrinsic interest, the Elephantine papyri assure us that Nehemiah was no longer governor of Judah in 407 B.C.; most probably he had been succeeded by Bagoas some years previously.

11. FROM EZRA TO ANTIOCHUS IV

We have almost no direct information covering the period between 427 B.C. and 167 B.C.; in other words, between the memoirs of Ezra and 1 Maccabees there is a lacuna of two and one-half centuries. All we know is that Jewish life continued along the pattern set by Ezra and Nehemiah and that during these centuries much of the Old Testament, as we know it, took final shape. (The last of the prophets appeared in this period: Joel and the author of Zechariah 9-14.)

1) The Background

Since we know so little of the Jewish history of this period it will not be possible to link up wider issues with conditions in Judah. However, a general grasp of the events of world history is necessary for the understanding of such books as Daniel.

THE END OF THE   Artaxerxes II had lost Egypt and had
PERSIAN EMPIRE   nearly lost his throne to his younger brother Cyrus; but his successor, Artaxerxes III Ochus (358-338 B.C.), vigorous and cruel, reconquered Egypt in 342 B.C. Yet despite appearances, the Persian Empire was finished. Artaxerxes III died by poison and was succeeded

by his son Arses (338-336 B.C.), a minor, who was poisoned in his turn. The next king, Darius III Codomanus (336-331 B.C.), came to the throne in the same year that Alexander became king of Macedonia; in five short years the immense Persian Empire was to fall to the Macedonian conqueror. In 333 B.C. Alexander defeated the Persian army at Issus. In 331 B.C. Darius made his last stand at Gaugamela in Iran. Defeated once again, he was assassinated by one of his satraps. This was the end of the Persian Empire.

ALEXANDER THE GREAT   It is no part of our purpose to
(336-323 B.C.)   treat in any detail the career of
Alexander the Great. He succeeded his father Philip in 336 B.C. In 334 B.C. he began his campaign and won control of Asia Minor. In 333 B.C. he defeated the Persians at Issus and advanced along the Mediterranean coast towards Egypt where he was welcomed as a liberator. Palestine was now under his control. In 331 B.C. Alexander moved into the heart of the Persian Empire and brought it to an end. In 326 B.C. he had advanced into India, beyond the Indus, but his troops refused to go any farther. In 323 B.C., at the age of thirty-three, he fell ill and died in Babylon. His brief career had changed the whole pattern and life of the East, a change that ultimately was to affect the history of the Jews.

THE SUCCESSORS   When Alexander died in 323 B.C. his
OF ALEXANDER   generals disputed possession of the empire. In 315 B.C., after seven years of struggle, four outstanding leaders had appeared. These were: Antigonus, the most prominent, who held all the territory from the Mediterranean to Central Asia; Cassander, who ruled in Macedonia; Ptolemy Lagi, who possessed Egypt and southern Syria (in connection with him must be mentioned Seleucus, his foremost general); and Lysimachus in Thrace. Antigonus aspired to be the sole successor of Alexander, with the natural result that the others allied against him; in the ensuing struggle Seleucus came to the fore. In 302 B.C., at Ipsus in Phrygia, Antigonus was defeated and slain. Seleucus won possession of Babylonia and Syria, and

though assassinated in 280 B.C., was succeeded by his son,
Antiochus I. Ptolemy remained in possession of Egypt, his
empire reaching as far as Damascus. By the year 281 B.C.
we find the empire of Alexander divided into three great
kingdoms: the kingdom of the Ptolemies (Egypt); the
kingdom of the Seleucids (Asia); and Macedonia. The
Ptolemies and the Seleucids alone interest us and, even at
that, it will suffice to list the kings of the two dynasties.

THE PTOLEMIES		THE SELEUCIDS	
Ptolemy I Soter	323-285	Seleucus I Nicator	312-280
Ptolemy II Philadelphus	285-246	Antiochus I Soter	280-261
		Antiochus II Theos	261-246
Ptolemy III Euergetes	246-221	Seleucus II Kallinikos	246-226
		Seleucus III Keraunos	226-223
Ptolemy IV Philopator	221-203	Antiochus III (the Great)	223-187
Ptolemy V Epiphanes	203-181	Seleucus IV Philopator	187-175
Ptolemy VI Philometor	181-146	Antiochus IV Epiphanes	175-163

2) The Jews under the Ptolemies

It seems that Palestine had quietly accepted Alexander's
control and the political and religious constitution of Judah was not changed in any respect. When the political
situation had at last been stabilized after the death of
Alexander, Palestine was ruled by the Ptolemies until 198
B.C. The position of Judah seems to have remained just the
same as it had been under Persia. The high priest was regarded as head of the community and increasingly took
on the character of a secular prince. It was a period of
peace and relative prosperity. Inevitably, Greek cultural influences made inroads into the Jewish society and the
seeds of a future violent conflict were sown.

At this time the Jewish population of Egypt grew rapidly. The greatest concentration of Jews was in the new
city of Alexandria which soon became a center of Jewish

life. Early in the third century the Greek-speaking Jews of
Alexandria translated the Torah into Greek, and the rest
of the Bible followed in due course; this was the Septuagint Version (LXX).

3) The Jews under the Seleucids

There were frequent wars between the Ptolemies and the
Seleucids, but the former were able to retain their hold
on Palestine and Phoenicia for a long time. The situation
changed when Antiochus III (the Great) (223-187 B.C.)
came to the throne of Antioch. He extended his kingdom
to the frontiers of India and then turned to the West. His
first campaign (217 B.C.) began successfully, but he was
seriously defeated by Ptolemy IV at Raphia near the Egyptian border. Several years passed before he moved again.
Finally in 198 B.C., at Panium near the source of the Jordan, he routed the Egyptian army. Palestine was annexed
to the Seleucid Empire. According to the Jewish historian
Josephus, the Jews welcomed the change and Antiochus
treated them with great consideration, guaranteeing them
the right to live in accordance with their own law.

Meanwhile, the Carthaginian general, Hannibal, who
had been defeated by the Romans at Zama in 202 B.C., fled
to the Seleucid court. Antiochus advanced into Greece and
Rome declared war. Antiochus was driven back and in
190 B.C., at Magnesia in western Asia Minor, he was disastrously defeated. He had to hand over hostages and pay
a huge indemnity; desperate for money, he was killed in
187 B.C. while attempting to rob a temple in Elam. His
successor, Seleucus IV (187-175 B.C.) tried—through his
minister Heliodorus and with the connivance of certain
Jews—to get possession of funds deposited in the Temple
of Jerusalem, but the attempt was thwarted (2 Mc. 3).
The high priest Onias III was obliged to journey to the
court in order to clear himself of slanders brought against
him by a certain Simon (2 Mc. 4:1-6).

Seleucus IV was assassinated by Heliodorus who planned

to place on the throne Seleucus' minor son Antiochus, ig-
noring the claims of an older son Demetrius, who was a
hostage in Rome. But a third pretender appeared, Antiochus, brother of Seleucus IV, who had formerly been a
hostage. Antiochus landed in Syria with an army and expelled Heliodorus. He acted as regent for his young
nephew Antiochus, but with the title of king. The latter
was assassinated in 169 B.C. and the uncle ruled alone.
With the arrival on the scene of Antiochus IV Epiphanes
(175-163 B.C.) the very existence of Judaism was threatened. The danger that his policy was to offer to the Jewish
way of life was augmented by a tragic split within the
community.

During the later Persian period the impact of Hellenistic
culture was being felt in Western Asia. As a result of the
conquest and of the deliberate policy of Alexander the
Great, the spread of the Greek language and Greek ideas
proceeded at an amazing rate; Greek soon became the
lingua franca of the civilized world. Jews of the Diaspora
absorbed the Greek language and culture; the Jews of
Palestine could not escape the influence since the land was
dotted with Greek colonies. In the main, this influence was
not direct; Greek thought was in the air and it was inevitable that something of it should have been absorbed.
Some Jews, however, were swept off their feet and, faced
with Greek culture, grew ashamed of their own way of
life, to the point of repudiating it. As so often happens,
they proved more zealous for things Greek than the Greeks
themselves. The Syrian king, in his attempt, first to Hellen-
ize Judah and then to destroy the Jewish religion, found
enthusiastic allies within the Jewish community, especially
among the priestly classes.

4) *The Jewish Diaspora*[46]

The term *Diaspora* (Dispersion) is frequent in Judaism of
the Hellenistic period and is used to designate the totality
of Jews who lived outside of Palestine. There was nationalistic sentiment in the term: the Jews who had to live out-

side the holy land were "disseminated" among the Gentiles. But not all the Jews of the Diaspora were involuntary exiles.

Many of the Jews of the Exile had elected to stay on in Babylon; hence Babylon remained an important center of Judaism. With the spread of Hellenism new important centers appeared, notably Alexandria. The Jews had a privileged place there and their colony grew quickly. Alexandria was the chief port of the Mediterranean; from it the way opened to the Greek and Roman world and to Asia Minor. The Seleucid capital, Antioch, which came close after Alexandria in importance, was another center of Judaism; it commanded the eastern Mediterranean and was open to Syria.

A characteristic of the Diaspora was the close contact between the various cells. This contact was maintained despite the different characteristics of the communities; Jerusalem was always the center of the whole vast network. The constitution of the single communities varied according to place and according to the juridical position of each in a particular city or state. Everywhere, however, synagogues sprang up and the offices of *archōn* and *archisynagōgos* were constant elements. The *archōn* was a collective office, which varied as to number and also as to duration and range of power; it handled the administrative and juridical affairs of the community. The *archisynagōgos* was an official who presided over the cult.

In the third century B.C. the Hebrew Bible was translated into Greek at Alexandria. This version, the Septuagint (LXX), was the Bible of the Jews of the Diaspora. It was a development of capital importance not only for Judaism but for Christianity, since the Septuagint became the Bible of the early Church. But the providential role of the Diaspora is not limited to this: the active proselytism of many Jews prepared the way for the spread of Christianity. Gentiles who had been attracted by the monotheism and the high moral code of Judaism found in the new religion all that they had sought.

12. THE MACCABAEAN REVOLT AND THE HASMONAEAN DYNASTY

1) The Background: Antiochus IV to Antiochus VII (175-129 B.C.)

Antiochus IV Epiphanes (175-163 B.C.) was anxious to unify his realm. This is the chief reason why he pushed forward so vigorously a policy of Hellenization. In 170 B.C. he invaded Egypt. He captured the young Ptolemy VI at Memphis and then moved on Alexandria where Ptolemy VII (brother of the other) had been declared king; Antiochus declared himself regent of his prisoner. He eventually agreed to retire, laden with immense booty, and left both Ptolemies reigning—in Memphis and Alexandria respectively. In 168 B.C. Antiochus was back in Egypt, but this time the Romans intervened—as protectors of Egypt. Antiochus was met by the legate, Popilius Laenas, who bluntly presented him with an ultimatum from the Roman senate; Antiochus retired. When the Maccabaean revolt had taken a serious turn in 165 B.C., Antiochus was committed to a campaign against the Parthians, leaving his regent, Lysias, to take care of the Palestinian situation. Early in 163 B.C. he died at Tabae in Persia. The subsequent history of the Seleucids is very involved.

Antiochus IV had designated his young son Antiochus V Eupator (163-161 B.C.) as his successor and had appointed his friend Philip as regent. Lysias, however, declared himself regent and took the young king into his charge; together they moved against Judas Maccabaeus. But soon they had to advance against Philip who had arrived in Syria from the East; he was quickly driven out of Antioch. In 161 B.C. another pretender appeared: Demetrius, son of Seleucus IV, who had been a hostage of Rome. He captured and killed Lysias and Antiochus V and assumed power.

Demetrius I Soter (161-150 B.C.) was an ambitious king who planned to restore Seleucid power. He failed to win the full support of his subjects and was regarded suspiciously by the Romans. Eventually a rival appeared: Alexander Balas, backed by Attalus II of Pergamum, put himself forward as an illegitimate son of Antiochus IV and was promptly recognized by the Romans. In 152 B.C. he landed at Ptolemais (Acre) and in 150 B.C. he defeated and killed Demetrius I. Alexander Balas (150-145 B.C.) married Cleopatra, a daughter of Ptolemy VI of Egypt. In 147 B.C. Demetrius (son of Demetrius I) arrived in Cilicia and was supported by his father's friend, Apollonius, governor of Coelesyria (the territory between the Lebanon and Mt. Hermon). In 145 B.C. he won an unexpected ally in Ptolemy VI (who had turned against his son-in-law); together they defeated Alexander near Antioch.

Demetrius II Nicator (145-138 B.C.) was now king of Syria. Before long he had to deal with a revolt in Antioch; and then Trypho, a general of Demetrius, supported the claim of a young son of Alexander Balas, whom he named Antiochus VI. The kingdom of Syria was divided between the rival kings, Demetrius II and Antiochus VI (145-142 B.C.). Trypho (142-138 B.C.), who had been acting as regent, killed his young charge in 142 B.C. and took the crown. Demetrius II had to campaign against the Parthians; in 140 B.C. he was taken prisoner by the Parthian king Mithradates I. (Released by Mithradate's successor, Arsaces, Demetrius reigned for a second period: 129-125 B.C.) In 138 B.C. Antiochus, brother of Demetrius, appeared on the scene, and Trypho was at last defeated and killed. Antiochus VII Sidetes (138-129 B.C.) brought the short-lived Jewish independence to a temporary end in 134 B.C. In 130 B.C. he reconquered Babylonia and Media, but the following year (129 B.C.) he was killed in battle against the Parthians. The successors of Antiochus VII, occupied in domestic rivalry, lost control of Palestine.

2) *The Maccabaean Revolt*[47] *(1,2 Mc.; Dn.)*

THE PERSECUTION The determined policy of Antiochus
OF ANTIOCHUS IV IV (175-163 B.C.), the Hellenization of his kingdom, sooner or later was bound to drive the

Jews into rebellion. At first, however, the king got all the
support he could have wished for from Hellenized Jews.

Jason, brother of Onias III the high priest, went to Antiochus and, in return for the high-priestly office, offered a
large sum of money and undertook to carry through the
Hellenization of Jerusalem; he was promptly confirmed as
high priest. His work of Hellenization was supported by
many elements in the city and by the powerful Tobiad
family of Ammon. In 172 B.C. Antiochus was approached
by a certain Menelaus (brother of Simon, an enemy of
Onias III) who offered him a huge bribe; again money
spoke and Menelaus obtained the high priesthood. He entered Jerusalem and Jason fled to Ammon. Onias III, in
Antioch, was assassinated by Andronicus, minister of the
king.

Antiochus IV entered Jerusalem in 169 B.C. on his return from his first campaign in Egypt and, with the connivance of Menelaus, plundered the Temple. Next year
the king invaded Egypt again, but he had to retire when
faced with an ultimatum of the Roman Senate. Meanwhile, at a rumor of the king's death, Jason attacked Jerusalem; Menelaus was able to hold out in the citadel north
of the Temple. At the approach of Antiochus, Jason fled;
his subsequent fugitive course ended with his death in
Sparta. Antiochus interpreted the action of Jason as a revolt and decided to deal with it as such.

In 167 B.C. he sent his commander, Apollonius, against
Jerusalem with a large force. Many of the people were
massacred, the city was partly destroyed, and its walls were
razed. A fortress, called the Acra, was built; it dominated
the Tyropoeon valley and the Temple and was manned
by a strong Syrian garrison. The Acra was, in fact, a colony
of Hellenized pagans and renegade Jews, with the constitution of a Greek *polis*. The decree of Antiochus III,
which guaranteed the free observance of Jewish law, was
abrogated; instead, Jewish religion was proscribed. The
Temple was dedicated to Olympian Zeus (Antiochus presented himself as a visible manifestation of Zeus; he is so
depicted on coins and his name Epiphanes means "[the
god] manifest"), and a pagan altar (the "abomination of

desolation" [Dn. 9:27; 11:31; 12:11]) was erected over the altar of holocausts. On 25 Chislev (December 8), 167 B.C., pagan sacrifices were offered in the Temple. About the same time the Samaritan temple on Mt. Gerizim was dedicated to Zeus Xenios. Antiochus' actions stiffened Jewish resistance and drove the hesitant into rebellion. A veritable reign of terror launched against the Jews only meant that the explosion came more speedily than it might have.

THE HOLY WAR Mattathias, a priest of Modein, west of (167-164 B.C.) Jerusalem, gave the signal for revolt. With his five sons he fled to the mountains of Judaea and was soon joined by other rebels. Particularly valuable support was provided by the Hasidim (Hasidaeans), a group entirely dedicated to the Law. The elderly Mattathias died in 166 B.C., but not before he had entrusted the leadership of the rising to his son Judas Maccabaeus (166-160 B.C.).

Judas organized "flying columns" and harassed the enemy by successful guerilla tactics. Philip, the Phrygian commander of the Acra garrison, had to seek reinforcements from Apollonius, governor of Samaria. In the mountains of Ephraim, Judas intercepted these reinforcements and killed Apollonius. Next, Seron, military commander of Coelesyria, moved against Judas—only to be disastrously defeated at Beth-horon. At this time Antiochus IV was obliged to take action against the Parthians, but he instructed his deputy Lysias to crush the rebellion in Judah. Large forces, under the generals Nicanor and Gorgias, were sent against Judas (165 B.C.); in a night attack on their camp near Emmaus he put the Syrians to flight. In 164 B.C. Lysias himself moved into Palestine, but he was defeated at Bath-zur. As a result an agreement was reached with Antiochus IV on 15 Xanthicus (April 15), 164 B.C. (see 2 Mc. 11:27-33): a general amnesty was declared and the ordinances that had caused the revolt were abolished. On 25 Chislev (December 8), 164 B.C.—three years to the day after the pagan profanation—Judas had the Temple purified and sacrifice offered.

PUNITIVE EXPEDITIONS   The concessions of the king gave
(164-163 B.C.)   rise to a wave of anti-Jewish feeling among the Hellenists, and orthodox Jews suffered. Judas decided to undertake punitive expeditions. He and
Jonathan went to the aid of Jews who were besieged in
Dathema and then subdued several other towns in Gilead
while they were about it. Simeon was equally successful in
Galilee. In a foolhardy move, a contingent which Judas
had left in Jerusalem attacked Jamnia and was defeated.

REVERSES AND   Antiochus IV died in 163 B.C. and
RESPITE (162 B.C.)   was succeeded by his young son
Antiochus V Eupator (163-161 B.C.), though the real ruler
was Lysias. Judas attacked the Acra—an action contrary to
the accord of 15 Xanthicus—and Lysias and the young king
moved against him. Judas met them at Beth-zechariah; he
was defeated and his brother Eleazar fell in the battle.
Lysias advanced on Jerusalem, where Judas had retired,
and besieged it. The fall of the city was imminent when
Lysias heard that Philip (the regent designated by Antiochus IV) had arrived in Syria, and he made a hasty peace
with Judas. The Jews were granted full religious freedom;
in return they recognized the king. Lysias had executed
Menelaus and had appointed as high priest Alcimus, a
Hellenized Jew who was not accepted by the Maccabees.

THE WAR OF ALCIMUS   In 161 B.C. Demetrius I Soter
(161-159 B.C.)   (161-150 B.C.) came to power in
Syria. He recognized Alcimus as high priest and sent
Bacchides, governor of the province Beyond the River
(the Afar-nahara of the Persians) to insure that he took
office. Judas, fearing treachery, refused to be drawn into a
meeting with Bacchides. The Hasidim accepted Alcimus,
though some of them were massacred for their pains.
When Bacchides retired, Judas commenced to harass the
Hellenists; Alcimus went to Antioch and appealed to the
king. Nicanor (who had earlier been defeated at Emmaus)
was entrusted with the task of subduing Judas, but after
some skirmishing a truce was arranged. Alcimus de-
nounced the truce and Nicanor was forced to act. On 13
Adar (March), 160 B.C., Nicanor was defeated and killed

at Adasa, five miles north of Jerusalem; the "Day of Nicanor" was celebrated thenceforth as an annual feast. Judas entered into an alliance (couched in very vague terms) with the Romans.

The war was not over, however. Bacchides advanced into Palestine and in April, 160 B.C., Judas was defeated and killed at Beerzeth, about twelve miles north of Jerusalem. The triumphant Hellenists carried out savage reprisals and the spirit of resistance was fanned to flame again. Jonathan (160-143 B.C.) proved a worthy successor to Judas and began a guerilla war. In May, 159 B.C., Alcimus died and Bacchides returned to Antioch.

A BREATHING-SPACE Jonathan and his followers had re-
(159-152 B.C.) treated to the desert of Judah and studiously avoided open conflict. The Hellenists appealed to Bacchides, but his attempts to take Jonathan failed. Eventually the peace proposals of Jonathan were accepted by Bacchides who thereupon returned to Antioch. Jonathan established himself at Michmash and gradually consolidated his position. He was accepted as the political and religious head of the people.

THE BALANCE OF In 152 B.C. Alexander Balas
POWER (152-143 B.C.) landed at Ptolemais. Demetrius I hurriedly offered Jonathan the right to raise troops and declared him his ally, ordering the Jewish hostages held in the Acra to be released. Jonathan at once occupied and fortified Mt. Sion, while the Syrian garrisons set up by Bacchides, except those at Beth-zur and in the Acra, were withdrawn. Alexander Balas now approached Jonathan and offered him the high priesthood, the title "Friend of the King," and the right to wear a purple cloak and a golden crown; Jonathan promptly changed allegiance. For the rest of his career he was to keep up this shrewd, and often dangerous, double game between the rival claimants to the Syrian throne. On the Feast of Tabernacles 152 B.C. Jonathan officiated as high priest for the first time.

In 150 B.C. Alexander Balas (150-145 B.C.) defeated Demetrius. Jonathan was appointed general (*stratēgos*) and governor (*meridarchēs*) of Judaea. When Demetrius

II appeared on the scene, Apollonius, the governor of Coelesyria who supported him, moved on Jonathan, but he was defeated at Azotus (146 B.C.). Jonathan was further honored and was given the territory of Ekron. In 145 B.C. Demetrius, in alliance with Ptolemy VI of Egypt, defeated Alexander Balas. Demetrius II Nicator (145-138 B.C.) decided that Jonathan would make a valuable ally. He summoned Jonathan to a conference at Ptolemais and confirmed the titles he had received from Alexander; he also ceded to him the districts of Lydda and Rathamin (west of Jerusalem) and Aphairema (north of the city). Some time later Jonathan helped Demetrius to put down a revolt in Antioch, following an assurance that the garrison of the Acra would be evacuated. The king did not keep his promise.

Meanwhile, Trypho, a general of Alexander Balas, supported the claim of a young son of Alexander, Antiochus VI (145-142 B.C.). Jonathan switched his allegiance to Antiochus VI and found himself appointed the supreme military commander in Syria; his brother Simon was general of the whole Palestinian coast. Jonathan held the generals of Demetrius in check in northern Syria and, at home, fortified Jerusalem. He sent letters to Rome and Sparta. Trypho, who had designs on the throne, was alarmed by the growing power of Jonathan; in 143 B.C. he had the Jewish leader treacherously arrested in Ptolemais.

Simon (143-134 B.C.) now became high priest and governor. Trypho invaded Palestine and made a pact with Simon who had intercepted him. This pact was conveniently forgotten when Trypho was urgently pressed to come to the relief of the Acra. Heavy snow prevented this move and he was forced to retire; but he killed Jonathan before he left the country. Next year (142 B.C.) Trypho assassinated Antiochus VI and reigned in his stead (142-138 B.C.).

INDEPENDENCE   Simon now turned to Demetrius II (who still held part of the kingdom) and was confirmed as high priest and governor. The year was 142 B.C., henceforth regarded as the year of Jewish independence: "The yoke of the Gentiles was removed from Israel, and the people began to write in their documents and contracts, 'In the first year of Simon the great high priest and commander and leader of the Jews'" (1 Mc. 13:41 f.). That same year the Acra fell. The hated symbol of foreign domination was gone at last.

In 140 B.C. Demetrius II was taken prisoner by the Parthians and two years later he was succeeded by his brother, Antiochus VII Sidetes (138-129 B.C.), who disposed of Trypho. The new king demanded of Simon that he should relinquish Joppa, Gazara, and the Acra, all of which he had taken beyond the terms of agreement with Demetrius. When Simon refused to yield, Antiochus sent his general Cendebeus against him; Cendebeus was defeated by John and Judas, the sons of Simon.

Then tragedy befell the Jews: Simon was treacherously murdered by his son-in-law Ptolemy. With his sons, Mattathias and Judas, the high priest had gone to inspect the fortress of Dok near Jericho, and there, at a banquet, he fell victim of a plot, while his two sons and their mother were held as hostages. Ptolemy then appealed to Antiochus VII for troops and asked to be appointed governor. An attempt to assassinate John, the remaining son of Simon, failed; instead, John was acclaimed in Jerusalem and accepted by the people as high priest and governor.

3) The Hasmonaean Dynasty[48]

From John Hyrcanus onwards the Maccabaean princes are known as the Hasmonaeans (after Hashmon, an ancestor of the family); though it might be said that the dynasty had really begun with Simon Maccabaeus who had achieved independence.

JOHN HYRCANUS I, HIGH   With the survival of John and
PRIEST (134-104 B.C.)   his acclamation by the people,
the plans of Ptolemy were set at nought. Very soon the latter found himself besieged in the same fortress of Dok. However, he managed to escape to Transjordan, though

not before killing his hostages. Jewish troubles were only beginning. In 134 B.C. Antiochus VII, whose attempt to cow Simon had failed, advanced into Palestine; he took Joppa and Gazara and besieged Jerusalem. John was obliged to surrender, and though he still remained high priest and governor, he had to pay tribute. As a vassal of Antiochus he took part in a campaign against the Parthians. The short-lived days of independence seemed at an end.

Nevertheless circumstances favored the Jews. In 129 B.C. Antiochus VII was killed in action against the Parthians, and the Seleucids lost control of Palestine. John Hyrcanus was free to act. He conquered Moab (from the Nabataeans), won control of Samaria—promptly destroying the temple on Mt. Gerizim—and campaigned in Idumaea. He was warmly supported by the Hasidim, now beginning to be known as Pharisees. John Hyrcanus died in 104 B.C. The subsequent history of the Hasmonaeans is a sorry page of Jewish history. Fortunately, for our purpose, since it falls outside the canonical histories, it can be treated even more briefly than the preceding stages.

ARISTOBULUS I, HIGH PRIEST AND KING (104-103 B.C.)   John Hyrcanus had arranged that his son Aristobulus should be high priest and that the civil power should be shared by all five sons under the authority of their mother. Aristobulus, however, seized power: he threw his mother into prison, where she died, killed Antigonus, and imprisoned the other three brothers. He claimed the title of king and annexed Galilee and Ituraea. When Aristobulus died in 103 B.C. his wife Alexandra (Salome) released the three brothers; the eldest, Alexander Jannaeus, became king and her husband.

ALEXANDER JANNAEUS, HIGH PRIEST AND KING (103-76 B.C.)   Determined to extend his territory, Alexander attacked Ptolemais, with the support of Cleopatra of Egypt. He captured Gaza and became master of the whole littoral, except Ashkelon. On the other hand, Alexander broke with the Pharisees and estranged the people. When officiating at the Feast of Tabernacles he was insulted by the people; he retaliated by turning his mercenaries on them and 6,000 of his people perished. Later, a defeat in Transjordan at the hands of the Nabataeans was the signal for revolt, and civil war dragged on for six years. Alexander at last put down the revolt with great cruelty. After this he conquered the Hellenistic cities of Pella, Gerasa, etc. (later known as the district of Decapolis). Alexander Jannaeus died in 76 B.C. and was succeeded by his wife Alexandra.

ALEXANDRA, QUEEN (76-67 B.C.) Alexandra's son, John Hyrcanus II, was high priest (76-67 B.C.; 63-40 B.C.). Her second son, Aristobulus II, received the military command. The queen placated the Pharisees and won their support. Hyrcanus II became king on the death of his mother, but was at once opposed by his brother Aristobulus who defeated him near Jericho. Hyrcanus fled to Jerusalem and was there besieged and forced to surrender.

ARISTOBULUS II, HIGH PRIEST AND KING (67-63 B.C.) Hyrcanus still had much support; the most effective was that of the governor of Idumaea, Antipater. In 65 B.C. John Hyrcanus II (supported by Antipater) and Aretas II, king of the Nabataeans, besieged Aristobulus in Jerusalem. Meanwhile, Pompey, who had conquered Asia Minor, had sent his legate Scaurus to Syria. Both parties appealed to him, but Scaurus ordered Hyrcanus and Aretas to raise the siege. Aristobulus inflicted a heavy defeat on the retreating force. Pompey entered Palestine in 63 B.C. Aristobulus surrendered personally, but Jerusalem resisted and was taken after a siege of three months. This marked the end of Jewish independence. Hyrcanus was established as high priest and received the title of ethnarch. Pompey carried Aristobulus and his son Antigonus off to Rome; Alexander, a second son, escaped on the way.

JOHN HYRCANUS II, HIGH PRIEST AND ETHNARCH (63-40 B.C.) The territory of the ethnarch had been reduced by Pompey and now comprised: Judaea, part of Idumaea, Galilee, and Peraea. The presence of Rome assured internal and external peace, while Antipater, minister

of Hyrcanus, was the real ruler. In 57 B.C. Alexander, son
of Aristobulus II, appeared and rallied the partisans of his
father. Gabinius, procurator of Syria, moved against him;
he was besieged in the Alexandreion (a fortress over the
Jordan valley) and surrendered. Gabinius divided the territory of the ethnarch into five toparchies which were
answerable to the procurator; Hyrcanus retained only the
administration of the Temple and an empty title. Aristobulus II, with his sons Alexander and Antigonus, escaped
from Rome in 56 B.C. and arrived in Palestine. Gabinius
quelled the attempted revolt; Aristobulus was captured and
sent back to Rome. In 55 B.C. Alexander attempted another
revolt but was defeated near Tabor.

The civil war between Caesar and Pompey began in
49 B.C. Caesar freed Aristobulus, planning to send him to
Palestine to stir up trouble there; Aristobulus, however, was
poisoned. Antipater persuaded Pompey to execute Alexander, who was being held prisoner at Antioch. Pompey
was defeated in 48 B.C. at the battle of Pharsalus. Antipater
went to the aid of Caesar in Egypt, and in 47 B.C. Julius
Caesar was in Palestine. Hyrcanus was confirmed as ethnarch and Antipater was made procurator of Judaea; the
sons of Antipater were governors: Phasael in Jerusalem
and Herod in Galilee. In 44 B.C. Caesar was assassinated
and Antipater supported Crassus, who had come to Syria.
Antipater was poisoned and was succeeded by Herod
(43 B.C.). The battle of Philippi took place in 42 B.C. and
next year Mark Anthony was in the East. Herod and
Phasael, who supported him, were named tetrarchs and
Hyrcanus remained high priest.

The Parthians invaded Syria in 40 B.C. and Antigonus
(son of Aristobulus II) seized his chance. With the help
of the invaders he besieged Herod and Phasael in Jerusalem. Herod managed to escape, but Phasael committed
suicide; Hyrcanus had his ears cut off, a mutilation which
barred him from the office of high priest.

ANTIGONUS, HIGH PRIEST   The Roman reaction to the
AND KING (40-37 B.C.)   Parthian invasion was rapid:

by 39 B.C. Asia Minor and Syria had been recovered. Herod had made his way to Rome where he was recognized as "King of the Jews" by Octavian and Anthony—and given the task of winning his kingdom. In 39 B.C. Herod, at the head of Roman legions, landed at Ptolemais. The war against Antigonus went on for three years; Herod laid siege to Jerusalem in 37 B.C. (and married Mariamme, a Hasmonaean princess, during the siege). Antigonus was captured and sent to Antioch where he was executed. The Hasmonaean dynasty was at an end. The subsequent history of Herod and his successors forms the background of the New Testament and is treated in Volume Three of this series.

[1] For a selection of Sumerian texts see J. B. Pritchard, *Ancient Near Eastern Texts* (relating to the Old Testament) (Princeton University Press, 1955[2]). Henceforth this book will be abbreviated ANET.

[2] See *ibid.*, passim.

[3] See *ibid.*, pp. 405-10, 441-44.

[4] See *ibid.*, pp. 161-63, 159-61.

[5] See *ibid.*, pp. 60-72.

[6] See *ibid.*, pp. 163-80.

[7] See *ibid.*, pp. 219-20.

[8] See *ibid.*, pp. 414-19, 18-22.

[9] J. Bright, *A History of Israel* (Philadelphia: Westminster Press, 1959), pp. 47 f.

[10] See ANET, pp. 483-90.

[11] See *ibid.*, pp. 199-203.

[12] Bright, *op. cit.*, p. 85.

[13] See Roland de Vaux, "The Hebrew Patriarchs and History," *Theology Digest*, 12 (1964), 227-40.

[14] See ANET, pp. 376-78.

[15] See *ibid.*, pp. 129-55.

[16] Bright, *op. cit.*, p. 108.

[17] See P. Lemaire and D. Baldi, *Atlante Storico della Bibbia* (Rome: Marietti, 1955), p. 85. Henceforth this book will be abbreviated *Atlante Biblico* (Biblical Atlas).

[18] Bright, *op. cit.*, p. 120.

[19] See *Atlante Biblico*, pp. 103-12.

[20] See *ibid.*, pp. 120-23.

[21] See Roland de Vaux, *Les Livres des Rois* (BJ) (Paris, 1958[2]), p. 14.

[22] See Vol. 2, p. 60.

[23] See ANET, pp. 277-79.

[24] See J. B. Pritchard, *The Ancient Near East in Pictures* (Princeton University Press, 1954), plate 355. Henceforth this book will be abbreviated ANEP. See ANET, pp. 280 f.

[25] See ANET, pp. 287 f.

[26] The two-campaign theory has been adopted.

[27] See ANET, pp. 60-99.

[28] See *ibid.*, pp. 320 f.

[29] See *ibid.*, pp. 284 f.

[30] See *ibid.*, p. 283.

[31] See *ibid.*, p. 501 (inscription of Barrakab).

[32] See *ibid.*, pp. 287 f.

[33] See ANEP, plates 371-74.

[34] The fall of Azekah is poignantly illustrated by one of the Lachish Letters (ostraca discovered at Lachish): an officer in charge of an observation post writes to the commander in Lachish that the fire signals of Azekah can no longer be seen (see ANET, p. 322).

[35] See Wilfrid J. Harrington, *Record of Revelation: The Bible* (Chicago: The Priory Press, 1965), p. 76, for the text of the "Prayer of Nabonidus" found in Qumran (4Q).

[36] Cyrus' account of his Babylonian triumph is recorded on the Cyrus Cylinder; see ANET, pp. 315 f.

[37] See Bright, *op. cit.*, p. 355.

[38] See *ibid.*, p. 363. For a note on the Elephantine texts see pp. 159-60.

[39] This chronology is followed, for example, by Heinisch-Heidt, *History of the Old Testament* (Collegeville, Minn.: The Liturgical Press, 1952), pp. 330-40; L. H. Grollenberg, *Atlas of the Bible*, trans. Joyce M. Reid and H. H. Rowley (Camden, N.J.: Nelson, 1959), p. 100.

[40] This order is followed, for example, by the following (though the probability of the other positions is always acknowledged): G. Ricciotti, *History of Israel*, trans. C. della Penta and R. Murphy (Milwaukee: Bruce, 1955), II, nn. 108-20. *Atlante Biblico*, p. 164; BJ, p. 405.

[41] See Bright, *op. cit.*, pp. 275-386; see IB, I, pp. 713 f.

[42] See pp. 160-61.

[43] Bright, *op. cit.*, p. 370.

[44] See ANET, pp. 491 f.

[45] See Bright, *op. cit.*, p. 327; *Atlante Biblico*, p. 166.

[46] See Ricciotti, *op. cit.*, nn. 180-200.

[47] See *Atlante Biblico*, pp. 176-88.

[48] See *ibid.*, pp. 188-97.

SEVEN

AN OUTLINE HISTORY OF
NEW TESTAMENT TIMES

THE GRAECO-ROMAN WORLD
THE JEWISH WORLD
CHRONOLOGY OF THE LIFE OF JESUS
THE APOSTOLIC AGE
ST. PAUL: CHRONOLOGY AND MISSIONARY JOURNEYS

This chapter is meant to sketch, in outline form, the historical, religious, and cultural background of the New Testament. Christianity did not, any more than the religion of Israel, come into being in a vacuum. Although essentially something new, Christianity is also a phenomenon of the first century A.D. and can be fully understood only in the setting of that century.

1. THE GRAECO-ROMAN WORLD
1) *The Roman Empire*

Roman history is usually divided into three parts: the period of the Kings; the period of the Republic; and the period of the Empire. Traditionally, Rome was founded in 753 B.C.; the first period reached from that year until 510 B.C. when Tarquinius Superbus, last of the kings, was deposed. The period of the Republic (509-27 B.C.) is the age in which Rome won her position in Italy, and then in the Mediterranean, and in which she gained political and administrative experience and learned from the civilization of other peoples—particularly from the Greeks. The years 133 B.C. onwards was a time of commercial expansion but political disorder. The third period, that of Imperial Rome, dates from the accession of Augustus in 27 B.C. It is true

that Augustus himself wished to be known as *Princeps* or
"first citizen," carefully avoiding the title of Emperor; but,
in reality, the Roman Empire did begin with him. Here
we are interested only in the last years of the Republic
and the first years of the Empire.[1]

In 66 B.C. Pompey, armed with the greatest powers a
Roman general had ever enjoyed, marched to the East.
He conquered Asia Minor and led his troops to the foot
of the Caucasus and to the shores of the Caspian Sea. In
the spring of 63 B.C. he was in Damascus and late that
same year he besieged and took Jerusalem, thus bringing
to an end the last period of Jewish independence. Pompey
celebrated his triumph in Rome in 61 B.C. Rivalry between
him and Julius Caesar (who had meanwhile conquered
Gaul) flamed into civil war in 49 B.C. Caesar won control
of Italy and Spain and followed Pompey into Greece; the
decisive battle of Pharsalus in 48 B.C. resulted in complete
victory for Caesar. Then, on the Ides of March, 44 B.C.,
Julius Caesar was assassinated. Again there was civil war:
Mark Antony and the young Octavian (Caesar's adopted
son), supported by Lepidus, faced the conspirators, Brutus
and Cassius; the latter were disastrously defeated at
Philippi in 42 B.C. The Triumvirs, Antony, Octavian, and
Lepidus, divided the Roman dominions among them—but
Octavian soon took over the army and territory of Lepidus.
The West declared for Octavian, while Antony, in Egypt,
dallied with Cleopatra. Soon there was open conflict and
Antony's fleet was destroyed at the battle of Actium in
31 B.C. Antony and Cleopatra committed suicide, leaving
Octavian as sole ruler of the Roman world. In 27 B.C. he
received from the Senate the new name Augustus and
until his death in 14 A.D. was unchallenged ruler of the
most powerful Empire the world had known. He restored
peace, order, and justice throughout the Empire. His beneficial rule seemed all the greater blessing in contrast to
the long years of civil strife.

Augustus was succeeded by his stepson Tiberius (14-37
A.D.). He was an able and experienced ruler but his suspicious temperament found vent, in his last year, in a reign
of terror. His successor, the young Caligula (37-41 A.D.)

was depraved and ruled as a capricious despot. On his assassination, the unwilling Claudius became emperor (45-54 A.D.) and proved a not incompetent ruler. He was succeeded by Nero (54-68 A.D.), the first great persecutor of Christians. His assassination was followed by a period of civil strife and the appearance of the ephemeral emperors: Galba, Otho, and Vitellius. At this point it became clear that real power now lay with the army. The legions of the Danube and the East chose as emperor the general Vespasian, then engaged in Palestine. Vespasian (69-79 A.D.) proved a happy choice. His son and successor, Titus, reigned for two years only (79-81 A.D.), the days of Nero returning under the rule of the latter's son, Domitian (81-96 A.D.)—the second great persecutor of Christians. An elderly lawyer, Nerva (96-98 A.D.), was appointed by the Senate after the murder of Domitian. He adopted as his son the able general Trajan who soon, in fact, succeeded him. The reign of Trajan (98-117 A.D.) marked a new era for Rome.

At the death of Augustus, the Roman Empire, stretching from Italy, took in Spain, Gaul, much of Germany, the Balkans, Asia Minor, Syria and Palestine, Egypt and North Africa. The Mediterranean had become a Roman lake and the authority of Rome extended to all its shores. During the first century A.D. the Roman legions pushed ever farther afield. Throughout the Empire the different ethnic groups were juxtaposed rather than amalgamated; national characteristics and traditions were preserved. Yet, many contacts in the economic, cultural, and religious spheres tended to offset the differences. In the cities the most common spoken language was the *Koine* (common or current) Greek, but in rural areas the native languages were still in possession. The Empire was divided into provinces. The older provinces were called senatorial and were governed by a proconsul appointed by the Senate; the other provinces were called imperial and were governed by a legate appointed by the emperor. Palestine was ruled by a procurator who was subject to the legate of Syria. A vast network of roads linked the wideflung provinces of the Empire. Along these roads, in a world governed by a sin-

gle power, the preachers of a new faith were soon journey-
ing. And the followers of this faith before long would
clash with that power.

A feature of Roman society was the enormous number
of slaves: there were almost as many slaves as free citizens.
A slave could be set at liberty by his master or by the state
and so become a freedman, but he did not thereby become a citizen. Roman citizens alone enjoyed the fullest
civil rights. Among other privileges, they were immune
from corporal punishment and could not be executed by
crucifixion if condemned to death; and they had the right
to appeal to Caesar's tribunal. Roman citizenship could be
given as a reward for services rendered, or it could be
bought (cf. Acts 22:25-28) and was hereditary.

2) Philosophical Trends[2]

In the Graeco-Roman world the metaphysics of Plato and
Aristotle had lost their appeal. Now the emphasis was on
the problems of human life, notably the conduct and happiness of the individual. The philosophers of the first Christian century were in fact eclectics (i.e., they chose elements from a variety of philosophical systems), but
Stoicism and Epicureanism contributed most to their gen-
eralized philosophy.

EPICUREANISM   Epicureanism has suffered from a misunderstanding of its ethical idea. The founder of the system
was Epicurus of Samos (342-270 B.C.), who did indeed
make pleasure the end of life; but we must understand
what he meant by *pleasure*.

> Two facts are to be noted: first that Epicurus
> meant, not the pleasures of the moment, individual
> sensations, but the pleasure which endures through-
> out a lifetime; and secondly, that pleasure for Epi-
> curus consisted rather in the absence of pain than in
> positive satisfaction. This pleasure is to be found pre-
> eminently in serenity of soul.[3]

Since the only durable pleasure is health of body and
tranquility of soul, moderation and self-control are neces-

sary on the one hand, and the avoidance of embroilment in political and public affairs on the other. Epicurus admitted the existence of the gods, but the gods stood apart from the world and were indifferent to human affairs. Although the appeal of Epicureanism was always limited, even in the first century B.C., its views were adopted by such thinkers as Lucretius and Cicero and by poets like Vergil and Horace, and its influence continued into the next century at least.

STOICISM The founder of the Stoic school was Zeno (336-264 B.C.). The influence of Stoicism continued after his death and was the dominant philosophy in the Graeco-Roman period. Since the sincere Stoic was a man of outstanding moral integrity, he, and the challenge of self-discipline and asceticism demanded by the Stoic way of life, appealed to many in an age of prevailing low moral standards in public and private life.

The Stoic divinity is material; he existed from eternity in the form of primeval fire, and yet he is the mind or soul of the universe that has emerged from him. God, the Logos, is the active principle which contains within itself the forms (the "seeds") of all things that are to be. The soul of man is part of the divine Fire which descended into men at their creation; personal immortality is not possible because all souls return to the primeval Fire at the conflagration when the universe is consumed to be burn anew—the cycle goes on eternally. Since the human soul is essentially one with the divine element, to live in accordance with the highest dictates of one's own being is to live in harmony with the divine purpose and so to attain to virtue.

The Stoic ethic is largely a struggle against the passions and affections, an attempt to reach a state of moral freedom and independence of externals. Since man is necessarily a social being, to live in society is a dictate of reason. Division of mankind into warring states is wrong and all men have a claim to our good will. "The ethical ideal is attained when we love all men as we love ourselves or when our self-love embraces all that is connected with the self, including humanity at large, with an equal intensity."[4]

Stoicism was the principal element of what might be termed the "popular" philosophy of the first century A.D. This philosophy was propagated by Stoic preachers—highly regarded by the people—who had a special teaching method: doctrinal or moral expositions in dialogue form, with questions and answers, apostrophes and exclamations —the *diatribe* (cf. Rm. 3:1-9). These later teachers no longer shared the pantheistic views of the earlier Stoics; rather, they preached a universal God, the soul and reason of the world, father of gods and men. They proclaimed the equality and brotherhood of all men; they taught that superiority lay only in the practice of virtue, and that virtue alone, entailing asceticism and self-control, can bring happiness. In short, a philosophic system had taken on something of the character of a religion.

3) *Religious Trends*[5]

THE MYSTERY   Even before the Hellenistic era the tradi-
RELIGIONS   tional worship of the Olympian gods had
declined among the Greeks. After Alexander, its influence, at least on the minds of cultivated men, grew less and eventually disappeared altogether. The Roman attitude toward the national religion was more conservative; but in the first century A.D. it too, at least in the cosmopolitan capital, had to yield to other influences. In fact, men were seeking something that the traditional religions could not offer: personal religious feeling and the prospect of immortality. This longing was promised fulfillment in the mystery cults. By mystery cults are meant sacred rites by which one was initiated into religious and divine secrets; knowledge of these secrets guaranteed the protection of the god or goddess of the mystery religion in question, and assured the eternal bliss of the initiate.

The Eleusinian mysteries had developed around the myth of Demeter. Persephone, the daughter of Demeter, goddess of the earth, had been carried to the underworld by Hades. Through the intervention of other gods, Persephone was restored to her mother, but must return to the underworld for four months of every year. The mysteries celebrated at Eleusis re-enacted the mourning of Demeter and the joyous return of Persephone—symbolizing the revival of nature in spring. Originally, the cult of Demeter would seem to have had the purpose of guaranteeing good crops; but later, the cycle of the life and death of nature was seen as a symbol of man's life and death, and participation in the Eleusinian mysteries would assure new life in a world beyond death.

The oldest and most popular of Hellenistic mystery cults was that of Dionysus, and in the beginning of the Christian Era the Dionysian mysteries were celebrated throughout the Graeco-Roman world. Dionysus was god of wine. His devotees, mostly women, after preparatory fasting and purification, were, by means of night-long ceremonies and the drinking of wine, overcome by a "divine" frenzy. In the rapture of their ecstasy, they achieved mystical union with the deity for a moment, a foretaste of eternal bliss.

In Rome, the Egyptian mysteries of Osiris had won a footing. The myth tells of Isis wandering over the earth searching for the dismembered body of her consort Osiris, who had become the god of the underworld. In the mysteries, the initiate, by re-enacting the sufferings and journey to death of Osiris, became united with the god of the dead. As a consequence, he had no further fear of death and was assured of life beyond the grave.

The secret of full initiation into the mysteries has been well kept and no more than a general outline of these religions is known to us. However, it is clear that the emphasis was on external rites which had to be carried out scrupulously. Salvation was guaranteed merely by a ceremony of initiation. Hence, the mystery cults had no really beneficial influence on moral conduct; they offered no challenge to a change of life. Indeed, in this sphere, the contribution of Stoicism was much more effective. But, on the other hand, the mysteries did foster belief in a life beyond the grave and did promote recourse to "savior" gods, and did give rise to a sense of personal unity with the divinity. All this emphasized the yearning of men for something more satisfying than the traditional religions could offer, and goes far to explain the appeal of Christianity to those who were also prepared to live up to its demanding standard.

THE IMPERIAL The notion of the divinity of kings was an
CULT ancient and common one in the East.
Alexander the Great found that his Eastern (and Egyptian) subjects regarded him as a god, and his successors, Seleucids and Ptolemies both, complacently assumed divine titles—for instance, Antiochus IV was "Epiphanes" ([god] manifest). The practice was slower to find a foothold in Rome, but was eventually seized upon as a valuable political factor. In the Hellenistic age, Rome itself had attained the status of a deity and the cult of the *Dea Roma* (the goddess Rome) had grown up. In the East it was soon accompanied by the cult of the emperor.

After his death in 44 B.C., Julius Caesar, by decree of the Senate, was declared one of the divine protectors of the state. Augustus did not claim divine honors in Rome, but he was worshiped as a divinity in the East where temples were raised to him (like the temple of Augustus built by Herod the Great in Sebaste, the restored Samaria). Later emperors openly claimed divine honors during their lifetime. The imperial cult had secured a firm grip and was nowhere more enthusiastically propagated than in Asia Minor.

The common emperor cult served as a unifying principle, a point of contact for the varied peoples of the Empire —and Rome, somewhat cynically, fully realized and exploited its political value. But there was one religious group which could not and would not give even token recognition to the divinity of the emperor. The Roman emperor was "Savior" and "Lord"—divine titles. In the eyes of Christians the claim was blasphemous: Jesus Christ was the only Savior and Lord. In Asia Minor more than elsewhere their singular attitude was manifest. The Roman authorities could not ignore their refusal to participate in the imperial cult, and Christians could not honor the emperor as god. A clash was inevitable. The Apocalypse bears witness to the bitter trials of those who "held fast the Name"—who would grant the title of "Lord" to Jesus Christ alone.

2. THE JEWISH WORLD

1) Palestine under the Romans[6]

THE HERODIAN DYNASTY[7] 1. *Herod the Great (37-4 B.C.).* Although Herod never gained the affection, or even the respect of his Jewish subjects (who regarded him as a "half-Jew" because of his Idumaean origin), he was an able and energetic ruler—at least in Roman eyes. In relation to Rome his status was that of *rex socius,* or allied king, enjoying autonomy and freedom from tribute, but subject to Rome in matters of foreign policy and obliged to furnish troops to the imperial army in time of war.

Herod, in the spring of 37 B.C. had married the Hasmonaean princess Mariamne, and was persuaded (against his will) by his mother-in-law, Alexandra, to appoint her son Aristobulus as high priest. That was early in 35 B.C. Late that same year Aristobulus was drowned in Jericho at the instigation of Herod. From Egypt, Cleopatra cast envious eyes on Herod's territory and won from Antony (who had been in Egypt since 40 B.C.) the coastal plain and the region of Jericho. Herod was already guarantor for the Nabataean[8] payment of tribute to Cleopatra: the queen had astutely set the two most important rulers at her Asiatic frontier at loggerheads. As it happened, the situation turned to the advantage of Herod. When civil war between Antony and Octavian broke out in 32 B.C., Herod was prepared to bring aid to Antony, but Cleopatra insisted that he move against the Nabataeans. Thus, he was saved from taking the field against Octavian—a move that might have prejudiced his career beyond recovery. Herod's campaign was successful, but the defeat of Antony at Actium (31 B.C.) seemed fatal to his position. However, he appeared before Octavian in Rhodes in the spring of 30 B.C. and was confirmed as king of the Jews. Later in the year he helped Octavian in the latter's march from Ptolemais to Egypt. The coastal strip and Jericho were restored to him and Samaria was added to his kingdom.

Before Herod died, his territory had come to include Idumaea, Judaea, Samaria, the coastal plain (to Caesarea), Galilee, Peraea (in Transjordan), and Gaulinitis-Ituraea-Batanaea-Trachonitis-Auranitis (districts north and east of the Sea of Galilee).

The reign of Herod was marked by great constructions which permitted him to give expression to his admiration for things Greek and enabled him to express his devotion to Augustus. He built temples to Augustus in Hellenistic cities; he restored Samaria and renamed it Sebaste (Greek *Sebastos* = Augustus); he rebuilt Strato's Tower and renamed it Caesarea. In Jerusalem he built the palace of Herod on the west side of the city and the tower of Antonia north of the Temple enclosure. He provided an amphitheater, and constructed gymnasia, theaters, and stadia throughout the land. In 20 B.C. he began his most ambitious project, the rebuilding of the Temple. Work was still in progress forty-six years later (cf. Jn. 2:20) and the restoration was not finished until 63 A.D., a few years before its total destruction (70 A.D.).

In the domestic sphere, Herod's reign was very troubled. He was of a suspicious nature (in 29 B.C. he had his favorite wife, Mariamne the Hasmonaean, executed for alleged adultery). He was jealous of his power and reacted violently against any attempt on it. In 28 B.C. his mother-in-law Alexandra was put to death on the charge of plotting against him. In 7 B.C. Alexander and Aristobulus, his sons by Mariamne, were strangled at Sebaste. A few days before his death, the king had his son Antipater executed. Herod died at Jericho in March/April, 4 B.C., and was buried on the Herodium near Bethlehem.

2. *The Sons of Herod.* In his will Herod had divided his kingdom among his sons Archelaus (whom he named king), Antipas, and Philip (both named tetrarchs). The will was subject to the approval of Augustus, but already Archelaus had to face disorders in Jerusalem and crushed an incipient rebellion at the cost of many lives. He went to Rome to plead his cause and a delegation of Jews set out to oppose his claim (cf. Lk. 19:14). Sabinus, the procurator sent by Augustus to take charge of the territory

of Herod until the succession had been settled, overstepped his authority and stirred up a revolt which was promptly and savagely put down by Varus, legate of Syria. Eventually Augustus did approve Herod's will; but Archelaus was named ethnarch, not king, and all three sons were vassals of Rome and subject to the legate of Syria.

1. Archelaus (4 B.C.-6 A.D.), Ethnarch of Judaea, Idumaea, and Samaria. In 6 A.D. Archelaus was summoned to Rome to answer charges of misgovernment. He was deposed and exiled to Vienne in Gaul, and his former territory was placed under a Roman procurator.

2. Philip (4 B.C.-34 A.D.), Tetrarch of Gaulanitis, Ituraea, Batanaea, Trachonitis, and Auranitis. His reign was peaceful. He restored Panias, renaming it Caesarea Philippi, and rebuilt Bethsaida-Julia. He married his niece Salome, daughter of Herodias, and left no descendants; at his death his territory was annexed to the province of Syria. (In 37 A.D. Caligula granted it to Agrippa I.)

3. Antipas (4 B.C.-39 A.D.), Tetrarch of Galilee and Peraea. He restored Sepphoris in Galilee, and by the southeast corner of the Lake of Gennesareth built the new town of Tiberias. He had married the daughter of Aretas IV, king of the Nabataeans, but repudiated her in order to marry Herodias (formerly the wife of his brother Herod Philip)—a union condemned by John the Baptist (Mt. 14:3 f. parr.). In 36 A.D. Antipas suffered a severe defeat at the hands of Aretas who was bent on avenging the insult to his daughter. Antipas (urged by Herodias who was jealous of the favor shown by Caligula to her brother Agrippa) went to Rome in 39 A.D. to request the royal title, and found himself exiled to Gaul. (His territory was given to Agrippa.)

3. *Agrippa I, King (41-44 A.D.).* In 37 A.D., when Caligula had become emperor, he granted to Agrippa, grandson of Herod the Great, the former territory of Philip, plus Abilene (between Damascus and Anti-Lebanon). In 39 A.D. Agrippa received, in addition, the former territory of Antipas. Agrippa was in Rome in 41 A.D. when Caligula was assassinated and he helped in the appointment of his friend Claudius. The new emperor

granted him the title of king and added to his realm the territory formerly ruled by the Roman procurator. In other words, Agrippa I was now (41 A.D.) master of the whole kingdom of Herod the Great. His brother, Herod, was made king of Chalcis, a small state between Lebanon and Anti-Lebanon (41-48 A.D.).

The reign of Agrippa I was peaceful and prosperous. Although himself a sceptic, he was careful to respect the religious scruples of the Jews and supported the Pharisees. In order "to please the Jews," he judged it politic to take action against the Christians and executed James the brother of John (Acts 12:1-3). He planned to fortify Jerusalem, but his "third wall" was not completed by the time of his sudden death at Caesarea in 44 A.D. (Acts 12).

4. *Agrippa II*. The son of Agrippa I (also named Agrippa) did not inherit his father's kingdom, but in 50 A.D. he was given Chalcis, the territory of his late uncle Herod; and was, at the same time, appointed supervisor of the Temple with the right of appointing the high priest. In 53 A.D. he exchanged Chalcis for the former territory of Philip, plus Abilene. When in 60 A.D., accompanied by his sister Berenice, he visited Caesarea, he was invited by the procurator Festus to hear Paul (Acts 25:13–26:32). He was a faithful subject of Rome, and although he had sought to prevent rebellion, he supported the Romans in

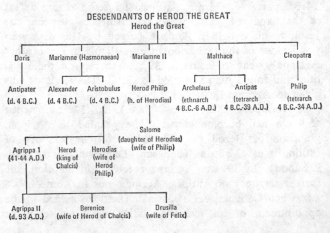

DESCENDANTS OF HEROD THE GREAT
Herod the Great

the Jewish revolt (66-70 A.D.) once it had broken out. He died in 92/93 A.D., the last of the Herodian kings.

THE ROMAN   After the deposition of Archelaus in 6 A.D.,
PROCURATORS his territory (Idumaea, Judaea, and Samaria) was annexed to the province of Syria and was governed by a Roman procurator subject to the legate of Syria.
The procurator had troops at his disposal and his powers
included the appointment and removal of the high priest.
His official residence was in Caesarea, but he moved to
Jerusalem for the great feasts—to be on the spot in case of
trouble. Procuratorial government was interrupted from
41 A.D. to 44 A.D. during the reign of Agrippa I and ended
with the outbreak of the Jewish revolt in 66 A.D.

We know scarcely anything of the first three procurators: Coponius (6-9 A.D.), Marcus Ambivius (9-12 A.D.),
and Annius Rufus (12-15 A.D.). Tiberius appointed Valerius Gratus (15-26 A.D.), who deposed the high priest
Ananus (Annas of Lk. 3:2; Jn. 18:13), and eventually
appointed Caiaphas (18-36 A.D.). Valerius was succeeded
by Pontius Pilate (26-36 A.D.), who continually irritated
and provoked the Jews. He tried to bring the imperial
standards (carrying the image of the emperor) into Jerusalem and later placed shields with the emperor's name
on the walls of Herod's palace; these were removed by
order of Tiberius. He requisitioned funds from the Temple
treasury to construct an aqueduct to the city. All this, and
his general attitude, were sore points with the Jews, but the
policy of Tiberius was to leave his representatives in office
as long as possible. Eventually Pilate overreached himself
by a senseless massacre of Samaritans; in 36 A.D. he was
suspended from office by Vitellius, legate of Syria (35-39
A.D.), and sent to Rome for trial. Pilate arrived in Rome in
37 A.D. and was condemned to exile (or suicide) by
Caligula (37-41 A.D.).

Pilate's successors were Marcellus and Marullus, of whom
nothing is known—it is even possible that only one man is
in question. In 39 A.D. the Jews of Jamnia destroyed an
altar to Caligula that had been set up in the town. The
enraged emperor ordered his statue to be placed in the

Temple of Jerusalem. Fortunately the legate of Syria, P. Petronius (39-42 A.D.), who had received the order in 40 A.D., was able to delay its execution until the assassination of Caligula in January, 41 A.D. The new emperor, Claudius, granted the procuratorial territory to Agrippa I.

On the death of Agrippa (44 A.D.), Claudius again placed Palestine under a Roman procurator, but added the regions of Gaulanitis, Ituraea, Batanaea, Trachonitis, and Auranitis. (This, the former tetrarchy of Philip, was assigned to Agrippa II in 53 A.D.) The political situation in Palestine, which had eased somewhat under Agrippa I, now became still more troubled. National sentiment grew stronger under foreign domination, and the extreme party of the Zealots became active.

Cuspius Fadus (44-46 A.D.) was sent to Claudius to take possession of the territory of Agrippa I. He came into open conflict with the Zealots. Tiberius Alexander (46-48 A.D.) was an apostate Jew, a nephew of the philosopher Philo. He took action against the Zealots and crucified James and Simon, the sons of Judas the Galilean, one of the original leaders of the group. During his term of office there was a severe famine (Acts 11:27-30). Vemtidius Cumanus (48-52 A.D.) supported the Samaritans in a clash with the Jews and had many Jews executed. The legate of Syria, Quadratus (50-60 A.D.), removed Cumanus from office and sent him to Rome. Antonius Felix (52-60 A.D.) was a freedman, yet he married Drusilla, sister of Agrippa II. Felix was extremely venal (cf. Acts 24:26—he hoped to receive a bribe from Paul) and unscrupulous. There was mounting tension in the land, fanned by false messianic hopes and claims; the procurator's reaction was ruthless and he was recalled by Nero. Porcius Festus (60-62 A.D.) was an honest and prudent magistrate who, unfortunately, died in office. He was the one who sent Paul to Rome after the latter had invoked his privilege as a Roman citizen and had appealed to the imperial tribunal. The death of Festus left the way open for the persecution of Christians by the high priest Ananus II (Ananias), and James the "brother of the Lord" was stoned in 62 A.D.

Meanwhile, the situation in Palestine was getting more

and more out of hand and the new procurator, Albinus (62-64 A.D.), did nothing to improve matters. A venal man, he became a tool in the hands of the high priest Ananias whom St. Paul had called a "white-washed wall" (Acts 23:2 f.). The Zealots were now much more active. The last procurator, Gessius Florus (64-66 A.D.), was possibly the worst of the lot. When in 66 A.D. he realized that his unscrupulous and ruthless conduct would not go unpunished in Rome, he incited the Jews to rebellion. In June of 66 A.D. organized revolt against Rome did break out.

THE JEWISH WAR   Agrippa II tried to dissuade the Jews AND AFTERMATH   from the final irrevocable step, but in vain. In Jerusalem the extremist party, led by Eleazar, gained the upper hand and openly rebelled against Rome. The Roman troops in the city surrendered, and were massacred. In October, 66 A.D., Cestius Gallus, the legate of Syria, attacked Jerusalem. Deciding that he lacked sufficient forces for an effective siege he retired; he was ambushed and disastrously defeated at the pass of Beth-horon. This victory stirred up all Jews against Rome, but, unhappily, hatred of a common foe was not enough to overcome the divisions that soon began to prove suicidal.

The defense of Jerusalem was entrusted to the ex-high priest Ananias and to Joseph ben Gorion. The Zealots, led by Eleazar, were dispatched to Idumaea, apparently with the hope of keeping them out of the way. Flavius Josephus, the future historian, became governor of Galilee and found himself opposed by John of Giscala and his band of Zealots. Nero sent his most experienced general, Vespasian, to quell the rebellion in Palestine. In 67 A.D. Vespasian was in Ptolemais at the head of three legions, together with auxiliary troops—a total of 60,000 men. Galilee was conquered in the course of the year, but John of Giscala and his Zealots escaped to Jerusalem. These and other refugees from Galilee increased the extremist element. In the ensuing conflict the aristocratic leaders were executed or assassinated and John of Giscala became master of the city.

Vespasian was content to let the Jews destroy one another, and turned to Peraea (68 A.D.). He was about to invade Judaea when he got word of Nero's death (June 9, 68 A.D.) and suspended operations. This unexpected respite proved disastrous for the Jews. In the spring of 69 A.D. Simon bar-Giora, leader of a band of Zealots, entered Jerusalem and immediately came into conflict with John of Giscala. In July of 69 A.D. the legions of the East acclaimed Vespasian as emperor; he, leaving his son Titus in command in Palestine, went to Alexandria and, early the following year, to Rome. Meanwhile, a third party, led by Eleazar, son of Simon, had taken a hand in the civil strife that raged in the capital; he was overcome by John of Giscala.

In March, 70 A.D., Titus, at the head of four legions, moved from Caesarea against Jerusalem. Famine, in addition to civil strife, had by now become another ally of his within the walls. On May 25, 70 A.D., the Romans broke through the "third wall" (the unfinished fortifications of Agrippa I had been hastily completed), but the city still held out and Titus waited for famine to do its work. In a fresh assault the fortress of Antonia fell on July the twenty-fourth, and finally, on August the ninth, the Temple was taken and destroyed by fire. Still the Jews resisted, but by the end of September the whole city was in Roman hands and both John of Giscala and Simon bar-Giora were prisoners. The war was not quite over: the fortresses of the Herodium and Machaerus had to be taken and the strongest position of all, Masada by the Dead Sea, fell only in April of 73 A.D. This was the end of the disastrous Jewish War.

Palestine, under the name of Judaea, became an independent imperial province governed by a legate, and the Tenth Legion was stationed in Jerusalem. Gradually the Jewish survivors began to regroup around their spiritual leaders, the scribes and Pharisees. A rabbinical school was established at Jamnia where the oral traditions that had grown around the written Torah were collected and shaped, eventually to take their place in the Mishna. Jerusalem lay in ruins and the Temple was gone, but Judaism survived. Not only that, but the Jews, in little more than half a century, were again rising in a final desperate revolt.

In 130 A.D. the Emperor Hadrian (117-138 A.D.) ordered the rebuilding of Jerusalem as Aelia Capitolina; a temple to Jupiter Capitolinus was to be erected on the site of the Temple. This decision, joined to an imperial decree forbidding circumcision, fomented another rebellion (132-135 A.D.). Its leader was Simon bar Kochba ("son of the star"; cf. Nb. 24:17) whose real name was Ben Koseba. He was supported by Rabbi Akiba who hailed him as the messiah. The ruins of Jerusalem were, for a time at least, occupied by the rebels; we also know that insurgents lived in the caves of Wadi Murabba'at and elsewhere in the desert of Judah. In 1950 two letters of Bar Kochba were found at Wadi Murabba'at; in 1960 a further fifteen letters of the Jewish leader were found in a cave farther south, near the Dead Sea.[9] The details of the struggle are not clear, but the fact that it dragged on for over three years—even though the Romans had dispatched four legions with auxiliaries under the command of Julius Severus, recalled from Britain for the purpose—indicates the seriousness of the rebellion.

The losses on both sides were very heavy; the surviving Jews were sold into slavery. Jerusalem, now named *Colonia Aelia Capitolina*, became a Roman colony, which no Jew might enter, and the temple of Jupiter was built on the site of Yahweh's Temple—just as Hadrian had ordered in the first place. The words of Lk. 21:24, which in their present form may be colored by the events of 70 A.D., find their most literal fulfillment after the Second Revolt: "They will fall by the edge of the sword, and be led captive among all nations; and Jerusalem will be trodden down by the Gentiles, until the times of the Gentiles are fulfilled." But the final note of hope should not be overlooked (cf. Rm. 11:25 f.).

2) *Jewish Religious Sects*[10]

PHARISEES AND SADDUCEES[11]

1. *The Pharisees.* The Hasidim movement of the Maccabaean period sur-

vived, in later times, in two branches: Pharisees and Essenes. The Pharisees (whose name means the "separated
ones") emerged during the reign of John Hyrcanus (135-
104 B.C.). During his reign and that of his successor, Alexander Jannaeus (104-76 B.C.), they cut themselves adrift
from, and stood in opposition to, the Hasmonaean dynasty.
Later they refused to take an oath of allegiance to Herod
the Great; they practiced passive resistance but avoided
embroilment in political affairs; and they maintained a
similar attitude toward the Roman authorities. However,
they also "separated" themselves from the *'am ha-ares,*
the "people of the land"—the mass of the people "who
knew not the law" (Jn. 7:49). Like the Hasidim before
them, they were champions of the Torah and, since they
had withdrawn from political activity, their religious character became more and more marked.

On the whole, the Pharisees came from the middle
classes. According to Josephus, the members of the party
numbered 6,000 in the time of Herod, and those in sympathy with their views must have been more numerous.
What set them apart was an exact and detailed knowledge
of the Mosaic Law and of the "traditions of the Elders,"
the oral interpretation of the Torah. Insistence on the oral
tradition was at once the strength and the weakness of
pharisaism. On the one hand it offered a means of adapt-
ing the prescriptions of the Torah to changing circumstances. It also meant that the Pharisees were more open
to the acceptance of new ideas; thus, they readily gave as-
sent to doctrines such as personal immortality, judgment
after death, the resurrection, and the existence of angels.
While stressing the action of divine Providence they also
insisted on human freedom. They looked forward eagerly
to the establishment of the kingdom of God on earth and
they had a lively messianic expectation. As moral theologians they were much more open and progressive than
the Sadducees.

On the other hand, preoccupation with the oral prescriptions—which they set on a par with the written Law
—could and did lead to legalism and even to puerile casu-
istry. The severe indictment of the Pharisees in Mt. 23

lists some of the extremes of their legalistic interpretation. They had turned the observance of the Torah into an insupportable burden and since, in their view, faithfulness to God was expressed through faithfulness to the whole Torah (written and oral) they had effectively "shut the kingdom of heaven against men" (Mt. 23:13). Besides, pride in their knowledge and observance of the Law led to self-righteousness, an attitude strikingly illustrated in the parable of The Pharisee and the Publican (Lk. 18:9-14). The Pharisee believed that he was the author of his own salvation, that he was justified by his observance of the Law. St. Paul—the former Pharisee—came to realize that perfect observance of the whole law was not possible (Rm. 7); he bluntly stated that the Pharisees did not, in fact, observe the Law (Rm. 2:17-24).

Even though the Pharisees despised "the common breed without the Law," their influence over the people was immense. They were zealous for the Law, their religious ideals were high, and their moral conduct was often exemplary. Paul himself bears witness to the sincerity of his former life: " . . as to the law a Pharisee . . . as to righteousness under the law blameless" (Phil. 3:5 f.). Besides, their independent attitude toward the Roman authorities appealed to the people. Not that the Pharisees were extremists; indeed, they cautioned against open revolt.

The trust of the people (in one sense at least) was not misplaced, for it was the Pharisees who saved Judaism from extinction. Their stand had always been on the Torah (understood in the wider sense), even though they did not despise the Temple cult. When the Temple was destroyed in 70 A.D., they were able to rebuild on the basis of the Torah alone. Their belief had always been that the destiny of the Jews was religious rather than political. Thus, political disaster did not spell the end of everything. Although their faults were glaring and although their opposition to and rejection of the Messiah was a national tragedy, we cannot but admire the faith and the courage that survived the shattering experiences of the two Jewish wars and we cannot but marvel at the spirit, bequeathed by them, that

has enabled Judaism to survive (against all reasonable expectation) to the present day.

2. *The Sadducees.* The Sadducees (their name probably
means "Zadokites," descendants or partisans of Zadok,
Solomon's priest—1 Kgs. 2:35) first appear as an organized
party in the time of John Hyrcanus. It was due partly to
the conflict of Sadducees and Pharisees that the Jews eventually lost their political independence: the appeal of both
parties to Rome led to Pompey's intervention in 63 B.C.
The conflict was not surprising; the two parties differed
widely in social structure as well as in outlook and practice.

> In general the Pharisees belonged to the middle
> classes, the Sadducees to the wealthy priestly aristoc-
> racy. The Pharisees claimed the authority of piety and
> learning, the Sadducees that of blood and position; the
> Pharisees were progressive, the Sadducees conserva-
> tive; the Pharisees strove to raise the religious stand-
> ards of the masses, the Sadducees were chiefly con-
> cerned with Temple administration and ritual, and
> kept themselves aloof from the masses.[12]

The Sadducees stressed the importance of the Law of
Moses, especially the regulations governing the priesthood
and sacrifice. However, they are not simply to be identified with the priesthood; they also included members of the
lay aristocracy. In fact, they took their stand on the Torah
alone (in the strict sense) and rejected the oral tradition.
Hence, they denied the resurrection of the dead, personal
immortality, and recompense beyond the grave, as well as
the existence of angels and devils (cf. Acts 23:8). Since
they interpreted the Law very literally, in moral matters
they held extremely rigid views. Politically, they easily accepted Roman rule because the preservation of the status
quo was to their advantage. It is readily understood that
they did not have the sympathy of the people and had little
or no influence in the religious and moral sphere. When
the Temple and its cult came to an end, they had no further *raison d'être* and they, too, disappeared from history.

3. *The Scribes.* Scribes first appear in the reign of Solomon as educated civil servants; they are the originators

and the authors of the wisdom literature in Israel. In post-exilic times, the scribe was one versed in the Law, like Ezra (Ez. 7:6, 11 f.; Neh. 8:1). In the first century A.D., the scribes, who were lawyers, moralists, and theologians, were the guides and teachers of the Jewish community: "The scribes sit on Moses' seat; so practice and observe whatever they tell you" (Mt. 23:2). They were named "lawyer," "teacher," "doctor of the Law," and were given the title of *rabbi* ("my master"). Some of them were celebrated founders of schools like Hillel and Shammai in the early part of the first century A.D.; others had great authority, like Gamaliel, St. Paul's master (cf. Acts 5:34-39; 22:3).

Although in the Gospels the scribes are most often associated with the Pharisees, the term "scribe" and "Pharisee" are not identical. For one thing, the scribes, even in the narrower sense of doctors of the Law, were in existence long before the Pharisee party emerged. Then, too, there were scribes with Sadducee leanings who held and taught the tenets of that party. However, it remains true that the great majority of scribes inclined to Pharisaism and their position as teachers of the people greatly increased the influence of the Pharisees.

This seems a convenient point to insert a word of explanation about the Talmud, for its compilation was the work of later scribes. The earliest written codification of oral law is called the *Mishna* ("repetition"). The *Mishna* is essentially a collection of *halakoth*—rules of conduct deduced from the Law—that are earlier than the year 200 A.D. The *Tosephta* ("complement") is a body of material similar to the *Mishna* in form and content. Finally, the *Gemara* ("completion") contains traditions not incorporated in the *Mishna*, the solutions of later rabbis as well as moral exhortations and legends. *Mishna* and *Gemara* together make up the Talmud—the compilation of rabbinical oral traditions. There are two Talmuds, differing widely in content and extent: the Jerusalem Talmud (fifth century) and the Babylonian Talmud (seventh century).

4. *The Sanhedrin.* The beginnings and original composition of the Sanhedrin are not clear, but, under the Ro-

man procurators, it had assumed a precise form and character. It was a senate of priests and laymen with seventy members—not counting the high priest who was *ex officio* president of the assembly. The sanhedrites were divided into three groups: the heads of the priestly families, the elders (representing the lay aristocracy), and the scribes. The third group was Pharisaic in spirit, the others were Sadducees. Paul skillfully played on this division when he was brought before the Sanhedrin (Acts 23:1-9).

Under the procurators, the Sanhedrin had considerable power. It could handle all cases involving infringement of the Torah: this included the civil as well as the religious sphere since Judaism knew one Law only. The council had its own police force and could arrest malefactors and punish them when convicted. It might pass sentence of death; but the sentence had to be ratified by the Roman procurator (cf. Jn. 18:31).

Outside of Jerusalem, in the communities of Palestine and throughout the Diaspora, local tribunals were also called "sanhedrin." They settled local affairs in the light of precedents established by the great Sanhedrin of Jerusalem, whose decisions were communicated to the various Jewish groups.[13]

THE ESSENES Josephus (the Jewish historian of the late first century A.D.), who presents the Jewish sects as "philosophies," describes the Essenes as a "third philosophy" —after the Pharisees and Sadducees. He gives the impression that they emerged during the reign of Jonathan (160-142 B.C.), and it seems that we may regard the sect as an offshoot of the Hasidim. Philo asserts that the Essenes dwelt in large numbers in many towns and villages of Judaea, and he interprets their name as meaning the "pious ones." Essenianism, as presented by Josephus and Philo[14] is seen as a monastic movement of priestly ascetics. All things were held in common, the members of the sect being charitably received in any of their settlements. Although Josephus knew a group of Essenes who permitted marriage, the sect as a whole observed perfect continence.

A candidate for admission to the order first had to undergo a postulancy of one year, after which he was admitted to the purification rites. Only after a further novitiate of two years was he admitted to the common religious meal and so received into the community. He also had to swear "dread oaths" to revere God, to act justly toward men, and to do harm to no man; he had to hate the wicked and take the part of the just; he had to be obedient to his superiors, avoid lies and theft, and keep the community teachings secret. Each community had a superior and was arranged in hierarchical order. The sectarians had very great respect for the Torah and were notably meticulous in observance of the sabbath. They sent offerings to the Temple, but did not themselves participate in the Temple cult; it would appear that they regarded the assumption of the high priesthood by Jonathan (and his successors) as a usurpation, and even as a profanation; this may have been the reason for their withdrawal from normal Jewish life.

Another ancient writer, Pliny the Elder, a Roman, tells of an Essene settlement on the western shore of the Dead Sea, between Ain Gedi and Jericho: "A lonely people, the most extraordinary in the world, who live without women, without love, without money, with the palm trees for their only companions." Pliny is undoubtedly referring to Qumran (which is the only important ruin in the area indicated by him). He named his "lonely people" Essenes. The majority of scholars agree that the Qumran sectarians, if they are not identical with the Essenes, are closely related; we shall regard them as identical. At this point we shall indicate the importance of Qumran (that is to say, of the Essene movement) for an understanding of the New Testament.[15]

The age immediately before the coming of Jesus, the last century B.C., is a relatively obscure period of Jewish history. The recently discovered Essenian texts have raised the veil to some extent, so that we now know something of a corner of that Jewish world into which Jesus was born. We are aware of an unexpected aspect of Jewish theology: a theology based on a dualism, a doctrine of two spirits, the spirit of God and the spirit of Belial (the

devil). Light and darkness stand in opposition: they fight
in the world, and the same conflict takes place within every
man. But this dualism is monotheistic, for God is the creator of both spirits. It is dualism of a moral order: the
influence of the spirit of truth is seen in the practice of
virtue, while vice shows the hand of the spirit of iniquity.
The combat is not unending, but will close with the utter
destruction of evil and the victory of the "children of
light."

Certain elements of the Qumran organization and certain tenets of the sect show an analogy with those of the
primitive Christian community: there may be an Essenian
influence on nascent Christianity. It is just possible that
John the Baptist may have been an Essene. According to
Lk. 1:80, John "was in the wilderness [i.e., in the desert
of Judah] until the day of his manifestation to Israel."
The only necessary conclusion from this statement, however, is that John must have known the Qumran settlement. Besides, if he had ever been an Essene, he had
broken with the sect: his baptism, public and not repeated,
differed radically from the daily ritual baths of the Essenes; and his universal call to repentance contrasted
sharply with their marked exclusiveness.

At first sight there is a striking resemblance in external
organization between the Essenes and the primitive Jerusalem community. According to Acts 2:44 f.; 4:32, 34-37;
5:1-11, the first Christians held all things in common. Each
day (Acts 2:46) they partook of a common meal. The
three stages to be observed in fraternal disciplinary correction (man to man; before one or two witnesses; before
the assembled community [Mt. 18:15-17; cf. Ti. 2:10])
are paralleled in Qumran procedure. In doctrinal matters,
the Pauline Epistles and the Fourth Gospel show some
contacts with Essenian doctrine.

It is with John that the greatest number of points of
contact, both literary and doctrinal, have been discovered.
In John a form of dualism is expressed in contrasts: light-
darkness, truth-falsehood, life-death; on the evidence of
the Qumran texts, such dualism is authentically Jewish and
is not due to gnostic influences (as had formerly been sug-

gested by certain scholars). The evangelist treats light, truth, and life as kindred, and often as identical, images; the same holds true for darkness, falsehood, and death. The meaning of these expressions is very close to that of similar ones in the Qumran texts, where they occur a number of times in practically the same sense.

In these texts, too, stress is laid on a spirit of unity and fraternal love. Such ideas are frequent in John, but with notable differences. Thus, the fraternal love so insisted upon in Qumran is limited to members of the sect; all others must be hated as enemies of God. This is not Christian charity. It is the word "Christian" indeed that underlines the essential difference between the Scrolls and the Gospel. The occurrence of the various themes in the Fourth Gospel and in the Essene writings points to a common Jewish background, but in John these same ideas have been quite transformed by the impact of Christian revelation and of Christian faith. There is also a wider relationship between Qumran and the primitive Christian community: a religious awakening marked by a spirit of exultation before the gift of salvation, and marked, too, by intensity and by generosity.

But the differences that separate the Essene movement and Christianity run far deeper than any mutual contacts. A most notable difference is the extreme exclusiveness of the sectarians. They are the Remnant, the true people of God, the Israel of the end-time. By the practice of the moral virtues, by their common life, by prayer and meditation, and also by the meticulous observance of the Law and the strict discipline of their order, they strove to be an authentically priestly community. In order to become the immaculate people of God, they cut themselves off, not only from any contact with sinners—from all, that is, who did not belong to the sect—but also they would accept no one with a bodily deformity into their community; only priests without blemish might officiate in the liturgy of the New Covenant.

> No man afflicted in such a way as to be unable to take a place in the congregation, and no one with a

bodily affliction, crippled in feet or hands, lame or blind, or deaf or dumb, or afflicted with a bodily disfigurement visible to the eye, or tottering with age so as to be unable to support himself among the congregation—these may not enter to take a place in the congregation of the Name; because holy Angels are in the congregation.[16]

How very different the outlook and practice of Jesus. He came to seek out and save the lost (Lk. 19:10). He associated with sinners and welcomed and healed the sick and the lame and the blind. And he never tired of teaching that the self-righteousness of men, reliance on their own efforts, cut them off from God. Salvation is not a distant goal which a man must reach by his own striving, it is the gift of a loving God. But it presupposes repentance, the tears of the prodigal son. And the gift is offered to all who will accept it.

In short:

[The Qumran texts] set in unexpected relief the contrast between Jesus and the religion of his time. There below, in that Dead Sea monastery, the small army of ascetics, the saints of God, the militia of the Most High, live a life of the most severe penance. Striving after perfect purity, engaged in the strictest legal observance, they hate, without quarter, the enemies of God, holding themselves apart from the reprobate, excluding even the sick and the blind. Here, Jesus proclaims to the poor, the miserable, the destitute of Yahweh, the incomprehensible, the infinite love of God, the dawn of that joyous time when the blind see, the crippled walk, and the poor have the Good News preached to them. Two worlds are there, face to face. On the one hand, the universe of the Law and of observance; Qumran had pushed to the extreme both its admirable sincerity and the limitation of its love. On the other hand the world of the Good News—the preaching of the limitless love of God and the joy of children forgiven by their Father. Better than ever before we see the splendor and the originality of the message of Jesus: that is the service, the great service, that the new texts have rendered us.[17]

OTHER GROUPS
1. *The Zealots.* When in the year 6 or 7 A.D. the legate Quirinius[18] set in operation a general census in Palestine, the exasperated Jews rebelled; the leaders of the revolt were a Pharisee called Sadduk and a Galilean named Judas of Gamala. These men gathered a group of insurgents around them and carried on a campaign against the Romans, first in Galilee and later in Judaea. This was the origin of the Zealots: ardent patriots who regarded themselves as the agents of God's wrath and the instruments of the deliverance of his people. Although the initial revolt was crushed, the party survived—men who owed allegiance to God alone, the sole Master.

The Zealots cut themselves adrift from the Pharisees who, in their eyes, were too conciliatory and too passive. They made use of any means, not excluding assassination, to free themselves from the foreign oppressor and to punish Jews suspected of collaboration. Since, in getting rid of their enemies, they usually used a short dagger called a *sica*, they were known as *sicarii* by the Romans. The Zealots were largely responsible for goading their countrymen into the fatal rebellion of 66 A.D. And the supporters of Bar Koseba in the final desperate rising of 132-35 A.D. were animated by the Zealot spirit: they were men who preferred death to pagan domination.

2. *The Herodians.* The Herodians are named three times in the New Testament (Mk. 3:6; 12:13; Mt. 22:16) and are also mentioned by Josephus. They were not a religious sect nor an extremist party like the Zealots, but the friends and supporters of the Herod family. They were found principally in Galilee, the dominion of Herod Antipas, although some Jerusalem families had remained attached to the Herods. It appears that, under the procurators, the Herodians allied themselves with the Pharisees. Although they were soon to disappear from the Palestinian scene, the Gospels would suggest that, at the time of Jesus, they were an important factor in the existing situation.

3. *The Samaritans.* The Samaritans were not a Jewish
sect or group, but it is convenient to consider them here.
The Samaritans of New Testament times were descendants
of the heterogeneous people planted in Samaria after
721 B.C. The seeds of the enmity between them and the
Jews were sown in the early days of the return from the
Exile; the final break came in the time of Alexander the
Great when (according to Josephus) the schismatic temple
was built on Mt. Gerizim. When their temple was destroyed by John Hyrcanus in 128 B.C., they continued to
maintain their cultic autonomy and to celebrate their Pasch
on the sacred mountain—a rite that they have faithfully followed to the present day. Their sacred Scripture was the
Pentateuch alone.

In the time of Jesus they formed a small group localized
in Samaria. With regard to doctrine they were monotheists,
and they venerated Moses as the prophet *par excellence*
who had given them the Torah. They believed that, from
the days of the high priest Heli, God had been angry with
his sinful people. However, they looked for the coming of
a messianic figure—the *Taheb*—another Moses (cf. Dt.
18:15). Jn. 4:25 makes allusion to this messianic expectation. Several Gospel texts reflect the bitter feeling between
Jews and Samaritans (e.g., Jn. 4:9; 8:48; Lk. 9:52-54).
With supreme courtesy Jesus held up a Samaritan as the
model of Christian charity; and Acts 8 relates how Samaria
welcomed the Good News.

3) *The Jewish Diaspora*[19]

The term *Diaspora* ("dispersion"; cf. 2 Mc. 1:27) is frequent in the Judaism of the Hellenistic period as a technical
term for the settlement of Jews abroad. The movement began in the sixth century B.C. when many of those exiled
in Babylon elected to remain there, but it really got under
way from the time of Alexander the Great. In the first
century A.D., the total number of Jews settled throughout
all the countries of the Mediterranean world may have
been in the neighborhood of four million; Acts 2:9-11
gives an idea of their geographical distribution. Charac-

teristic features of the Diaspora were, first of all, the strict community life of Jews living in the different centers; and then the close contact maintained between the various cells, with Jerusalem as the focal point of the whole vast network.

The constitution of the individual communities varied according to place and according to the juridical position of each in a particular city or state. Each community was governed by a *gerousia* ("council") formed of "Elders." Everywhere synagogues sprang up and the offices of *archisynagogos* ("president over the cult") and of *archontes* ("chief magistrates") were constant elements in the communities. Roman law not only recognized and protected this special organization, but also granted special privileges to Jews. Their right to collect the Temple tax and to dispatch it to Jerusalem was scrupulously safeguarded. They were dispensed from participation in pagan ceremonies and from swearing on the name of the emperor —they were expected to pray for the emperor—and the sabbath observance was respected.

One of the most important Jewish communities was that of Alexandria. There, beginning in the third century B.C., the Hebrew Bible was translated into Greek. This version, the Septuagint, became the Bible of the Greek-speaking Diaspora. In Roman times, the Jews of Alexandria enjoyed a considerable degree of autonomy (the Jews had welcomed Octavian's conquest of Egypt and had shown themselves openly in favor of Rome), although they did not possess full Alexandrian citizenship. They were disliked by their Gentile neighbors for their exclusiveness and for their pro-Roman tendencies. Serious disturbances occurred during the reign of Caligula (37-41 A.D.), but order was restored by Claudius (41-54 A.D.). The Jewish war in Palestine (66-70 A.D.) had repercussions in Alexandria, and many thousands of Jews lost their lives.

Jews in the cosmopolitan and intellectual atmosphere of Alexandria were conscious of the influence of the Hellenistic milieu in which they lived and their reaction was not only defensive. True, they did defend the Jews and Judaism from the attacks of pagans, but they also sought to prove the superiority of the Jews and Judaism over the nations and their religions. The most outstanding figure in this work of propaganda was the philosopher Philo.[20] Born about the year 20 B.C. of a prominent family, Philo was leader of a Jewish embassy to the emperor Caligula in 39 A.D.; he died some time after 40 A.D. His great achievement was his attempt to present Judaism in terms of contemporary Hellenistic philosophy. This involved a thoroughgoing allegorical exegesis of the Torah (by seeking a deeper meaning beneath the plain surface of the narrative): he strove to show that the biblical writers were saying the same thing as the philosophers of his own day. The influence of Philo is visible in at least one New Testament writing, the Epistle to the Hebrews, for the unknown author of the Epistle was almost certainly an Alexandrian Jewish convert.

For Philo, God is absolute Being who, by reason of his transcendence, is outside the scope of human knowledge. This supreme Being has used intermediaries in his work of creation and continues to make use of them in his conservation of the world; the intermediaries are ideas (*logoi*). The highest of them and the nearest to God is the *Logos,* the original Idea which contains all the others. The Logos, shadow and image of God, the exemplar of all created things, stands between the absolute Being and sensible creation: it is through the Logos that the human soul can attain to God in mystical contemplation. Philo had no intention of changing Judaism: he wished to make it relevant in a milieu imbued with intellectual speculation. The God of Philo is still the Yahweh of the Old Testament, yet there is a great distance between the Alexandrian philosopher and the views of the Palestinian rabbis.

Jews had, naturally, settled in Rome, but the colony in the capital was not as large or as compact as that of Alexandria and did not enjoy the same civil autonomy. In recognition of Jewish support in Judaea and in Egypt, Julius Caesar had looked with favor on the Roman colony; Augustus also regarded the Roman Jews favorably. Such an occurrence as the expulsion order of Claudius (Acts 18:22) would have been unusual, and that particular decree does not appear to have been very effective; at least, Jews were soon able to return.

A notable characteristic of Judaism in this period was proselytism (cf. Mt. 23:15). In Alexandria especially a deliberate attempt was made to propagate Jewish beliefs by means of such works as 1 (3) Esdras, the Letter of Aristeas, and the Jewish Sibylline Oracles. Philo, we have noted, presented Judaism in terms of Greek philosophy. But a similar approach would have had a limited appeal and the real attractive power of Judaism lay in its superiority over the other religions of the Graeco-Roman world and in the high moral standards and conduct of Jews.

Many Gentiles who had wearied of the pagan religions and who were prepared to admit the principle of monotheism, were drawn to Judaism. They were freely admitted to the synagogue worship. They came to know and to appreciate the main tenets of the religion, and began to observe certain Jewish practices. If they were prepared to accept circumcision, a ritual baptism, and Jewish citizenship, they became true proselytes (incorporated into the Israel of God) and were subject to all the prescriptions of the Law. It seems, however, that the number of proselytes was not great—and the bulk of them would have been women. A much larger class was formed of "God-fearers" (cf. Acts 13:43, 50; 17:4; Rm. 2:19 f.). They accepted monotheism and certain Jewish practices, but objected to circumcision and to Jewish citizenship, and hence would not take the final step of full incorporation into the Jewish religion. For, despite praiseworthy efforts to remove barriers, Judaism remained a nationalistic religion. The Christian message of true universalism offered something that Judaism could never really give, and Christian missionaries made many converts among the God-fearers of the synagogues. In two ways at least, by producing the Septuagint, which became the Christian Bible, and by the good seed sown among the Gentiles, the Jewish Dispersion had prepared the way for the Christian Church.

This sketch of Jewish influence may give a wrong impression unless seen against a somber background. If some Gentiles came to appreciate the qualities of Judaism, many more were suspicious of and hostile to the exclusive communities in their midst. The Jews were known to have a supreme contempt for any cult other than that of the God of Israel and they held themselves aloof from the religious and social life of the cities in which they dwelt (almost always in closely-knit colonies). Misunderstanding and misrepresentation were only too easy: their religion had no place for temple, statue, or sacrifice (Were they atheists?); they practiced the "mutilation" of circumcision; and the sabbath observance was taken as a proof of indolence on their part. The privileges they enjoyed gave more cause for resentment. Reaction not infrequently took a violent turn. In the first century A.D., the phenomenon that we term anti-semitism reared its ugly head in many parts of the Mediterranean world. In Alexandria in 34 A.D. and in Caesarea and Antioch in 66 A.D. many thousands of Jews were massacred. These crimes might be put down to the exasperated reaction of paganism to a religion and a code of morals whose very presence was a constant irritant.

3. CHRONOLOGY OF THE LIFE
OF JESUS

The evangelists, who had no intention of writing a biography of Jesus in the modern sense, were not worried about precise chronology. We can date few of the events of our Lord's life, and even then we have to be content with approximations. No date can be established with absolute certainty, because the evidence at our disposal is meager and open to conflicting interpretations. We shall be content to indicate a chronology based on a reasonable evaluation of the available data.

1) *The Birth of Jesus*

Jesus was born during the reign of Herod the Great. This is attested to by Mt. 2:1 and Lk. 1:5. Hence, the birth occurred not later than 4 B.C., the date of Herod's death.[21]

According to Lk. 2:1 f., Jesus was born at a time of a

census ordered by Augustus and carried out by Quirinius, governor of Syria[22] Augustus was emperor (27 B.C.-14 A.D.). The general census of the Roman Empire ("all the world" = the *orbis Romanus*) was in view of tax assessment; Luke sees it as the providential means of ensuring that Jesus would be born in Bethlehem. There is evidence for a census in Gaul in 12 B.C., and there was provision for the taking of a census in Egypt every fourteen years; the series seems to have begun in 10/9 B.C. According to Tacitus,[23] a *Breviarium Imperii*, in Augustus' own hand, found at his death, gave not only the numbers of regular and auxiliary troops and the strength of the navy, but provided statistics on the provisions of dependent kingdoms, direct and indirect taxation, and recurrent expenditures. This information must have resulted from a general census which, of course, need not have been carried out simultaneously in all parts of the Empire. The possibility of a Roman census in the domain of Herod the Great has been questioned. But Augustus knew that Herod, a puppet king, must bow to his wishes, and besides there was a distinct coolness in their relations following Herod's unauthorized campaign against the Nabataeans (9/8 B.C.). In view of the evidence it is reasonable to suppose that Luke is standing on sound historical ground when he refers to the edict of Augustus.

The celebrated chronological difficulties raised in Lk. 2:2 are still unsolved. It is widely accepted, on the sole authority of Josephus,[24] that a census was held in 6/7 A.D., when Publius Sulpicius Quirinius was legate of Syria and was resisted by the Zealots under John the Galilean.[25] If this dating is accepted, we must look for an earlier census carried out by Quirinius. On the evidence of inscriptions from Tivoli and Antioch of Pisidia, it has been argued that he was legate of Syria between 4 and 1 B.C. and also that he had a special commission to carry out a census in Palestine during 10-8 B.C. Tertullian[26] attributed the nativity census to Sentius Saturninus, legate of Syria (8-6 B.C.); he could well have completed a census begun by Quirinius. On the evidence, the best we can say is that Jesus was born between 8 B.C. (the census of Quirinius) and 4 B.C. (the death of Herod). The years 7 or 6 B.C. are commonly proposed as the most probable.

2) *The Public Ministry*[27]

In Luke 3:1 f., the evangelist is at great pains to date exactly the ministry of the Baptist; his real purpose is thereby to date the beginning of our Lord's ministry. His elaborate synchronization serves to set the Gospel event in the framework of world history and to describe the political situation in Palestine. Unfortunately, however, only one element is of any use to us: the fifteenth year of Tiberius Caesar. The reign of Tiberius began on August 19, 14 A.D.; the fifteenth year would be—in the Roman system—from August 19, 28 A.D. to August 18, 29 A.D. It is more likely that Luke follows the Syrian calendar with its year beginning on October 1. In this case the short period August 19-September 30 would be reckoned as the first year of Tiberius; the fifteenth year of his reign would be October 1, 27 A.D.-September 30, 28 A.D. Thus, it seems that we can put the beginning of the ministry of Jesus, coming shortly after the inauguration of the Baptist's mission, in the year 28 A.D.

An incidental indication of importance is that of Jn. 2:20: "It has taken forty-six years to build this temple." Herod began his reconstruction of the Temple in 20 B.C.; forty-six years later would be 27 or 28 A.D., thus agreeing with the indication of Lk. 3:1.

We would gather from the Synoptics that the public ministry lasted not more than one year, although there are some indications that it may have been longer. The Fourth Gospel, by clearly distinguishing three Passovers, leaves us in no doubt that the ministry really lasted more than two years.[28] After his encounter with the Baptist and the miracle of Cana, Jesus went to Jerusalem for the Passover (Jn. 2:13, 23). Back in Galilee, he multiplied the loaves by the lake "when the Passover was at hand" (Jn. 6:4), obviously a year later. He was in Jerusalem for the feasts of Tabernacles (Jn. 7:2) and Dedication (Jn. 10:22); thus, his visit to Bethany, "six days before the Passover" (Jn. 12:1), took place in the following year, the year of his death.

3) The Death of Jesus[29]

All four Gospels agree that Jesus died on the *parasceve* of the sabbath, that is, on a Friday (Mk. 15:42; Mt. 27:62; Lk. 23:54; Jn. 19:31), but the date (the day of the month) of his death is disagreed upon by the Synoptics and John.

Synoptics: Jesus ate the Passover on 15 Nisan (according to our reckoning the evening of 14—the Jewish day began immediately after sunset) and died on the afternoon of 15 Nisan.

John: Jesus died on 14 Nisan (at the hour that the Passover lambs were immolated in the Temple).[30]

In detail, we observe that, according to the synoptists, the last supper eaten by Jesus with his disciples was a Passover meal. He had the preparations made for the Passover on the "first day of Unleavened Bread," that is, on 14 Nisan (Mk. 14:12 parr.; cf. 14:14 parr.). On taking his place at table, he remarked: "I have earnestly desired to eat this passover with you before I suffer" (Lk. 22:15).

But, John begins his account of the passion in this way: "Before the feast of the Passover" (Jn. 13:1); and at the trial scene before Pilate he remarks that the Jews refused to enter the praetorium "so that they might not be defiled, but might eat the passover" (Jn. 18:28). Jesus was condemned to death on the "day of the Preparation for the Passover" (Jn. 19:14) and was crucified on the same day (Jn. 19:42). John's dating is confirmed by 1 Cor. 5:7: Jesus *died* on the day the paschal lamb was immolated, that is, 14 Nisan.[31]

When we look again at the Synoptics we find that the day of the death of Jesus was not a day of sabbath rest. The guards who took part in the arrest carried arms (Mk. 14:47). Simon of Cyrene came from the fields where, apparently, he had been working (Mk. 15:46 parr.). The shops were open: Joseph of Arimathea could buy a winding-sheet (Mk. 15:46 parr.) and the women could buy spices (Lk. 23:56). All such activity could not have taken place on the solemn day of the Pasch, 15 Nisan. It may be that the Paschal character of the Last Supper, stressed in the Synoptic tradition, has upset the chronological perspective, and that the perspective has been restored in the Fourth Gospel. We recognize with John that Jesus died on 14 Nisan and with the synoptists that the Last Supper was a paschal meal—although it anticipated by twenty-four hours the Passover of the Jews. Various explanations of this last factor have been proposed,[32] but it seems best to acknowledge that Jesus freely anticipated the paschal meal. "Since he would be unable to celebrate the Passover on the morrow, except in his own person on the Cross (Jn. 19:36; 1 Cor. 5:7), Jesus instituted his own new rite in the course of a meal which had all the characteristics of the Jewish Passover."[33]

The crucifixion must have taken place between 26 and 36 A.D.—the term of Pilate's procuratorship. Since we have accepted the view which dates the death of Jesus to Friday, 14 Nisan, we can limit our scope to the years in which these factors were verified: 27, 30, and 33 A.D. When we consider that the public ministry opened in 28 A.D. and lasted more than two years, but less than three years, we see the years 27 and 33 are eliminated. Hence, we may assert, with some confidence, that Jesus died on Friday, 14 Nisan, 30 A.D., that is to say, on April 7, 30 A.D.

In conclusion, we may set in tabular form our relatively exact chronology of the life of Jesus:

7/6 B.C.	Birth of Jesus
28 A.D. (before Passover)	Beginning of the public ministry
April 7, 30 A.D.	Crucifixion
April 9, 30 A.D.	Resurrection (and Ascension)

4. THE APOSTOLIC AGE[34]

In this and the next section we shall be content to follow the main lines of the Acts of the Apostles. The whole of the chapter offers no more than the broad background and general historical outline of New Testament times.

1) The Jerusalem Community

The first Christian community was founded in Jerusalem where the group of Galileans, Apostles and disciples of Jesus, were gathered. They had been commanded to await the promise of the Father (Acts 1:4, 8); and the outpouring of the Spirit on Pentecost 30 A.D. marked the birth of the Church.

THE TWELVE The Twelve, naturally, took the first place in the community. As companions of Jesus, hearers of his words, witnesses of his works and of his resurrection, their position was unique. From the beginning it was recognized, spontaneously—though it may not have been fully grasped until later—that the Twelve were the foundation of the Church: "The wall of the city had twelve foundations, and on them the twelve names of the twelve apostles of the Lamb" (Ap. 21:14). It is not surprising, then, to find them functioning as a group in the early days of the Church. Their first act was to fill the vacancy left by Judas and to restore the sacred symbol of the twelve tribes of the New Israel. If it was Peter who spoke on Pentecost, he was not alone, but stood "with the Eleven" (Acts 2:14); and at the close of his discourse those who heard turned to "Peter and the rest of the Apostles" (Acts 2:37). It was the Twelve who selected and laid hands on the new ministers (Acts 6:2 f.). When the Good News had reached Samaria and had been welcomed there, "the apostles at Jerusalem . . . sent to them Peter and John" (Acts 8:14). All the while the Twelve had been busy at "the ministry of the word" (Acts 8:14) in Jerusalem. But they were Galileans; besides, their mission was to be witnesses of Christ to the "ends of the earth" (Acts 1:8); it was the task of others to rule the church of Jerusalem.

THE ELDERS A council of Elders was set up under the direction of James the "brother of the Lord"; its responsibility was to watch over the spiritual and material interests of the Jerusalem community. This arrangement was modeled on the council of Elders of the Jewish synagogues in Palestine and throughout the Diaspora. Acts bears ample witness to the influence of the Elders (Acts 11:30; 15; 16:4; 21:18).

PETER   Peter, first of the Twelve, was undoubtedly head of the Christian community; Acts 1-12 leaves no room for doubt on that score. He made decisions, presided over, and governed the infant Church. We see him act in the election of Matthias (Acts 1:15-26); he was the first preacher (Acts 2:14-36; 3:12-26) and the spokesman before the Sanhedrin (Acts 4:8-12); he took the initiative in the case of Ananias and Sapphira (Acts 5:3-11); he went on an official visit to the Samaritan converts (Acts 8:14-24) and undertook an apostolic journey to the coastal region (Acts 9:32-43); he baptized Cornelius (chap. 10). The role of Peter is confirmed by the testimony of Paul. Peter was the first disciple to see the Risen Christ (1 Cor. 15:5). When Paul visited Jerusalem three years after his conversion, it was with the sole purpose of meeting Peter (Gal. 1:18). Eleven years later, at the "council" of Jerusalem, it was Peter who upheld Paul's case—and appealed to his own experience with Cornelius.

Although the evidence leads to the conclusion that Peter was leader of the Twelve and head of the primitive community, yet, "to see him as someone apart from the apostolic group is to sever the head from the body. Peter's role in 'confirming his brethren' (Lk. 22:32) should not lead us to overlook the fact that those to be confirmed are his 'brethren'—and so much his 'brethren' that one of them, Paul, did not hesitate to rebuke Peter at Antioch (Gal. 2:11-14)."[35]

JAMES, THE   A James is named "brother of the Lord"
"BROTHER OF   in Mk. 6:3 and Mt. 13:55; and we learn
THE LORD"   that the Risen Lord appeared to him (1 Cor. 15:7). He is certainly not to be identified with the Apostle James, son of Zebedee, who was martyred in 44 A.D. (Acts 12:2). His identification with the Apostle James, son of Alphaeus, is possible, but is generally re-

jected by modern scholars. It is clear that his authority in the church of Jerusalem was second only to that of the Twelve.

Acts 1:14 informs us that the "brethren" of Jesus were with the Apostles in the "upper room" on the day of Pentecost; hence, James was, from the first, a member of the Church. Obviously, his position as head of the family of the Lord marked him out as natural leader of the Hebrew Christians. When Paul visited Jerusalem three years after his conversion—he had come to see Peter—he also made a point of meeting James (Gal. 1:19), whom, with Peter and John, he names one of the "pillars" of the Church (Gal. 2:9). In his account of the council of Jerusalem (Acts 15), Luke brings out the eminent position of James. In 44 A.D., when Peter had fled Jerusalem as a result of the persecution of Herod Agrippa I, he clearly designated James as head of the Jerusalem community (Acts 12:17). James was able to remain on in the city because his zeal for the Law was well known and because he was respected by the Jews as head of the Hebrew group. Finally, when Paul returned to Jerusalem in 58 A.D., after his third missionary journey, he found only James (Acts 21:18).

For information on the death of James we depend on Josephus.[36] He relates that the high priest Ananias had James stoned in 62 A.D., in the interval between the death of the procurator Festus and the appointment of his successor, Albinus. The tradition of Hegesippus that James was cast from the pinnacle of the Temple is secondary. It is said that James was succeeded by his brother Simeon, who, before the disaster of 70 A.D., led the Hebrew community to Pella in Transjordan.

THE TWO   Acts 6:1 speaks of two groups in the primitive
GROUPS   Jerusalem community: "Hebrews" and "Hellenists." The Hebrews were Palestinian Jews who spoke Aramaic and who read the Bible in Hebrew in their synagogues. James, we have noted, was leader of the converts from among the Hebrews. They were distinguished by their zeal for the observance of the Law and were treated tolerantly by orthodox Jews. These Hebrew converts were

not, as such, "Judaizers," that is, converts from Judaism who held that full observance of the Mosaic Law was necessary for salvation. It is understandable, however, that there were some among them with Judaizing leanings and that some of them may indeed have been Judaizers (cf. Acts 15:1, 5; Gal. 2:4). They did tend to look askance at the freedom from observance of the Law enjoyed by Gentile converts (cf. Acts 11:1-3, 22; 21:21). It is not surprising that missionary activity sprang not from this group but from the other.

The Hellenists (cf. Acts 6:1; 9:29) were Jews of the Diaspora who lived outside Palestine and who had synagogues of their own in Jerusalem where the Bible was read in Greek. They normally spoke Greek rather than Aramaic. Faithful to the Law and its observance, proud of their Jewish blood, they, at the same time, had a broader outlook than their Palestinian brethren and did not share their aversion for pagans. Acts 2:8-11 testifies to the presence of many Hellenistic Jews in Jerusalem on the fateful Pentecost. We gather that the converts from their ranks were not fewer than from among the natives of Jerusalem. The Hellenists did not at once break with the Law or with the Temple; all the brethren—Hebrews and Hellenists—assembled daily in the Temple (Acts 2:46). However, friction soon arose between the two groups; the Hellenists complained that their widows were being neglected in the daily distribution (Acts 6:1). Accordingly, the Twelve asked them to designate seven of their own group who were then appointed to the service of alms. (The title "deacon" does not occur in the text, but the verb *diakonein,* "to serve," is used in Acts 6:2.) The seven bear Greek names, and one of them, Nicolaus, was a proselyte from Antioch.

2) *The Spread of the Church*

The plan for the expansion of his Church was traced by Christ himself in a charge to the Twelve before his definitive ascension: "You shall be my witnesses in Jerusalem and in all Judaea and Samaria and to the end of the earth" (Acts 1:8).

JERUSALEM The coming of the Holy Spirit transformed the Twelve and those with them. Peter began to preach the Good News boldly and confidently. Those who heard, and repented, were initiated into Christianity by baptism in the name of Jesus, for the remission of sins and by the gift of the Spirit (Acts 2:38). On the first day there were over 3,000 converts. At the close of a summary statement Luke can declare: "And the Lord added to their number day by day those who were being saved" (Acts 2:47); and afterwards repeatedly refers to the numerical increase of the Church. The first Christians were assiduous in following the teaching of the Apostles. They were of one heart and one soul; they frequented the Temple daily and were united in the breaking of bread and in prayer. All things were in common among them and they were highly thought of by the people (Acts 2:42-47; 4:32-35; 5:12-16). Barnabus, a Levite of Cyprus, was specially commended for generosity (Acts 4:36).

The Jewish authorities could not fail to react to the growing strength of the Church. The Apostles were arrested (Acts 5:17 f.); miraculously delivered from prison (Acts 5:19-21), they were summoned before the Sanhedrin where the prudent counsel of Gamaliel prevailed (Acts 5:27-42). Friction within the community itself was allayed by the appointment of seven "deacons" (Acts 6:1-6). One of these, Stephen—probably of Alexandrian origin—at once became prominent and was bitterly opposed by some of the Hellenistic Jews; he was brought before the Sanhedrin (Acts 6:8-15). In an impassioned speech he showed how the Old Testament prophecies had been fulfilled in the person of Jesus of Nazareth. He ended by attacking the emptiness of the Temple cult, the formalism of the scribes, and the blindness of the religious authorities of Jerusalem (Acts 7). The enraged hearers dragged him outside the city and summarily stoned him (Acts 7:57-60); and Saul approved of the murder (Acts 8:1).

The martyrdom of Stephen seems to have been the first episode in a violent persecution (Acts 8:1). It appears to have been aimed at the Hellenists; the Twelve were undisturbed. The execution of Stephen and the persecution—

highhanded and quite illegal action on the part of the Jewish authorities—would not have been possible under Pilate. He was recalled to Rome in the autumn of 36 A.D.; the legate of Syria, Vitellius, a man favorable to the Jews, was in immediate charge until the appointment of a new procurator. We may with some justification put the death of Stephen and the outbreak of persecution in the winter of 36 A.D. The Hellenists were dispersed and went from place to place, preaching the Good News (Acts 8:4): Christian missionary activity had begun—born of persecution.

JUDAEA AND   Another of the seven, Philip, preached the
SAMARIA   Gospel in Samaria with great success (Acts 8:5-13); this was the first missionary activity outside of Jerusalem. When the Twelve had heard of Philip's success, they sent Peter and John, who not only approved but themselves carried on the work of evangelization (Acts 8:14-25). Philip baptized the eunuch minister of Candace, queen of the Ethiopians (i.e., of Nubia, the modern Sudan); the man was obviously a "God-fearer" (Acts 8:26-39). Philip continued to evangelize the coast area (Acts 8:40) and, indeed, seems to have settled in Caesarea (Acts 21:8 f.). Other Hellenist Christians were busy elsewhere: there were many converts. Meanwhile, the greatest of them all had been converted by the Risen Lord in person (Acts 9:1-19).

The conversion of Paul seems to have been followed by a period of tranquillity for the churches: "So the church throughout all Judaea and Galilee and Samaria had peace and was built up" (Acts 9:31). The inclusion of Galilee is significant: the Church had spread there. Peter availed of the calm to visit the brethren of Judaea and the coastal plain. He remained for a time at Joppa (Jaffa) in the house of Simon a tanner. Providentially, his steps had been guided toward an event, simple in itself, but of capital significance: the reception, by the leader of the Christian community, of the first Gentile convert. The conversion of the Roman officer Cornelius, a "God-fearer"—but still a Gentile—was, in the accompanying circumstances, not an individual case but an event of universal import; it was to be a deciding factor at the assembly of Jerusalem (Acts 15:7-11, 14). Peter (Acts 10) had learned a twofold lesson: God had shown him that pagans must be received into the Church without being constrained to the observance of the Law; God also had made clear to him that he ought to accept the hospitality of the uncircumcised. One senses the problem of relations between Christians of Jewish and of pagan origin. True enough, Peter was called upon, by Hebrew Christians, to justify his action (Acts 11:1-18).

Some time after this event, when Agrippa I was king of Judaea and Samaria (41-44 A.D.), he "laid violent hands upon some who belonged to the church" and had James, son of Zebedee, beheaded (Acts 12:1). In order to please the Jews still further, Agrippa had Peter arrested, but the latter was miraculously delivered and departed for "another place" (Acts 12:3-17). All this happened during the Passover season (Acts 12:3). The death of the king, reported in Acts 12:20-23, seems to have followed soon after his return to Caesarea from Jerusalem (where he had attended the Pasch). This would date his repressive measures to the year 44 A.D. Peter returned to Jerusalem, for he was back there at the assembly of 49 A.D.

Shortly after Paul and Barnabas had returned to Antioch from their journey in Asia Minor (45-49 A.D.), certain brethren came from Jerusalem and taught that circumcision was necessary for salvation (Acts 15:1; Gal. 2:4). The church at Antioch decided to send Paul and Barnabas, with some of their own number, to Jerusalem (Acts 15:2; Gal. 2:1). In Jerusalem they were received by the community and by the Apostles and Elders (Acts 15:4); but some converts from pharisaism immediately demanded that Gentile converts should be subjected to circumcision (Acts 15:5). The Apostles and Elders examined the question (Acts 15:6). Peter brought forward the case of Cornelius: it would be "tempting God" to impose any burdens on the converts since he had manifested his will so clearly. It was by the grace of the Lord Jesus alone that Jews and Gentiles were saved (Acts 15:7-11). James, arguing from the Old Testament for the call of the Gentiles, agreed fully with Peter on the question of circumcision. However, he added the "James-clause": the Gentile Christians were to abstain from meat sacrificed to idols, from marriage within the forbidden degrees of kindred (*porneia*), from strangled animals, and from blood (Acts 15:13-21); this would be a gesture to the Hebrew Christians. A letter was drawn up, addressed to "the brethren who are of the Gentiles in Antioch and Syria and Cilicia." It was sent with Paul and Barnabas, who were accompanied by two distinguished members of the Jerusalem church, Judas and Silas (Acts 15:22-29). Thus was the authority of the mother-church invoked to settle a problem that had troubled the great missionary church of Antioch and had imperiled the future of Christianity. Jerusalem had approved the "Gospel" of Paul; and Paul himself was officially recognized as Apostle of the Gentiles (Gal. 2:7-9).

It is not our intention to linger over the difficulties raised in Acts 15—especially in its confrontation with Gal. 2—but it would be well to indicate them. In general, we should recognize that the Epistle and Acts represent, from different points of view, the relations of Paul with the Jerusalem Apostles. Paul wrote an *apologia*, defending his apostolate; Luke had no such concern. Paul took his stand on personal recollection, and his statements have an importance all their own; Luke was obliged to compile details from different sources. There is no question of setting Paul and Luke in opposition or in contradiction.[87] It is likely that the journey of Barnabas and Saul to Jerusalem, with help for the famine-stricken brethren (Acts 11:27-30), is identical with that of Acts 15:2 (cf. Gal. 1:18; 2:1 f.). The famine is the one mentioned by Josephus as having occurred during the procuratorship of Tiberius Alexander (46-48 A.D.); it was aggravated by the sabbatical year of 47/48 A.D. In that case, Barnabas and Saul carried the alms from Antioch on their journey to the assembly in Jerusalem in 49 A.D.[88]

With regard to Acts 15, it seems probable that Luke has fused two accounts. One concerned a dispute about circumcision and the attitude of Gentile converts to the Mosaic Law. Paul and Barnabas went up to Jerusalem and the matter was settled on the authority of Peter. This is described by Paul in Gal. 2:1-10 and by Luke in Acts 15 and Acts 11:27-30. The later controversy, in which James (in the absence of Peter) played the decisive role, concerned the problem of social contacts between converts from Judaism and from paganism (Acts 15:13-21; cf. Gal. 2:11-14). A letter, embodying the decision on this question, was sent to the churches in Syria and Cilicia.

Luke's rearrangement of the material may be explained by his intention of bringing out more effectively the approval by the Jerusalem church of the Gentile mission.

> He probably wishes to show (a) that James and the "apostles and elders" disapproved of the Judaizing party, who claimed to speak in their name; (b) that they recognized the divine approval of Paul's Gentile mission, both in the signs and wonders done in Asia Minor and also in the prophetic scriptures rightly interpreted; (c) that Paul was scrupulously loyal to the authorities at Jerusalem in carrying out his Gentile mission.[39]

The pre-eminence of the Jerusalem church was short-lived. In 62 A.D. James was stoned, and a few years later all Palestine was in a ferment as the Zealots rose against Rome. Before the catastrophe of 70 A.D., Simeon led his flock to Pella in Transjordan. Later, some few returned to live in and near the ruins of the city. The last survivors disappeared under Trajan (98-117 A.D.). Thus, in fact, Judaeo-Christianity ended with the City and the Temple.

THE END OF THE EARTH   Some of those who had been dispersed after the death of Stephen went farther afield, to Phoenicia and Cyprus and Antioch (Acts 11:19). In the latter city they preached to Gentiles as well as to Jews (Acts 11:20), thus giving a decisive turn to the work of spreading the Good News. Antioch, at the mouth of the Orontes, was capital of Syria and the third city of the Empire. It was a busy commercial city with a cosmopolitan population. Converts were won from the first. When news of the new trend had reached Jerusalem, Barnabas was sent to investigate. He wholly approved of the work that had been done, and his influence gave a fresh impetus to the spread of the Gospel (Acts 11:21-24). Barnabas went to Tarsus to fetch Saul (who had retired to his own city after his apostolic efforts at Damascus and Jerusalem had been blocked by the Jews), and the two spent a year together preaching in Antioch where "the disciples were for the first time called Christians" (Acts 11:25 f.).

Antioch became the headquarters of Paul, the source of missionary expansion. From chapter 13 of Acts onward we are concerned almost exclusively with the mighty figure of the Apostle. Paul is Luke's hero, but he is also much more: the incarnation of the dynamism of the Church. Luke had taken the plan of his book from Christ's own words (Acts 1:8) and, tracing the expansion of the Church from Jerusalem, he leads the Apostle of the Gentiles to the capital of the Roman Empire, the heart of the world. There, with high dramatic effect, he leaves Paul—technically a prisoner—"preaching the kingdom of God and teaching about the Lord Jesus Christ quite openly and unhindered" (Acts 28:31). The book is not principally a study of personalities; it is the story of the Church.

> Acts is the history not of Paul nor of the Apostles, but of the Holy Spirit and the Church. In these lines Paul is not Paul alone, he is the Church, the Church which although hemmed in by a hostile world goes on with its task of preaching openly and fearlessly to all who come to it. So the Acts ends as it began, with Christ and the Kingdom.[40]

5. ST. PAUL: CHRONOLOGY AND MISSIONARY JOURNEYS[41]

The literary work of Paul will be treated in some detail in later chapters. It is convenient, at this point, to sketch the framework of his life and to outline his missionary activities.

1) Chronology

CHRONOLOGICAL INDICATIONS   1. *Proconsulate of Gallio in*
FROM PROFANE HISTORY   *Achaia.* An inscription
found in Delphi in 1905 gives a rescript of Claudius in
which Lucius Junius Gallio (brother of Seneca) is named
as proconsul of Achaia. The rescript was written after
Claudius had been acclaimed—a special honor decreed for
the emperor after a victory—for the twenty-sixth time, that
is, very probably between January 25 and August 1, 52
A.D. Achaia was a senatorial province; the proconsul was
in office only one year, from spring to spring. It is likely
that Gallio was proconsul in Achaia from the spring of
52 A.D. to the spring of 53 A.D. Paul's appearance before
him (Acts 18:12-17) was, plausibly, early in the proconsul's term of office—the Jews were attempting to take advantage of his inexperience—and toward the close of the
Apostle's one and one-half year stay in Corinth; in other
words, the summer of 52 A.D. Thus, we may, with some
confidence, date Paul's stay in Corinth during his second
missionary journey: winter 50 A.D.-summer 52 A.D.

2. *Recall of Felix and Appointment of Festus.* Antonius
Felix took office as procurator of Judaea in 52 A.D. He
was recalled by Nero, according to many scholars, in 60
A.D. His successor was Porcius Festus (60-62 A.D.). According to Acts 24:27, Paul was arrested at Pentecost two
years before Felix was recalled. His case was reopened by
Festus soon after he had taken office; Paul's appeal to
Rome forestalled a protracted trial. We may date Paul's
departure for Rome to the autumn of 60 A.D.; and his imprisonment in Caesarea to the years 58-60 A.D.

CHRONOLOGICAL INDICATIONS   1. *Conversion of Paul.* The
IN THE NEW TESTAMENT   martyrdom of Stephen
seems to have been the first episode of a persecution on the
part of the Jews (Acts 8:1, 3). This would not have been
possible under Pilate, who would have welcomed such a
disturbance in order to pay off the Jews. He was recalled
in the autumn of 36 A.D., and the legate Vitellius, favorable

to the Jews, would have turned a blind eye to their activities. We may reasonably date the martyrdom of Stephen in the autumn of 36 A.D. The conversion of Paul followed soon after: during the winter of 36 A.D.

2. *Episodes Dating from the Conversion.* According to Gal. 1:8, Paul visited Jerusalem three years after his conversion. In Gal. 2:1 he tells us that he again visited the city fourteen years after his conversion. According to the manner of computation then in vogue, both first and last years of a period were reckoned, and, even when incomplete, were counted as full years. Hence, "three years" could be anything from one and a half to three years, and "fourteen years" could be from twelve and a half to fourteen. If we put the conversion at 36 A.D., three years after would be 38-39 A.D.; fourteen years after would be 49-50 A.D.

3. *Birth of Paul.* Here we have only the vaguest indications. In Philemon 9 (written about 62 A.D.) Paul is called *presbutēs,* an "old man"; and in Acts 7:58 (just before his conversion in 36 A.D.), he is called *neanias,* "young man." This would put his birth about 10 A.D.

2) *The Missionary Journeys*

FIRST MISSIONARY JOURNEY: SPRING 45 A.D.-SPRING 49 A.D. (ACTS 13-14)

Success in Antioch had fired the apostolic ambition of the Christians there. In the course of a liturgical reunion, Barnabas and Saul were "set apart" for a new venture farther afield. The first goal was Cyprus, homeland of Barnabas. Taking with them John Mark (cousin of Barnabas), they sailed from Seleucia, port of Antioch, and landed at Salamis, on the east coast of Cyprus and the chief port of the island. There they began to preach in the synagogues, thus setting a pattern that they were to maintain throughout; Paul would continue to preach the Good News to the Jews before turning to the Gentiles. At Paphos, on the west, the administrative capital of the island, they were favorably received by the proconsul, Sergius Paulus. At this point in

Acts, the Jewish name Saul is dropped, and Paul is named before Barnabas.

The apostles crossed to Asia Minor and came to Perga, capital of the province of Pamphylia. At this point, Mark left them and returned to Jerusalem—a step that Paul regarded as desertion (Acts 15:36-39). Paul and Barnabas moved on to Pisidian Antioch, a Roman colony by then incorporated in the province of Galatia. An important stage on the main route from Syria to Ephesus, it had a cosmopolitan character and a considerable Jewish population. The Good News was rejected by the Jews but gladly accepted by the Gentiles; the missionaries may have spent the best part of a year here. Eventually, the Jews succeeded in having them driven from the district. Paul and Barnabas went to Iconium, some eighty miles southeast of Antioch. Here they met with notable success among both Jews and Gentiles, but the inevitable opposition forced them to move on to the Roman colony of Lystra, twenty-three miles southwest of Iconium. There was no Jewish synagogue in Lystra, but it was the home of Timothy (Acts 16:1-3). Roused by the cure of a cripple, the people of Lystra hailed Barnabas and Paul as Zeus and Hermes. Later, at the instigation of Jews who had come from Antioch, they stoned Paul.

After this the missionaries went to Derbe, a frontier town of the province of Galatia, about thirty miles southeast of Lystra. The mission here was highly successful. After they had preached for some time, the apostles decided to retrace their steps. They organized the local administration of each of the churches they had founded. However, they did not revisit Cyprus, but from Attalia, port of Perga, sailed directly to Syrian Antioch. News of the remarkable success of the venture, especially among the Gentiles, disturbed some elements in Jerusalem; at a solemn assembly in Jerusalem, Gentile freedom from the Mosaic Law and the special apostolate of Paul were recognized (Acts 15; Gal. 2). It was a momentous decision: Christianity was now, in fact, established as a universal religion.

SECOND MISSIONARY JOURNEY: Heartened by the happy
AUTUMN 49-AUTUMN 52   solution of the problem
(ACTS 15:36—18:22)   that had threatened to
wreck his work, Paul soon began to look toward Asia
Minor again. On this new journey his companion was Silas. They traveled overland from Antioch, through the
Cilician Gates, and so reached Derbe and Lystra. At Lystra
he met Timothy (converted on the first visit: Acts 16:1-3)
and took him as a companion; Timothy would remain a
valued friend of Paul until the end.

When Paul had visited the churches already established,
he wished to go directly westward to the province of Asia,
but, receiving a prohibition from the Spirit, he went north
toward Bithynia instead. Here again he received a divine
prohibition and turned due west, on a route that must
lead to Troas, a port and Roman colony on the coast of
Mysia (near the site of ancient Troy). At last the mysterious directions were made clear: Paul had a vision and
heard the urgent cry of Macedonia.

At Troas the party was joined by Luke (the first "we-
passage" begins at Acts 16:10) and all set sail for Europe.
They landed at Neapolis (modern Cavalla), the port of
Philippi, and hurried on to that important Roman colony.
Apparently there was no synagogue in Philippi, the few
Jews who lived there meeting for prayer outside the town.
A God-fearer named Lydia, a native of Thyatira, was con-
verted, together with her household. Paul's cure of a pos-
sessed girl was the occasion of the arrest of himself and
Silas and their imprisonment as disturbers of the peace.
The incident had as a sequel the conversion of their jailer
and the apology of the magistrates who had flogged and
imprisoned Roman citizens without trial.

The missionaries then took the Egnatian Way through
Amphipolis and Apollonia to Thessalonica, the capital of
Macedonia. Paul and Silas preached in the synagogue and
converted many of the Gentile adherents of the synagogue
and some influential women. The Jews quickly stirred up a
rabble against the missionaries; the brethren prevailed on
Paul and Silas to slip away by night to Beroea, a small town
west of Thessalonica. Here many Jews were converted,

but the arrival of troublemakers from Thessalonica forced the brethren to send Paul (obviously the chief target) on to the coast and by sea to Athens, while Silas and Timothy remained behind.

In Athens, Paul spoke to Jews and God-fearers in the synagogues, and daily in the market place held disputations with passers-by and also entered into controversy with Epicurean and Stoic philosophers. He was called upon to justify his teaching before the Council of the Areopagus, the Athenian Senate. He won a few converts, notably a member of the Council of the Areopagus named Dionysius.

Soon afterwards Paul left for Corinth, capital of the province of Achaia, residence of the proconsul, and a major commercial center. Here he met the couple Aquila and Priscilla, converts from Judaism, and lodged with them. He preached in the synagogue sabbath after sabbath; and was soon joined by Silas and Timothy. Repulsed by the Jews, he turned to the Gentiles with considerable success. He spent a year and one-half in Corinth (winter 50 A.D.- summer 52 A.D.) and wrote 1 and 2 Thessalonians during his stay.

The Jews took advantage of the arrival of the new proconsul, Lucius Junius Gallio, to bring a trumped-up charge against Paul. The proconsul dismissed the charge without hesitation. However, soon afterwards Paul sailed for Ephesus, taking with him Priscilla and Aquila whom he left in that city. He himself preached briefly in the synagogue, promised to return, and sailed to Caesarea. He went to pay his respects to the church of Jerusalem and then returned to Antioch (autumn of 52 A.D.).

THIRD MISSIONARY JOURNEY: After a short stay in Anti-
SPRING 53-SPRING 58   och Paul decided to visit
(ACTS 18:23—21:16)   Asia Minor. Yet again: "He went from place to place through the region of Galatia and Phrygia, strengthening all the disciples" (Acts 18:23). But this time his jail was Ephesus, capital of the province of Asia, a city of wealth and magnificence, one of the great cities of the age. It was famed for its Artemesion—the temple of Artemis (Diana)—one of the

seven wonders of the world. In Ephesus, Paul was received by Aquila and Priscilla. He instructed and baptized a small group of the disciples of John the Baptist. As usual, he preached first in the synagogue—for three months —but, inevitably, he was eventually rejected by the Jews. For more than two years after this (his whole stay in Ephesus was nearly three years: Acts 19:8-10; 20:31) he carried on his mission among the Gentiles, using for this purpose the lecture hall of a certain Tyrannus. Meanwhile, his disciples worked throughout Asia (cf. Col. 1:7 f.; 4:12 f.). A striking testimony to the success of Paul's preaching is provided by the reaction of the silversmiths whose main business was the manufacture of silver statuettes of Artemis for devotees of the goddess. They recognized in Paul a serious threat to this lucrative business, and organized a riot in an attempt to get rid of him; soon afterwards (before Pentecost, 57 A.D.), Paul did leave the city. During his stay in Ephesus, the Apostle wrote 1 Corinthians (and, perhaps, Philippians). It seems likely that 1 Cor. had been followed by a brief visit to Corinth (cf. 2 Cor. 1:23—2:1; 12:14; 13), and that after his return to Ephesus he wrote the "letter written in tears" (2 Cor. 2:3 f., 9; 7:8 ff.). Galatians was also written in Ephesus; whether before or after 1 Cor. is not clear.

From Ephesus, Paul went to Macedonia where he wrote 2 Corinthians; and then went on to Corinth where he spent three months (winter, 57/58 A.D.). While there he wrote the Epistle to the Romans. He had planned to sail directly from Corinth to Antioch, but he was warned of a plot against him and he decided to travel overland by way of Macedonia instead. At Philippi he met Luke and they sailed for Troas just after Easter of 58 A.D. Paul was anxious to be in Jerusalem for Pentecost; in order to avoid inevitable delay, he bypassed Ephesus and had the Elders of the church come to meet him at Miletus, where he took a touching leave of them. Eventually the party landed at Tyre and spent a week with the brethren there. Then they continued the voyage to Caesarea, stopping off at Ptolemais on the way. In Caesarea they stayed with Philip, one of the seven deacons; there the prophet Agabus foretold the im-

minent imprisonment of Paul. On arrival at Jerusalem they
were warmly welcomed by the brethren. The next day
Paul was received by James and the Elders. As a concilia-
tory gesture to the Judaeo-Christians, it was suggested that
Paul should defray the expenses of four men under a
Nazirite vow; he agreed with alacrity. However, Jews from
Asia who had seen Paul in the company of the Ephesian
Trophimus—a non-Jew—accused him of bringing a Gentile
into the Temple; prompt action by the tribune Claudius
Lysias saved Paul from being lynched. Paul's address to
the mob only inflamed them the more, and the tribune,
not understanding Aramaic and believing that his prisoner
was provoking the crowd, was on the point of flogging
him when Paul appealed to his rights as a Roman citizen.
Next day the tribune had Paul brought before the Sanhedrin where he deftly set Pharisees and Sadducees at loggerheads. The Apostle's nephew warned him of a plot
against him; the tribune, without delay, sent Paul under
heavy escort to Caesarea where he was handed over to the
procurator Antonius Felix. After a preliminary trial, the
venal Felix, hoping for a bribe, held Paul a prisoner in
Caesarea during the remaining two years of his term of
office (58-60 A.D.).

JOURNEY TO ROME   In 60 A.D. Porcius Festus suc-
(AUTUMN 60-SPRING 61) ceeded Felix. The new procu-
AND LAST YEARS   rator, briefed by the Jewish
leaders, wanted Paul to stand trial in Jerusalem. But Paul,
realizing the murderous intention of the Jews, appealed to
the imperial tribunal. That settled the matter: the procurator was now bound to send his prisoner to Rome for trial.
Before leaving Caesarea, Paul had an opportunity of stat-
ing his case before Agrippa II and his sister Berenice who
had come on a state visit to Festus.

In the autumn of 60 A.D., Paul was handed over to the
custody of a centurion of the Augustan Cohort (imperial
couriers) named Julius. The party boarded a ship bound
for Asia Minor. When they had reached Myra in Lycia,
the centurion transferred his prisoners to a ship bound for
Italy. The voyage, described in dramatic detail in Acts

27-28, ended in shipwreck in Malta. The party spent the winter on the island and arrived in Rome in the spring of 61 A.D. There Paul was under house arrest for two years. He was able to carry on a fruitful apostolate; and he wrote his "captivity epistles": Colossians, Ephesians, Philemon, and, probably, Philippians. His enemies knew that it was useless to proffer their charges against Paul in the imperial tribunal. Hence, after the statutory two years, Paul was set at liberty.

We know little about the last phase of Paul's life (63-67 A.D.). He may have fulfilled his intention of visiting Spain (cf. Rm. 15:24 f.). The Pastoral Epistles indicate that he visited Ephesus (1 Tm. 1:3) and Crete (Ti. 1:5); while 1 Timothy and Titus appear to have been written in Macedonia about 65 A.D. From 2 Timothy we learn of a second Roman captivity, much more severe than the first (2 Tm. 1:8, 12; 2:9). Paul realizes that death is in store for him this time (2 Tim. 4:6-8). He was likely a victim of the persecution of Nero. The traditional date of his martyrdom is 67 A.D.

3) Chronological Table

c. 10 A.D.	Birth of Paul in Tarsus
after 30 A.D.	Jerusalem—disciple of Gamaliel
c. 36 A.D.	Conversion
36-39 A.D.	Damascus and Arabia
39 A.D.	Visit to Jerusalem
39-43 A.D.	Tarsus
43-44 A.D.	In Antioch with Barnabas
45-49 A.D.	First missionary journey
49 A.D.	Assembly in Jerusalem
50-52 A.D.	Second missionary journey
	Corinth: winter, 50 A.D.-summer, 52 A.D.
	1, 2 Thessalonians
53-58 A.D.	Third missionary journey
	Ephesus: autumn, 54 A.D.-spring, 57 A.D. [*Philippians*] *Galatians*
	1 Corinthians

	Visit to Corinth: 57 A.D.
	Macedonia: summer, 57 A.D.
	2 Corinthians
	Corinth, winter, 57/58 A.D.
	Romans
58 A.D. (Pentecost)	Arrest in Jerusalem
58-60 A.D.	Prisoner in Caesarea
60-61 A.D.	Journey to Rome
61-63 A.D.	Prisoner in Rome
	Colossians, Ephesians, Philemon
	[*Philippians*]
63 A.D.	End of first captivity
	Perhaps journey to Spain
c. 65 A.D.	Ephesus, Crete, Macedonia
	1 Timothy, Titus
c. 67 A.D.	Second Roman captivity
	2 Timothy
c. 67 A.D.	Death

---

[1] See A. A. M. van der Heyden and H. H. Scullard, editors, *Atlas of the Classical World* (London: Nelson, 1960), pp. 122-34.

[2] See R. H. Pfeiffer, *History of New Testament Times*, With an Introduction to the Apocrypha (London: A. & C. Black, 1963[2]), pp. 116-27; R. McL. Wilson, *Peake's Commentary on the Bible*, M. Black and H. H. Rowley, editors (London: Nelson, 1962), n. 624 a-d (henceforth references to this work will be abbreviated PCB); H. C. Kee and F. W. Young, *The Living World of the New Testament* (Englewood Cliffs, N.J.: Prentice-Hall, 1965[2]), pp. 15-19; F. Copleston, *A History of Philosophy* (New York: Doubleday Image Books, 1962[2]), I, Pt. II, Greece and Rome, pp. 145-71.

[3] Copleston, *op. cit.*, p. 151.

[4] *Ibid.*, p. 144.

[5] See Pfeiffer, *op. cit.*, pp. 127-65; Kee and Young, *op. cit.*, pp. 21-24; R. McL. Wilson, PCB, nn. 620-626; A. Tricot, *Introduction à la Bible*, A. Robert and A. Feuillet, editors (Tournai: Desclée, 1957; second edition, 1959), II, pp. 23-29 (henceforth references to this work will be abbreviated IB).

[6] See P. Lemaire and D. Baldi, *Atlante Storico della Bibbia* (Rome: Marietti, 1955), pp. 197-208. Henceforth references to this work will be abbreviated *Atlante Biblico* (*Biblical Atlas*); Pfeiffer, *op. cit.*, pp. 24-45; A. Tricot, IB, pp. 85-97.

7 For Herod's rise to power see Wilfrid J. Harrington, *Record of the Promise: The Old Testament* (Chicago: The Priory Press, 1965), pp. 96-98.

8 The Nabataeans were a powerful Arab nation with a territory stretching from north of Damascus, along the edge of the desert, to the border of Egypt. Their capital was the rock-hewn Petra, that "rose-red city, half as old as time."

9 See Y. Yadin, *The Biblical Archaeologist*, 24 (1961), 34-50, 86-95.

10 See A. Tricot, IB, pp. 67-74; M. Black, PCB, nn. 604 e-605 d; Kee and Young, *op. cit.*, pp. 39-45; Pfeiffer, *op. cit.*, pp. 54-59; F. V. Filson, *A New Testament History* (Philadelphia: Westminster Press, 1964), pp. 48-56.

11 Under this heading we may conveniently treat of the scribes, although they did not, of course, constitute a sect; and we may consider the Sanhedrin.

12 Pfeiffer, *op. cit.*, p. 56.

13 See A. Tricot, IB, pp. 63-65.

14 The relevant texts, together with the testimony of Pliny the Elder, all in English translation, are conveniently assembled by E. F. Sutcliffe, *The Monks of Qumran* (Westminster, Md.: Newman Press, 1960), pp. 224-38.

15 We follow the judicious assessment of J. Jeremias, "Qumran et la théologie," *Nouvelle Revue Théologique*, 85 (1963), 675-90.

16 IQSa, 2:3-9; see Sutcliffe, *op. cit.*, p. 151.

17 Jeremias, *art cit.*, 690.

18 See p. 39.

19 See A. Tricot, IB, pp. 98-105; Pfeiffer, *op. cit.*, pp. 166-96; W. D. Davies, PCB, nn. 598-603; *Atlante Biblico*, pp. 205-7; Harrington, *ibid.*, pp. 85 f.

20 See IB, pp. 103 f., 128 f.

21 According to Josephus (*Antiquities*, XVII, 8:1; 9:3; *Jewish War*, I, 33:8; II, 1:3), Herod died in Jericho a few days before the Pasch of 750 A.U.C. (= March/April, 4 B.C.). The monk Denis the Small, in the sixth century, erroneously fixed 754 A.U.C. as the beginning of the Christian Era.

22 See M.-J. Lagrange, *Évangile selon Saint Luc* (Paris: Gabalda, 1921), pp. 65 f.; G. Ricciotti, *Vita de Gesù Cristo* (Rome: Società Editrice Internazionale, 1951[14]), pp. 195-202; Tricot, *Initiation Biblique, op. cit.*, pp. 635-37; English edition, pp. 124-27; *Atlante Biblico*, pp. 219 f.; J. Schmid, *Das Evangelium nach Lukas* (Regensburg: Verlag F. Pustet, 1960[4]), pp. 66-70; G. Ogg, PCB, n. 635.

23 *Annals*, 1, 11.

24 *Antiquities*, XVII, 13:5; XVIII, 1:1; *Jewish War*, VII, 8:1.

25 See p. 29.

[26] See *Adversus Marcionem*, 4:19.

[27] See Tricot, *op. cit.*, pp. 638-43; G. Ogg, PCB, n. 636 a-b; *Atlante Biblico*, p. 220.

[28] An unidentified feast (Jn. 5:1) has sometimes been regarded as another Passover, thus giving a ministry of over three years. It is more likely that the feast in question is Pentecost, or possibly Tabernacles.

[29] See Tricot, *op. cit.*, pp. 643-46; G. Ogg, PCB, n. 636 c.

[30] Passover always fell on 15 Nisan, whatever day of the month it should happen to be. The paschal lambs were slaughtered in the Temple on the afternoon of 14 Nisan, i.e., after 2:00 P.M., and were eaten that same day after sunset—which was 15 Nisan by Jewish reckoning. From the second century B.C. this was always the rule when Passover and sabbath coincided.

[31] In fairness we should observe that a strong case can be made for the synoptic dating. In an important *excursus* (*Das Evangelium nach Markus* [Regensburg: Verlag F. Pustet, 1954³], pp. 268-73), J. Schmid argues that John had changed the date of the death of Jesus for theological reasons.

[32] A. Jaubert (*La Date de la Cène. Calendrier biblique et liturgie chrétienne* [Études Bibliques; Paris: Gabalda, 1957]) proposes the theory that, although 14 Nisan of the crucifixion year was a Friday, Jesus followed an older calendar (which was still in use at Qumran) in which 14 Nisan was Tuesday of Passion Week. For an excellent critique of Miss Jaubert's book, see P. Benoit, "La Date de la Cène," in *Exégèse et Théologie* (Paris: Cerf, 1961), I, pp. 255-61.

[33] *La Sainte Bible*, traduite en français sous la direction de l'École Biblique de Jérusalem (Paris: Cerf, 1957), p. 1325. See also the second revised edition in fascicle form. Henceforth references to this Bible will be abbreviated BJ; references to the fascicles will be abbreviated (BJ).

[34] See Tricot, *op. cit.*, pp. 811-38; *Atlante Biblico*, pp. 241-47.

[35] B. M. Ahern, "The Witness of Sacred Scripture to the Collegiality of Apostles and Bishops," *The Bible Today* (October, 1964), 860.

[36] *Antiquities*, XX, 9:1.

[37] See L. Cerfaux, IB, p. 352.

[38] See BJ, p. 1454.

[39] G. W. H. Lampe, PCB, nn. 791 f.; cf. BJ, pp. 1458 f.

[40] C. H. Rieu, *The Acts of the Apostles*, A New Translation with Introduction and Notes (Baltimore, Md.: Penguin Books, 1957), p. 176.

[41] See *Atlante Biblico*, pp. 247-54; L. Cerfaux, IB, pp. 377-84; B. Rigaux, *Saint Paul et ses Lettres* (Paris: Declée de Brouwer, 1962), pp. 99-138.

BIBLIOGRAPHY

This bibliography is obviously not meant to be exhaustive and has been restricted, as far as possible, to works in English.

GENERAL

(The works listed under this heading cover all, or most, of the field of this General Introduction.)

Articles in: *The Catholic Biblical Quarterly*. Washington, D.C.; *The Bible Today*. Collegeville, Minn.: Liturgical Press.

Castelot, J., *Meet the Bible*. Baltimore: Helicon, 1960. I.

Charlier, C., *The Christian Approach to the Bible*. Trans. H. J. Richards, and B. Peters; Westminster, Md.: Newman, 1958.

Daniel-Rops, H., *What is the Bible?* Trans. J. R. Foster; New York: Hawthorn, 1958.

Hunt, I., *Understanding the Bible*. New York: Sheed & Ward, 1962.

Robert, A., and Feuillet, A., editors, *Introduction a la Bible*. Tournai: Desclée, 1957. I.

Robert, A., and Tricot, A., editors, *Guide to the Bible*. Trans. E. P. Arbez, and M. R. P. McGuire; New York: Desclée, 1960². I.

Buttrick, G. A., ed., *The Interpreter's Dictionary of the Bible*. An Illustrated Encyclopedia in Four Volumes. Nashville: Abingdon, 1962.

Brown, R. E., Fitzmyer, J. A., Murphy, R. E., eds., *The Jerome Biblical Commentary*. Englewood Cliffs, N.J.: Prentice-Hall, 1968.

Fuller, R. C., ed., *A New Catholic Commentary on Holy Scripture*. London: Nelson, 1969.

Robert, A. and Feuillet, A., *Interpreting the Scriptures*. New York: Desclée, 1969.

CHAPTERS ONE AND TWO

Harrington, W., *What is the Bible?* New York: Paulist Press, 1963.

Jones, A., *God's Living Word*. New York: Sheed & Ward, 1961.

Levie, J., *The Bible, Words of God in Words of Men*. Trans. Roger Capel; New York: Kenedy, 1961.

Richards, H., *God Speaks to Us*. London: D.L.T., 1963.

Burtchaell, J. T., *Catholic Theories of Biblical Inspiration since 1810*, Cambridge: The University Press, 1969.

Harrington, W. and Walsh, L., *Vatican II on Revelation*. Dublin: Scepter, 1967.

Rahner, K., *Theological Investigations* VI. Baltimore: Helicon, 1969.

Vawter, B., *Biblical Inspiration*. Philadelphia: Westminster Press, 1972.

CHAPTERS THREE TO FIVE

Benoit, P., "Inspiration," *Guide to the Bible*. A. Robert and A. Tricot, editors; trans. E. P. Arbez, and M. R. P. McGuire; New York: Desclée, 1960². I. Pp. 9-52.

——, *Aspects of Biblical Inspiration*. Trans. J. Murphy-O'Connor and S. K. Ashe; Chicago: The Priory Press, 1965.

——, "Inspiration Biblique," *Catholicisme*. Paris: Letouzey et Ane, 1963. V, 1710-1721.

——, "Inerrance Biblique," *Catholicisme*. Paris: Letouzey et Ane, 1963. V, 1539-1549.

——, "Note complementaire sur l'inspiration," *Revue Biblique*, 63:416-22, 1956.

——, *Prophecy and Inspiration*. New York: Desclée, 1961.

Forestell, J. T., "The Limitations of Inerrancy," *Catholic Biblical Quarterly*, 20: 9-18, 1958.

Harrington, W., "The Inspiration of Scripture," *The Irish Theological Quarterly*, 29:3-24, 1962.

McKenzie, J. L., *The Two-Edged Sword*. Milwaukee: Bruce, 1956. Pp. 1-44.

——, *Myths and Realities*. London: Chapman, 1963. Pp. 37-82.

MacKenzie, R. A. F., "Some Problems in the Field of Inspiration," *Catholic Biblical Quarterly*, 20:1-8, 1958.

Rahner, K., *Inspiration in the Bible*. New York: Herder and Herder, 1961.

Smyth, K., "The Inspiration of the Scriptures," *Scripture*, 6:67-75, 1953-54.

Stanley, D., "The Concept of Biblical Inspiration," *Proceedings of the Thirteenth Annual Convention of the Catholic Theological Society of America*. Yonkers, N.Y.; 1958. Pp. 65-95.

Topel, L. J., "Rahner and McKenzie on the Social Theory of Inspiration," *Scripture*, 16:33-44, 1964.

Barr, J., *Old and New in Interpretation*. A Study of the Two Testaments. London: SCM, 1966.

Bauer, J. B., *Encyclopedia of Biblical Theology*. 3 vols. London: Sheed & Ward, 1970.

Bright, J., *The Authority of the Old Testament*. London: SCM, 1967.

Leon-Dufour, X., *Dictionary of Biblical Theology*. New York: Desclée, 1967.

McKenzie, J. L., *Dictionary of the Bible*. Milwaukee: Bruce: 1965.

Rowley, H. H., *The Unity of the Bible*. London: Carey Kingsgate Press, 1953.

Wright, G. E., *The Old Testament and Theology*. New York: Harper & Row, 1969.

Harrington, W. J., *The Path of Biblical Theology*. Dublin: Gill and Macmillan, 1973.

CHAPTER SIX

Beek, M. A., *Atlas of Mesopotamia*. H. H. Rowley, editor; London: Nelson, 1962.

Bright, J., *A History of Israel*. Philadelphia: Westminster Press, 1959.

Childe, V. Gordon, *What Happened in History*. Baltimore: Pelican, 1954².

* Daniel-Rops, H., *Sacred History*. Trans. K. Madge; New York: Longmans, Green, 1949.

Finegan, J., *Light from the Ancient Past*. Princeton University Press, 1952².

* Grollenberg, L. H., *Atlas of the Bible*. Trans. Joyce M. H. Reid and H. H. Rowley; Camden, N.J.: Nelson, 1959.

Gurney, O. R., *The Hittites*. Baltimore: Pelican, 1954².

* Heinisch, P., *History of the Old Testament*. Trans. W. Heidt; Collegeville, Minn.: Liturgical Press, 1952.

* Johnston, L., *A History of Israel*. London: Nelson, 1964.

* Lemaire, P., and Baldi, D., *Atlante Storico della Bibbia*. Rome: Marietti, 1955.

Pritchard, J. B., *Ancient Near Eastern Texts*. Princeton University Press, 1952².

———, *The Ancient Near East in Pictures*. Princeton University Press, 1954.

* Ricciotti, G., *The History of Israel*. Trans. C. della Penta and R. Murphy; Milwaukee: Bruce, 1955.

Wright, G. E., and Filson, F. V., *The Westminster Historical Atlas to the Bible*. Philadelphia: Westminster Press, 1956².

Negenman, J. H., *New Atlas of the Bible*. London: Collins, 1969.

Pedersen, J., *Israel: Its Life and Culture*. 2 vols. London: Oxford University Press, 1959².

Renckens, H., *The Religion of Israel*. New York: Sheed & Ward, 1966.

Ringgren, H., *Israelite Religion*. London: S.P.C.K., 1966.

Vriezen, T. C., *The Religion of Ancient Israel*. London: Lutterworth Press, 1967.

CHAPTER SEVEN

* Bonsirven, J., *Palestinian Judaism in the Time of Jesus Christ*. New York: Holt, Rinehart, & Winston, 1964.

Burrows, M., *The Dead Sea Scrolls*. New York: Viking Press, 1955.

——, More Light on the Dead Sea Scrolls. New York: Viking Press, 1958.

* Copleston, F., A History of Philosophy. New York: Doubleday, 1962². I.

Cross, F. M., The Ancient Library of Qumran. Garden City, N.Y.: Doubleday, 1958.

Cullmann, O., The Early Church. Philadelphia: Westminster Press, 1965.

Doresse, J., The Secret Books of the Egyptian Gnostics. New York: Viking Press, 1959.

Filson, F. V., A New Testament History. Philadelphia: Westminster Press, 1964.

Grant, R. M., and Freedman, D. N., The Secret Sayings of Jesus. Garden City, N.Y.: Doubleday, 1960.

Jeremias, J., Unknown Sayings of Jesus. London: S.P.C.K., 1964.

* Lemaire, P., and Baldi, D., Atlante Storico della Bibbia. Rome: Marietti, 1955.

* Milik, J. T., Ten Years of Discovery in the Wilderness of Judaea. Naperville, Ill.: Allenson, 1959.

Pfeiffer, R. H., History of New Testament Times. London: A. & C. Black, 1963².

Ramsay, W. M., St. Paul the Traveler and the Roman Citizen. Grand Rapids, Mich.: Baker Book House, 1960.

* Ricciotti, G., Paul the Apostle. Milwaukee: Bruce, 1953.

* Sutcliffe, E. F., The Monks of Qumran. Westminster, Md.: Newman Press, 1960.

Van der Heyden, A. A. M., and Scullard, H. H., editors, Atlas of the Classical World. London: Nelson, 1960.

Vermes, G., Discovery in the Judaean Desert. New York: Desclée, 1956.

Barrett, C. K., The New Testament Background. Selected Documents. London: S.P.C.K., 1956.

Davies, W. D., Christian Origins and Judaism. London: Darton, Longman & Todd, 1962.

Jeremias, J., Jerusalem in the Time of Jesus. London: SCM, 1969.

McNamara, M., Targum and Testament. A Light on the New Testament.